The Collected Works of
Marie-Louise von Franz

MLvF

Volume 11

General Editors

Steven Buser

Leonard Cruz

Marie-Louise von Franz
1915-1998

Volume 11

Alchemy

Marie-Louise von Franz

Translated by Alison Kappes-Bates

CHIRON PUBLICATIONS • ASHEVILLE, NORTH CAROLINA

Logo of the Foundation for Jungian Psychology, Küsnacht, Zürich, Switzerland:
Fons mercurialis from Rosarium Philosophorum, 1550 (Fountain of Life).

First published by Inner City Books

www.ChironPublications.com
Interior and cover design by Danijela Mijailovic
Translated by Alison Kappes-Bates
Cover image by Martina Ott
Printed primarily in the United States of America

ISBN 978-1-68503-670-6 paperback
ISBN 978-1-68503-671-3 hardcover
ISBN 978-1-68503-672-0 electronic
ISBN 978-1-68503-673-7 limited edition paperback
ISBN 978-1-68503-674-4 limited edition hardcover

A Note on the Compilation of The Collected Works of Marie-Louise von Franz

Marie-Louise von Franz was blessed with a keen intellect and an outstanding memory. As a classical philologist with a doctorate in Latin and Greek, she was familiar with the writings of the ancient philosophers. She was exceptionally well read. Her private library alone contained over 8,000 books and writings. She was also both diligent and conscientious in her work. She met C.G. Jung in her youth and found him to be an excellent teacher and mentor. She went on to become a close confidant and collaborator, particularly in his work on alchemy. Jung's psychological observations and the conclusions and hypotheses he drew from them about the structures of the unconscious psyche increasingly coincided with her own observations. Marie-Louise von Franz was imbued with an inexhaustible creativity that inspired her well into her old age. She devoted her last lecture to the rehabilitation of the feeling function, a subject that was of great importance to her and to C.G. Jung. Her unconditional devotion to the manifestations of the unconscious psyche was exemplary for all who met her during her lifetime, and for many who came to know her from her writings or their own dreams.

Only a few of her works survived in the form of finished manuscripts. Many of her books derived from transcriptions of her lectures, some of which were delivered in German, though most were in English. The English transcriptions were later translated into her native German. Her primary focus was always on the psychological context and background of her books, and less on their linguistic delivery. Some publishers therefore took the liberty of adding or changing certain things in her texts to make it easier for the reader, as they thought. After realizing what they had done, Marie-Louise von Franz indignantly insisted on her original text being used, claiming that what she had written was what she had wanted to express. Since then, many of her works have been translated into 23 languages, with editions of varying quality being used as the basis for translations into local languages.

In addition to the publishing rights, Marie-Louise von Franz left to the Foundation for Jungian Psychology a handwritten list in which she noted which editions of her books she considered to be the best and most accurate. After her death in 1998, the members of the Foundation decided to republish all of her works in German in accordance with her list. We have respectfully endeavored to remain as close as possible to her original tone, to correct obvious audio or transcription errors, to add footnotes to facilitate understanding, and to supplement texts when written records or tape recordings of her lectures were available. In some instances, this has resulted in greatly altered and revised publications, which we consider to be the basis for all new translations.

For the publication of the Collected Works of Marie-Louise von Franz by Chiron Publications, the Stiftung commissioned Alison Kappes-Bates, Hirzel, a professional translator who knew Marie-Louise von Franz for over 30 years and was a close companion until her death, to translate into English the newly-revised texts in German. Mark Kyburz, Zürich, an experienced translator of Jungian texts, re-edited the first three English volumes of Archetypal Symbols in Fairytales, translated Volumes 4 and 5, and will translate further volumes. The Foundation for Jungian Psychology is responsible for the content and the design, the latter having been created in close consultation with Chiron Publication, Asheville.

On behalf of the Foundation for Jungian Psychology,
Küsnacht, April 24, 2023
PD Dr. Hansueli F. Etter

Table of Contents

Foreword

What is alchemy? From beginners to experts, everyone finds themselves grappling with this question time and time again because alchemy is as mysterious as it is multifaceted. It was as elusive in its Greek beginnings as it was when it slipped into obscurity in the 19th century.[1] Alchemy has been referred to as "art and science," "sacred" or "divine art," "the mother of all sciences," and as the "ars magna."[2] When one first encounters it, it is unclear if the language of alchemy is designed to obscure or if it describes human experiences that simply cannot be expressed with everyday words. Alchemy occurred both in laboratory experiments and in the experimenter's own spiritual experience, and the latter called himself "adeptus" or "adeptus est," i.e., the one who "is wise." Alchemy spanned fields of knowledge as divergent as mining and medicine, and it was used successfully in both domains. Even the origin of the name cannot be traced with any certainty. Some argue that the word chymia has Greek provenance (a chymia is a metalworker or metal alloy maker), while others consider it to have Egyptian roots (chem = black)[3] or even Hebrew roots (kimi jah = because of God)[4]. The prefix "al" was added in Arabic. Thus, the word "alchemy" itself is difficult to define, and there is plenty of room for interpretation.

So what was it that fascinated people about this science, about a process that was as unsuccessful as it was expensive? After all, no alchemist was ever able to produce gold from other substances or managed to obtain the philosopher's stone by the end of their life, find the elixir of life, or attain eternal life and everlasting health in the here and now.

---

[1] The purely chemical-physical aspect of alchemy continued in the 19th century as "secularized alchemy" in the form of modern chemistry.

[2] Great, important, prestigious art.

[3] Jack Lindsay, *The Origins of Alchemy in Graeco-Roman Egypt*, Frederick Muller, London 1970, p.68ff.

[4] Gershom Scholem, *Alchemie und Kabbala*, Suhrkamp, Frankfurt on the Main 1994, p. 14f.

Although alchemy is shrouded by a great deal of mystery, we can nevertheless study its unique characteristics, as well as the premises and key tenets of alchemical philosophy. Even if they are only sketched, they can be useful guides when trying to decipher alchemical texts. The alchemists thought of themselves as microcosms, continually participating in the events that unfolded in the macrocosm around them. What transpired in the laboratory also happened within themselves and to the world. They were certain that a creative force must be at work in the natural world and that this force was driving all things toward completion. Therefore, if the alchemists had indeed managed to synthesize gold in the laboratory, they would have simultaneously reached fulfillment as human beings. In this way, every alchemist participated in God's everlasting work of creation. Success in the laboratory, however, was dependent on an act of grace, i.e., the alchemists needed God's help.

In their laboratories, the alchemists repeatedly observed that their own state of being seemed to correlate with the way in which matter behaved. This was the riddle they sought to solve. Von Franz reminds us that we have not yet solved this basic alchemical problem of the relationship between psyche and matter—neither in the personal nor in the collective realm. Here, in her view, we are touching on the great mysteries, and thus it would be "cheap to say that the old alchemist, i.e., the medieval natural scientist of antiquity, projected unconscious images into matter and nowadays we are enlightened."[5] We, too, have not found the answer to the alchemists' questions.

An alchemist saw himself as a creative individual who, in his quest for perfection, sought to transcend and expand the existing natural order. In his view, this creative process began in the material world, for it was in nature that he experienced the divine mystery of the creative spirit on a daily basis. His experiments with various substances in the laboratory were designed to reveal this entity. He had no doubt that nature was not only governed by cause and effect but that a teleological force[6] with a final intention was also at work,

[5] Marie-Louise von Franz, in this CW 11, p. XX.
[6] A force that is oriented toward a future goal.

i.e., that it was aimed at a goal, even if this goal was ultimately unknowable. An alchemist, therefore, saw himself as a collaborator of the divine on earth, seeking to complete the original process of creation.

The substances with which the alchemists experimented were not chemical compounds in a modern sense. They distinguished between materials according to the various colors that appeared over the course of an experiment. Changes that occurred in the laboratory were considered stages of a process primarily expressed by color change. This partially explains the language used to describe the important progression from black (nigredo) to white (albedo) and finally to red (rubedo), for example. Rather than being viewed as an elemental metal, as part of the periodic table as we do today, gold, the perfect metal of the highest value, was also identified by its color. Since colors express feelings, the color names they gave to substances and the importance of their color changes reflect that an alchemist's way of working was determined less by analytical thinking and more by emotional observation.

Again, this underscores the close connection between the alchemist himself and his work in the laboratory. To give another example, the term lapis, i.e., stone, was not used in the contemporary petrographic sense. In his *Lexicon Alchemiae*[7], Martin Ruland gives the following definition of stone: "What does not turn to smoke and remains solid, the chymists call a stone."

Cultural evolution since the time of the great Greek philosophers shifted the notions of "spirit" or "spirituality" further and further into the spheres of the divine. Spirit became transcendent, masculine, and numinous. The alchemists, however, conceived of the spirit as Mother Nature's feminine potential, which also had a dark, destructive side. After all, they had experienced how an entire laboratory could blow up during an experiment and how diabolical sulfur smells and caustic, poisonous vapors could be released! Jung pointed out that for the alchemists, "...the dark side of the world and

[7] Martin Ruland, Lexicon Alchemiae, Frankfurt 1612, Faksimile from Georg Olms Verlag, Hildesheim, Zürich, New York 1987, p. 273.

of life had not been conquered, and this was the task they set themselves in their work."[8]

The inherent contradictory nature of all things was recognized in the alchemists' work, as well as in the language they used. Alone, the oft-repeated maxim "solve et coagula"[9] clearly shows that "the alchemist saw the essence of his art in separation and analysis on the one hand and synthesis and consolidation on the other."[10] In his introduction to the contradictory nature of alchemy, Jung writes: "For [the alchemist] there was first of all an initial state in which opposite tendencies or focus were in conflict; secondly there was the great question of a procedure which would be capable of bringing the hostile elements and qualities, once they were separated, back to unity again. The initial state, named the *chaos*, was not given from the start but had to be sought for as the *prima materia*. And just as the beginning of the work was not self-evident, so to an even greater degree was its end. There are countless speculations on the nature of the end-state, all of them reflected in its destinations. The commonest are the ideas of its permanence (prolongation of life, immortality, incorruptibility), its androgyny, its spirituality and corporeality, its human qualities and resemblance to man (homunculus), and its divinity."[11] All these characteristics of the desired end product of the alchemical experiments point to a unification of opposites—of time and eternity, of male and female, of psyche and matter, of man and God.

The alchemists were almost exclusively men. The art of alchemy must, therefore, be considered from the perspective of masculine psychology. The alchemists were searching for the things their consciousness lacked, for what was difficult to grasp, and for the force that was mysteriously and creatively at work within them and also worked through them. By projecting it into matter, they were searching for their soul. Men embody the "heavenly spirit," which is why they seek the unknowable side of their soul in the material world. And what about women? Women have an earthy soul, which is why

[8] C. G. Jung, Mysterium Coniunctionis, CW 14, Routledge & Kegan Paul, London, 1981, § 49.
[9] Dissolve and coagulate.
[10] C. G. Jung, Mysterium Coniunctionis, CW 14/I, p. XIV.
[11] Ibid, p. XIV.

they seek the unfamiliar side of the spirit in the ether. For men, alchemy takes on feminine qualities: it becomes *Alchemia*. This representation of the feminine principle is the embodiment of the material vessel for transformation. A woman, Alchemia, *is* the *Athanor* (the alchemical furnace) in which chaos is organized by the *prima materia*. Thanks to the body's constant temperature, the secondary matter will be purified and cleansed, then it will increase and become creative in the dark vessel of her uterus, and, finally, it will come into existence in the form of new life. In the eyes of the alchemists, becoming a mother was an alchemical process in which the homunculus was mysteriously created, a process in which a man was involved but from which he was simultaneously also excluded. Thus, the kinship that alchemical language has to the erotic imagery of the sexual union between men and women is not surprising. For in love, opposites can become one in perfect harmony and create new life.

After the ancient Greeks, mainstream culture became increasingly dominated by a masculine spirit. Thus, the alchemists stood in opposition to the officially held beliefs. By doing so, they revitalized a cultural undercurrent that compensated for the thinking of their time. The ancient Greeks still believed that the natural world was animated and fertilized by a divine spirit, which they worshipped in the form of Pan. This archetypal figure harks back to the Egyptian god Thoth, the god of arithmetic and writing, dreaming and memory, as well as world order and lawfulness. In ancient Rome, Thoth lived on as Mercurius. From the eighth century onward, Muslim scholars developed and deepened the science of alchemy, and, via Spain, they brought their knowledge to Europe. Clerics and doctors embraced it with great enthusiasm and commitment and explored things further in their laboratories. The rational, reductionist, and causal thinking that would flourish in Europe during the Enlightenment would gradually strip nature of any trace of a soul, and by the 19th century, it would banish alchemy from the realm of recognized scientific inquiry. Seen in this light, alchemy is like a red thread that, via Islam, connects ancient cultures to Christianity. Jung argued that the alchemists of the West were ultimately suffocated by their own confusion.[12] With the help of symbolic thinking and by considering it from the perspective of depth psychology, Jung rescued alchemy from the dustbin of history and taught us how to give it new meaning! Thanks to the seminal works of C. G. Jung and Marie-Louise von Franz, alchemy was given a new lease of life.

In 1959, Marie-Louise von Franz gave a lecture in English at the C. G. Jung Institute in Zurich entitled "Introduction to the Symbolism of Alchemy." Mrs. Una Thomas completed a transcription, which Marie-Louise von Franz reviewed. In 1980, Daryl Sharp and Marion Woodman first published this text with Inner City Books, Toronto, Canada, in a slightly modified form. Hans-Ulrich Möhring did the first German translation, which was never published. Using Möhring's manuscript as a reference, Irene Gerber-Münch, Zurich, translated the Inner City Books' version into German, commissioned by the Foundation for Jungian Psychology. She diligently checked all the source texts discussed by Marie-Louise von Franz, which are listed in the footnotes. She also organized the text into chapters to make things more digestible; the nine lectures are nevertheless referred to throughout. Lastly, she added annotations, footnotes, images, an extended bibliography, and an index. The German version was published in 2008 by the Foundation for Jungian Psychology.

This 11th volume of Marie-Louise von Franz's Collected Works is a new English translation of the 2008 German edition. Alison Kappes-Bates, Ernen, has retranslated and adapted the German text into English based on both the original English and the new German versions and supplemented it further. She has completed this challenging task with her usual diligence and creativity, and once again, we owe her our heartfelt thanks. I would also like to thank Shannon Rea Kappes, London, for her sensitive translation of this foreword.

On behalf of the Foundation for Jungian Psychology
Küsnacht, June 6, 2024
PD Dr. Hansueli F. Etter, President

[12] Ibid, § 121.

Foreword to the German New Edition

Marie-Louise von Franz lectured on the *Introduction to the Symbolism of Alchemy* at the C. G. Jung Institute in Zurich in 1959. Miss Una Thomas made a transcription at the time that was looked over by the author. In a slightly modified form, it was published in 1980 by Inner City Books, Toronto, Canada, by Daryl Sharp and Marion Woodman with the title *Alchemy: An Introduction to the Symbolism and the Psychology.*

As it was important to the editors to publish the entire lecture to serve the purpose of documentation, this revised English edition has been adapted to conform to the revised German edition published by the Verlag Stiftung für Jung'sche Psychologie, Küsnacht, Zurich in 2008 that is based upon the original transcription by Una Thomas. (The 2008 German edition also drew upon an unofficial and unpublished German translation done by Hans-Ulrich Möhring, Göttingen, with annotations by René Malamud, that was based upon the above-mentioned English edition by Daryl Sharp and Marion Woodman.) It was decided not to correct what at first glance appear to be discrepancies in the writing. Summaries and repetitions at the start of a new lecture of what had been said previously were retained, along with insertions relating to different chapters. This seemed to be the best way to retain Marie-Louise von Franz's lively train of thought. The material was divided into chapters, for the benefit of the reader, while the nine lectures can still be identified as such. Annotations and bibliographical sources have been added to the footnotes, along with some illustrations, a complete bibliography and an index.

Careful attention was paid to the source of the texts cited by Marie-Louise von Franz in this book. Parts of the Greek text *Isis the Prophetess to her Son Horus* are available in English, partly in C. G.

Jung's 'The Visions of Zosimos', Collected Works Volume 13, and partly in Marie-Louise von Franz's book *On Dreams and Death*, and the citations are from these sources where possible. For citations from the Egyptian *Höhlenbuch*, the French version that was used by Marie-Louise von Franz has not been used, rather, the 1989 translation by Erik Hornung, the best authority on ancient Egyptian literature of the Beyond, *Die Unterweltsbücher der Ägypter.* Marie-Louise von Franz translated the text *Über die heilige Kunst* of Olympiodor from Greek to English herself. Consequently, the citations from this text are taken from the transcription of her lectures, although occasionally formulations found in *On Dreams and Death* have been taken into consideration.

At that time, Marie-Louise von Franz translated both texts of Muhammad Ibn Umail – *The Book of the Silver Water and the Starry Earth* and *Love Letter from the Sun to the Sickle Moon* – into English from the Latin text *De Chemia.* Translations of this originally Arabic text were not available at that time. Reference to studies that have been done since then in Arabic alchemy, in particular the translations of Muhammad Ibn Umail *Kitab al-Ma'al-waraqi wa-l-ard an-nagmiya* and *Risalat as-sams ila l-hilal* by Salway Fuad and Theodor Abt have been noted in the footnotes.

The excerpts in Part Three from *Aurora Consurgens* were taken from the English edition that was published by Inner City Books, Toronto in 2000. The footnotes that appear in this volume, however, have been omitted here.

Alison Kappes-Bates adapted the English edition to the new revised German edition, for which we sincerely thank her.

Küsnacht, January 2016

For the German New Edition
Irene Gerber-Münch

Lecture 1
Introduction

1 I have given much thought as to how I should give an introduction into the symbolism of alchemy, and I have decided to interpret many texts, instead of one text as I have done at other times. Of the nine lectures, I shall give three lectures on Old Greek alchemy, three on Arabic alchemy, and three on later European alchemy. In this way, one should get at least a glimpse of every phase in the development of this science.

2 As we know, Dr. Jung devoted many years of study to alchemy. He practically dug it up from the dunghill of the past for it was a forgotten and despised field of investigation that he suddenly revived. The fact that now the smallest pamphlet sells for about 100 Swiss francs, while about 10 years ago an excellent book on alchemy could be bought for two or three francs, is actually due to Jung because, except for the interest displayed by some Freemason circles, and later developments by Rosicrucians, nobody really knew anything about the subject when he began his work on it.

3 If you have such a text in front of you, it soon becomes clear why alchemy came to be forgotten, and why, even in Jungian circles, many people still say that they can follow Jung as far as myth interpretation is concerned, and all else he has written, but when it comes to alchemy, they have had to give up. Either they do not read these books at all, or they grumble while reading them. In itself, alchemy is tremendously dark and complex. The texts are very difficult to understand, and one needs an enormous amount of technical background knowledge to penetrate this field. I hope this introductory course may help one get into the material better. It

should give the readers of Jung's books some background knowledge that will help them to understand the material.

4 In *Psychology and Alchemy*, C. G. Jung, as it were, introduced alchemy into psychology, first by publishing a series of dreams of a natural scientist that contain a great amount of alchemical symbolism, and then by referencing them to old texts.[1] In this way, Jung hoped to show how important and modern this material is, and how much it has to say to modern man. He himself discovered alchemy absolutely empirically. He once told me that he frequently came across certain motifs in his patients' dreams that he could not understand until one day he started to look at old books on alchemy and noticed a connection. For example, a woman patient dreamt that an eagle was at first flying up to the sky, then it suddenly turned its head and began to eat its own wings and finally dropped back onto the earth. Jung was naturally able to understand the symbolism without historical parallels as the high-soaring spirit, or thought bird, so to speak. The dream indicates a sort of interpretation of enantiodromia, the return to earth through one's own strength. All the same, Jung was very much struck by the motif which one at once recognizes as archetypal and which one feels convinced must have parallels. It strikes one as a general motif, yet it was nowhere to be found. Then one day Jung discovered the *Ripley Scroll*[2] that includes a series of pictures of the alchemical process—partly published in *Psychology and Alchemy*[3]—that includes an image of an eagle with a king's head that turns back and eats its own wings.

5 The coincidence struck him very forcibly. He kept it in mind for years and felt that there was more to alchemy and that he should go into the subject. He hesitated to attack this most complex field, realizing how much work it would involve and that it would mean brushing up on his Greek and Latin and reading so much. Finally, however, he came to the conclusion that it had to be done, that there was too much buried in the subject which was important to us for a

[1] C. G. Jung, *Psychology and Alchemy*, 2nd ed., vol. 12, *Bollingen Series XX: The Collected works of C. G. Jung*, ed. Herbert Read, Michael Fordham, Gerhard Adler and William McGuire, trans. R. F. C. Hull (Princeton, NJ: Princeton University Press, 1993).

[2] In Elias Ashmole, ed., *Theatrum chemicum Britannicum*, vol. 1 (Hildesheim: Olms, 1968).

[3] Jung, *Psychology and Alchemy*, vol. 12, *CW*, § 30, § 92, §196, § 228,§ 251, § 257.

better understanding of the dream material of modern people. Jung was interested in alchemy not as a theoretical problem, but because he noticed the striking parallels to the material with which he was dealing. But why should alchemical symbolism be closer to the unconscious product of many modern people than any other material? Why would it not suffice to study comparative mythology, fairytales and the history of religions? Why has it to be alchemy in particular?

6 If we study the development of symbolism in the comparative history of religion—for instance, the many allegories of the Virgin Mary, or the tree of life, or the cross, or the symbolism of the dragon in medieval Christian material, or if, for example, we think of the mythology of the North American Indians, of the beliefs of the Hopis, the song of the Navaho, etc.,—in each case we are dealing with material that has been formed in shared collective life and handed down by a more or less organized culture. Among the North American Indians there were medicine men who handed down songs and rituals only to their pupils, while other things were known by the whole tribe who also participated in these rituals. The same holds true for Christian symbolism that is handed down in the tradition of the Church: the whole symbolism of the liturgy and of the Mass, with all its meaning, is transmitted through its dogma, through culture and through human organizations. This is also true of various Eastern yoga teachings and other forms of meditation. These symbols certainly originated in the unconscious, but they have since been worked upon and formed by tradition. One sees repeatedly how anyone who has had any original and immediate experience of unconscious symbols begins to work upon them afterward.

7 As an example, let us take Niklaus von Flüe, the Swiss saint, who had a vision of a wanderer, a divine figure, who came toward him wearing a shining bearskin and singing a song of three words.[4] From the original report it is obvious that the saint was convinced that it was either God, or Christ, who was appearing to him in this form.

[4] Cf. Marie-Louise von Franz, *Die Visionen des Niklaus von Flüe*, 3rd ed. (Zurich: Daimon, 1983), 70-71.

But the original report got lost, and until about 80 years ago, there was only a report made by one of his earliest biographers who told the story more or less correctly but omitted the bearskin! The three words of the song refer to the Trinity, the divine wanderer would be Christ visiting the saint, and so on. The biographer mentions all of this, but with the bearskin he could do nothing—for why should Christ wear a bearskin? So that item was dropped, and it was only by the chance rediscovery of the original report of the vision that it was afterward included. This is exactly what happens to original experiences that are handed down: A selection is made. What fits or coincides with what is already known is handed down, while other details tend to get dropped because they seem strange and one does not know how to deal with them.

8 It seems, therefore, that symbolism handed down by tradition is to a certain extent rationalized and purged of the scurrilities of the unconscious, of the funny little details that the unconscious tags on, that are sometimes contradictory or dirty. On a small scale, this happens within us, too. I recall a young doctor who was very skeptical about the way we write down our dreams, believing that a lot was falsified when one wrote down one's dreams in the morning. So he put a tape recorder by his bedside, and when he woke in the night, even if in a half sleepy state, he recorded his dream, and in the morning he wrote down the same dream as he remembered it and compared the two. He discovered that his skepticism was exaggerated. The reports we make of our dreams the next morning are almost correct, albeit we involuntarily introduce order into them. For instance, he dreamt that something happened in a house and that he later went into the house. In retelling the dream in the morning, he corrected the time sequence and wrote down that he went into the house and then experienced this and that. Actually, dreams that are recorded at once are more confused with regard to time, but otherwise they are fairly correct. So when a dream crosses the threshold of consciousness, consciousness does something to it in reporting it, amending it, and making it a little more understandable.

9 *Cum grano salis*, you could compare the above to the way in which religious experiences are handed down in a living religious system in that the immediate personal experience is usually purified, clarified and revised. For example, accounts of the personal inner life of Catholic saints speak, in most cases, of the saints having immediate experiences of the Godhead—this is included in the definition of a saint—or visions of the Virgin Mary, or Christ, and so on, but the Church has rarely published such reports without first expurgating them of what was considered to be personal material. Only what fitted with tradition was chosen.

10 The same thing happens not only in our culture, but also in free primitive communities. Even the North American Indians omit certain details that they find uninteresting to their collective conscious ideas. Australian aborigines celebrate a festival called Kunapipi that goes on for 30 years—a big rebirth ritual that lasts for a whole generation. For 30 years certain rituals are performed at specified times and when the 30 years are up, it starts all over again. The ethnologist who first described it took the trouble to collect dreams that referred to the festival.[5] He discovered that members of the tribe often dreamt about it, and that in those dreams—as one would expect and as would happen to us—there were variations in little details that did not quite fit with what actually took place. According to what the Australian aborigines said, if a dream contained a good idea, it was told to the tribe and adopted as a part of the festival, which in that way varied a little; in the main, though, they kept to the tradition that had been handed down.

11 I have often seen the same phenomenon with Catholic analysands, namely that they dream of the Mass, but something special happens, for instance, the priest distributes hot soup instead of the Host, or something like that. It is all quite correct except for the one detail. I recall a nun's dream in which, in the middle of the Sanctus—at the holiest moment when the transubstantiation was about to take place—the old bishop who was reading Mass suddenly stopped and

[5] Roland M. Berndt, *Kunapipi: A Study of an Australian Religious Cult*, (New York: International Universities Press, 1951).

said, "Now something more important is first necessary," and then gave a sermon on the Incarnation. Then he stopped again and said that now they would go on with the traditional Mass and handed it over to two young priests to finish. Apparently, this nun, like many other people, had not enough real understanding of the mystery of the Mass—to her it was just a mechanical repetition of the mystery. The dream showed that one should explain to the people what was *really* happening, for if they did not participate with their minds, it was of no help to them: They were just believing without comprehending. So, in her dream the bishop gave a long explanation, after which the classical Mass continued with younger priests, showing that it was a renewal. Renewal takes place according to the way in which the Mass is understood, and here the old man handed it over to the two young men. This illustrates how individual experience of religious symbols always varies a little from the official formula, which is only an average pattern. There is very little immediate manifestation of the unconscious in historical source material.

12 By observing dreams, visions and hallucinations, etc., modern man can look at the phenomena of the unconscious in an unprejudiced way for the first time. What comes from the unconscious can be observed through individuals. The past has handed down some rare reports of individual experiences, but most information about symbols of the unconscious reach us in the more traditional way. This is because people do not normally approach the unconscious individually, but rather, with few exceptions, relate to it indirectly through their own religious system. As far as I can see, this applies generally, except in the oldest and most primitive societies, and in certain other already codified forms of approach to the unconscious.

13 In a number of Inuit tribes there are, for instance, practically no contents of collective consciousness. There are a few ideas about certain ghosts and gods—Sila, god of the air, and Sedna, goddess of the sea, and so on—which are handed down orally, but the shamans or medicine men, the religious personalities of such communities,

speak only of their personal experiences. The Inuit lead such a hard life and have such difficulty surviving, owing to the terrific conditions under which they live, that normally everybody concentrates only on survival, with the exception of a few chosen individuals who have some commerce with ghosts and have inner experiences and dreams. These people relate to their own dreams and have their own thoughts about them, rather as a Jungian analysand does here. The only guidance they receive is in meeting other shamans and exchanging experiences, so that they may not be quite alone with their inner experiences. Generally, the younger ones look for older shamans, for they are afraid that they might go mad, just as we would. In communities like this there is a minimum of collective conscious tradition and a maximum of immediate personal experience of a few individuals.

14 I think it probable that this represents the remnants of an original condition, because, according to anthropological reflections, one can assume that mankind originally lived in small tribal groupings of about 20 to 30 people, among whom there were usually two or three gifted introverts who had personal inner experiences. They were the spiritual guides, while the strong hunters or fighters were the earthly guides. In these tribal groupings there is material about immediate inner experiences, though very little collective tradition.

15 There is also, however, the phenomenon of individuals meeting the unconscious immediately within the organized initiation rituals of their people. For example, in many of the North American Indian tribes, part of the initiation of a young medicine man consists in climbing a mountain, or going into the desert after fasting, and sometimes also after having taken drugs in order to have a vision or a hallucination, an experience that he then reports to his master, who is responsible for his initiation. If, for example, he says that he has seen a lizard, he is told that he belongs to the Thunderbird clan and will have to become such and such a medicine man. Here the interpretation of the individual experience is connected with collective conscious tradition and anything that is completely

individual or anything strange, a medicine man would just omit. Paul Radin has published dreams of Indians showing how they interpret them.[6] Here one sees that they just skip what they do not understand. They pick out of the dream what connects with conscious collective ideas and skip the funny details—just as beginners in Jungian analysis do when they begin to interpret their own dreams. If you suggest that they try their hand at interpreting their dreams, they usually pick out one motif which seems to connect with something they understand and say they know what that means and what it is referring to. I then ask, "But what about this detail and what about that one?" I ask about details that they simply omit.

16 Immediate experiences of the unconscious that certain individuals have had may later be codified, or interpreted, or built into a religious system. Naturally, there are sects in all religions that tend to revivify what were once immediate experiences. Wherever a religion seems to be too codified, a compensatory sect is usually formed to revivify truly individual experiences. This accounts for the many splits. For instance, there are the Sunnites and the Shiites in Islam, or the Talmudic school and the Kabbalah in the Jewish Middle Ages. The codified religious symbols are handed down, while the more recent group tends to give more value to individual experiences. One group claims to be orthodox, while the other claims to be more vibrant, to have the living spirit, which is also the contrast between extroverts and introverts. But even in the tradition of the introvert who claims to have the living spirit, there is very little real personal experience of the unconscious. There are always only a few individuals who have such experiences, probably because they are so dangerous and frightening. Only rare and unusually courageous people go this way, or fools who do not know how dangerous the thing is, and who are therefore driven mad by it.

[6] Paul Radin, "The Winnebago Tribe," first published in *Annual Report of the Bureau of American Ethnology* (Washington, DC, 1923). Later edition: Paul Radin, *The Winnebago Tribe* (Lincoln: University of Nebraska Press, 1970).

17 In some of his early lectures at the E.T.H., the technical college in Zurich[7], Jung wanted to exemplify and interpret the symbolism of the process of individuation. For this purpose, he discussed a series of images in an Eastern meditation text and the famous spiritual exercises, the *Exercitia Spiritualia*, of Ignatius of Loyola, as well as Hugh de St. Victor's *Benjoumin minor*. He showed that all these forms of codified meditation contain essential theories, or symbols, which normally appear in the process of individuation in individuals. But all of these approaches to the unconscious, and most forms of Eastern meditation as well as medieval Christian forms, contain a program. For instance, a person who goes through the *Exercitia* of St. Ignatus *must* concentrate on the sentence *Homo creatus est* in the first week, on the sufferings of Christ the following week, and so on. To think he would like some coffee in the middle of his contemplation would be a worldly disturbance by the devil that he has to restrain. But there might also be holy disturbances! He might, when meditating on the Holy Cross, suddenly see a blue light or a crown of roses around it. As that does not fit in, that thought also has to be banished for that would be the devil falsifying the process, for he should see the Holy Cross, not a bunch of roses, or something of that sort. He is therefore taught to reject those spontaneous irruptions of the unconscious and to adhere fanatically to the program.

18 Naturally, he is still concentrating on symbols of the unconscious, for the cross *is* a symbol of the unconscious, but his mind is driven into a definite channel given through collective tradition. If he tells his father confessor that he saw a bathtub instead of the cross, he will certainly be told that he was not concentrating properly, that he has digressed. The same thing applies to certain Eastern forms of meditation. If beautiful divas and goddesses appear and try to divert the Yogi from his goal, he must chase such thoughts away as disturbing factors. Thus, in these forms of approach to the unconscious, conscious direction and a prescribed way, or path,

[7] C. G. Jung, "Exercitia spiritualia" in *Modern Psychology: Notes on Lectures Given at the Eidgenössische Technische Hochschule Zurich*, 2nd ed., vol. 3 and 4 (privately printed).

must be conformed to, and certain thoughts that want to surface must be ignored. For this reason, the symbolism that appears in such forms is not quite of the same quality that *we* have, for we tell people who come to us to simply observe what comes up. This naturally produces slightly different material, so that we can only make a relative comparison of the two products.

19 The alchemists were in a completely different situation. They believed that they were studying the unknown phenomenon of matter—I will give details later on—and they just observed what came up within them and interpreted that somehow, but without any specific plan. If, for instance, they had a lump of some strange matter lying in front of them and did not know what it was, they made conjectures about it which, of course, were unconscious projections. But there was no definite intention or tradition. Therefore, one could say that in alchemy, projections were made most naively without any program, and they were left completely uncorrected.

20 Imagine an old alchemist's situation! A man in some isolated village builds himself a hut and cooks up all sorts of things that cause explosions. Quite naturally, everyone calls him a witch doctor! One day someone comes and says he has found a queer piece of metal, and would the alchemist be interested in buying it? The alchemist does not know the value of the metal but gives the man some money at a guess. He then puts what he has bought on his stove and mixes it with sulphur, or something similar, to see what happens, and if the metal were lead, he would have been badly poisoned by the vapors. He concludes, therefore, that this particular matter makes one feel sick if approached, and it nearly kills you. As a result, he will say that there is a demon in lead! Afterward, when he writes his recipes, he adds a footnote saying, "Beware of lead, for there is a demon in it that will kill people and make them mad," which would be quite an obvious and reasonable explanation for someone of that time and level. Therefore, lead was a wonderful subject for the projection of destructive factors, since its effects are poisonous in certain combinations. Acidic substances were also dangerous but,

being corrosive and as a means of dissolving things, they were nevertheless highly important for chemical operations. If you wished to melt something or have it in liquid form, it could be melted or dissolved in an acidic solution. Thus, the projection was that acid was a dangerous substance that dissolves things, but it also makes it possible to handle certain substances; it was also thought to be a medium of transformation for a metal with which you can otherwise do nothing can be made accessible to transformation by adding certain liquids. The alchemists wrote about it in the naïve form I am now describing and did not notice that that was not natural science but contained a lot of projection, if looked at from a modern chemical standpoint.

21 Thus, there is an astonishing amount of material from the unconscious in alchemy, produced in a situation where the conscious mind had no definite plan, no specified program, but was simply searching. C. G. Jung himself approached the unconscious in a similar manner, and we, too, try to get people to adopt an attitude of approaching the unconscious with no set program. When someone comes to us with a certain problem, we simply affirm the situation and suggest that we should look at the unsatisfactory condition the person is in from the lively phenomenon that we call the unconscious. We then consider together what something might represent and what it might be driving at. This approach of having no program corresponds to that of the alchemist, so that the unconscious responds in a very similar manner. This is why alchemical writings are especially helpful to our understanding of modern material.

22 ***Question:*** *In a volume of ancient dream material by A. Oppenheim, one feels that ancient dream interpreters were also interpreting on a collective basis.*[8] *Do you agree?*

23 Yes, in that they also chose specific dreams: They chose those that were connected to collective material. This also applies to

[8] Cf. A. Leo Oppenheim, *The Interpretation of Dreams in the Ancient Near East:* With a Translation of an Assyrian Dream-Book, Transactions of the American Philosophical Society, vol. 46 (Philadelphia: The American Philosophical, 1956), 179-373.

Artemidoros.[9] I know of only one document from antiquity in which there is a series of dreams that has not been selected—a text from the Serapeum of Memphis. Ulrich Wilcken published it in his book *Urkunden der Ptolemäerzeit.*[10] A man called Ptolemaeus got into some trouble, I believe for debts, and in order to escape being imprisoned, he elected to become a novice, a *katochos,* in the Serapeum—the Serapis sanctuary of Memphis. According to the regulations, a *katochos* must write down his dreams. In Ptolemaeus's papyrus—a unique papyrus in Hellenized Greek—in which there are the most amazing "modern" dreams, something like, "I met Mr So-and-So and said ..." followed by some banalities, and then the name again, and so on, which would be typical of our dreams. It is impossible to interpret such a dream for one does not know the associations. In a series of about 27 dreams, there are two or three in which the goddess Isis, for instance, appears. Collective dreams in which collective figures appear we can understand, but the others cannot be interpreted because we have no associations. Ptolemaeus says, for example, that he met his nephew, but nobody knows what his nephew meant to him!

24 There is something else which was of great importance to me when I discovered this document, namely that those people dreamt exactly as we do. If you read the Babylonian dreams, you feel that they did *not* dream as we do, for in the Babylonian dream material, dreams were selected to fit the traditional interpretation. For example, to dream about a black goat portends bad luck. Hundreds of other dreams that the same man perhaps had had were ignored, but because in collective tradition a black goat appearing in a dream means bad luck, that dream was recorded. That is still the case in our peasant countries where nobody takes any notice of ordinary dreams. But if anybody dreams about a coffin, or a wedding, or a snake, it is discussed, and they wonder if anyone in the family is going to die. This only applies to traditional motifs: All the other material goes down the drain.

---

[9] Artemiodoros von Ephosos, born in Daldis, second century A.D., wrote the most famous ancient dream book, *Oneirokritika* in 5 volumes.

[10] Ulrich Wilcken, ed., *Urkunden der Ptolemäerzeit (ältere Funde)*, vol.1 (Berlin: Gruyter, 1922-1957).

25 The fragments that we have of the dreams of Ptolemaeus, however, show something completely different from the dream literature of antiquity, and one realizes that the people of that time dreamt just as we do, though dream literature only relates the few dreams which fitted their theories—if you dreamt the house was on fire, then you were in love, etc. You can always see how they arrived at their interpretations, which, by the way, were not too bad, for it is quite likely that someone in love would dream of a house on fire! Such books are built up on average experiences, but all medieval dream material, as well as that of antiquity, is thoroughly concretistic. A dream is never taken as an inner thing, as an inner process, but is always projected onto the outer world.

26 Even nowadays simple people here in Switzerland often discuss their dreams, but only on a prognostic level. I analyze a charwoman, and the other day her brother rang me up and asked why I was making his sister even madder by analyzing her dreams, that dreams were all junk which he had proved himself, for he had dreamt of coffins last winter three times—and nobody in the family had died! This shows what nonsense it all is! He still thinks in the classical Greek-Egyptian-Babylonian way.

27 Let us go back to the original traditions of little primitive groups living together and say that a man among them has dreams or visions. There are two possibilities open to him: If he knows someone who is supposed to be a shaman or a medicine man or a priest, he goes to him and accepts his interpretations, or he can remain independent and build up his own interpretation, draw his own conclusions, and work out the whole system.

28 ***Remark****: So, it depends on the attitude and understanding of the person in authority. Ultimately it resolves into the question of whose authority is to be respected most, that of the interpreter according to tradition or of the person who has had the dream or experience.*

29 Yes, and ultimately it depends upon who has the most mana, upon who is the greater personality—who leads the more spiritual life and has greater authority. For instance, sometimes people keep their experiences to themselves even in these primitive countries

and develop their own system. But if then they fail in life, they are looked upon as fools. So the man who is arrogant enough to want to remain alone risks being regarded as someone possessed and a fool, instead of as a great medicine man. He has to run this risk, but only life can show who is correct. Nevertheless, even such tribes discriminate between fools who are possessed and medicine men.

30 ***Remark****: In Christian terminology, you could say that such a man carries his cross, but everything depends upon his motive.*

31 Yes, exactly. Or, if we take Catholic heresiology, someone may have a personal revelation of God that causes him to deviate from the dogma. Let us imagine that he has a vision of Christ in which Christ tells him that he is half animal; this person would then say that he knows that Christ not only incarnated as man but also even on the level of an animal. If a man believed this, the Inquisition would have condemned him to being burned at the stake, but they would have added that he might still be saved and still be right. He has to be burned because the orthodox creed must be defended, but a door is left open by their saying that the heretic might be right. Nevertheless, if he wanted to adhere to his personal truth, he had to accept being burned for it. It was not said that he had lost his soul, for God may accept him into Paradise, but it was also his fate to be burned. Such an approach shows a kind of spiritual modesty, for while condemning him to be burned, they neither condemn his soul, nor do they claim that he has forfeited salvation. Such a man was proud, or lonely, or spiritually independent enough to rely upon his own beliefs and personal experiences, but he had to accept the consequences, and the Catholic community did not accept him. In other circles, the attitude may have been different. Meanwhile, modern Catholic teachings have also been slightly modified, as I heard recently. A Jesuit told a friend of mine that you are allowed to believe something, like the man in the tribe mentioned above, provided that you do not tell anyone else about it and do not make a doctrine out of it or try to convert others to the same belief. If you just keep it to yourself and decide not to reject your inner vision, the Catholic Church will close its eyes to it.

32 **Remark**: *I think that applies not only to the Catholic Church, but also to any group of people. It depends on whether the individual believes that he can tell his group of this experience or not.*

33 Yes, which is why I often say to schizoid people that their madness does not consist in what they say and believe, but rather in telling it to the *wrong* people. If they kept it to themselves, it would be all right. I am thinking, for example, of a borderline case, a woman, who goes to every psychiatrist and accuses them all of being idiotic rationalists who do not believe in God and then tells them her visions. I think her only mistake is in telling these people, for that is simply being maladapted! Her visions in themselves are quite all right, and also what she thinks about them, but her extraverted feeling is inferior; she is socially maladapted. She should not speak of such things to a rationalistic psychiatrist who then only wonders whether he should have her committed!

34 **Remark**: *No, because his reputation is in turn at stake!*

35 Yes, of course. His colleagues would scoff at him if he started believing in his patients' visions. Colleagues always behave like that and speak of countertransference, etc. It is so often a question of ambition and prestige and of collective convention—just as it is with us.

36 There is a further reason why alchemy is of such importance to modern man. Alchemy is a natural science and therefore attempts to understand material phenomena in nature; it is a mixture of physics and chemistry of those early times and corresponds to the conscious mental attitudes of those who studied it and who concentrated on the mystery of nature, particularly of material phenomena. It is also the beginning of an empirical science. I will go into its specific history later. The average modern man, particularly in Anglo-Saxon countries, but also increasingly in European countries, is trained mentally in the observation of natural science phenomena, while the humanities, as you know, are increasingly neglected. This is a present-day tendency that places ever-increasing emphasis upon a "scientific" approach. If you analyze modern people, you find that their outlook on reality is very

much influenced by the basic concepts of natural science. Generally speaking, one is dealing with people who view the world in this way, and the compensatory or connecting material from the unconscious is accordingly similar. But this is only a superficial analogy, for the reason lies much deeper.

37 If one asks why natural sciences predominate to such an extent in our worldview, it can be seen as the result of a long and specific development. As we know, confined to our European context, natural science is regarded as having originated in the sixth century B.C., around the time of pre-Socratic philosophy. This was largely philosophical speculation about nature, for the early natural scientists did very little experimental investigation. It would be more accurate to say that the birth of natural science as a theory, or as a general concept of reality, took place at that time. Natural science, in the sense that man has always experimented with animals, stones, materials, matter, fire and water, is much wider, and in former times it was a part of those magical practices that are connected with all religions and that deal with material things. One might therefore say that with a view to life's ultimate realities, man is overwhelmed by ideas and concepts from within, by symbols and images, but that he also has to deal with outer life and material things. This explains why in most rituals there is something concrete representing a symbolic meaning, for instance, a bowl of water placed in the center for divination, or something of that kind.

38 Thus, matter and material phenomena are approached in a "magical" way. The religious histories of different peoples describe religious symbols that both embody and represent demons with half-personified aspects, as well as divinities or powerful factors that have a material aspect. We know that even historians of religion without a Jungian background compare the concept of mana to electricity. If an Australian rubs his churinga stone to get more mana, it is with the idea of refuelling his totem, or his life essence, like recharging an electric battery. The whole concept of mana bears the projection of semimaterial, divine electricity, of divine energy or power. Thus, a tree struck by lightning would represent mana.

39 Further, in most religious systems there are sacred substances, such as water, fire, or certain plants, and so on, as well as spirits, demons, and incarnated gods, who are more personified and who appear and speak in visions and behave in a half-human manner. At times the emphasis lies more upon the depersonalized nature power symbols, while at other times it is more upon personified powers. In some religions one aspect is more dominant while in others, the other.

40 An extreme example of the latter is the religious system in its decaying form that is mirrored in the Homeric poems. Mount Olympus and the half-personified Greek gods with their human deficiencies appear in them. By contrast, there was a counter-movement, for example, in Greek natural philosophy where suddenly the whole emphasis was placed upon symbols such as water, said to be the beginning of the world, or fire, in Heraclitus. This was a revivification of the mana idea on a higher level.

41 In Christianity, we have a mixture of both: God the Father and God the Son are usually represented in art as normal human beings, while the Holy Ghost, like God the Father, is sometimes represented as an old man with a beard —an absolute cliché—but frequently also as an animal, which is another form of personification. It can, however, sometimes be represented by fire, wind, water, or as the breath between God the Father and God the Son. So, even in the Bible, the Holy Ghost is likened to such natural phenomena as fire or water or breath. Thus, the Christian god image includes both aspects, and in other religions also there are either a number of human or other gods, so that we probably have to suggest the hypothesis that, in its ultimate, archetypal manifestations, the unconscious sometimes likes to appear symbolized in natural phenomena, while at other times it appears personified. What does this signify?

42 It is a very difficult question. Why, for instance, has someone a concept of God as an invisible, all-pervading fire, while another will imagine Him as having human form? As a small child, one usually thinks of God the Father with a white beard, while later, when one

has acquired a scientific approach to things—and if one thinks of God at all—it would be rather as a meaningful power in the cosmos, or something of that kind. But then we just project our own specific way of looking at things! So far as I can see, it is not true that personified manifestations or images of the gods, or the Godhead, are more infantile.

43 To be able to answer the question, we would be obliged to carefully study a lot of dream material and then, quite apart from this religious problem, ask ourselves what it means if an archetypal content manifests as a ball of fire, instead of as a human being. Let us say that one man dreams of a ball of fire that gives him comfort and enlightenment, while another dreams of a marvelous, wise old man appearing to him, and both are equally overwhelmed. Superficially, you could say that both images symbolize the Self, that is, the totality, the center, a manifestation of the image of God. What is the difference when one man experiences this as light or as a ball of fire, while the other experiences it as a superhuman wise man?

44 ***Answer**: The former would represent the abstract meaning.*

45 Yes, one is more abstract—lat. *abstrahere*—but it is *abstractus* from what?

46 ***Remark**: It would be further from the human.*

47 Yes, *per definitionem*, but how would you reply to an analysand who asked you such a question? We can never give an absolute answer, but we can nevertheless say something about it. I would make it simple and ask the patient and try to encourage him. You can talk to the wise old man —you can ask him questions or present him with all your human problems, for example, whether you should divorce, or if you should spend your money on this or that. Since he appears in this form, you can assume he might know something about that, even though he might say that he is far removed from such things! In any case, the primary feeling, or guess, or attitude that it evokes is that you can relate to such a figure on a human level. But you cannot talk to a ball of fire or make contact with it, except in some natural scientific form—perhaps by catching it in a glass bowl, if that is possible; or you might watch it and see what it does,

or go on your knees and worship it, and keep far enough away so as not to be burnt; or you might go into it and discover that it is a fire that does not burn. But it is not possible to relate to it in a human way.

48 So manifestation in a human form would demonstrate the possibility of conscious relation, whereas an inhuman form, or a natural power form, is just a phenomenon that can only be related to as such. Apparently, whatever the Divine is, it has both aspects, and this has been maintained in most theologies. What is a god to whom you cannot relate? If you cannot tell him anything about your human soul, of what use is he? On the other hand, of what use is a god who is merely a kind of human being, who does not extend beyond that? He also seems to be the completely mysterious Other to which you cannot relate, just as you cannot relate to mysterious phenomena in nature. Therefore, there have probably always been the two aspects of this ultimate, inner centre of the psyche: one that is completely transcendent, that manifests in something as remote as fire or water, and another that sometimes manifests in human form, which would mean that it is approaching in a form to which one could relate.

49 If someone dreams of the godhead as a human being, there will be a great deal of emotional and intuitive feeling experience of this divine presence. In a dream or vision, Niklaus von Flüe had a vision of Christ approaching him as a berserker, and in the same vision the berserker later told people the truth about themselves.[11] He saw into them and what they really were, and people ran away from him. After this vision, Niklaus knew at once what they wanted to ask him, and very often he did not even ask what they wanted but simply gave the answer. Obviously, Niklaus had the same quality as Christ had had in his vision, which illustrates that something belonging to the archetypal unconscious can enter a human being. If you dream of an archetype in a human form, it means that you can incarnate it to some extent. It can manifest in you and can express itself through you—which is the whole idea of the inner Christ. If you dream of a

[11] von Franz, *Niklaus von Flüe*, 81-90.

wise old man, it might happen that you get into an impossible situation where you are asked an impossible question, but suddenly a perfect answer comes to you! If you are honest, you feel obliged to admit afterward that it was not you speaking. "It" spoke through you. You could not claim to have had such a thought, but rather it was the wise old man manifesting in you—someone or something not identical with the ego, but helpful in a difficult situation.

50 ***Question:*** *Why do you necessarily deny identification with the ego?*

51 If you identify with this helpful figure, you get into an inflation. That is why you have to remain humble. If you have made a mental effort, you can say that it was your thought; but it has sometimes happened to me that I have said something, and afterward people have quoted it, saying that I saved their lives by saying that. If I am honest, I reply that I had not realized what I was saying in the moment; I simply said what came to me. That happened to be something much wiser than anything I could have thought. But even if you make the effort, and subjectively have the feeling that you thought it out, it actually came from the unconscious for without its cooperation, you cannot produce anything. Even if you say at 12 o'clock you must remember to do a certain thing, if the unconscious does not call, you will forget it.

52 Actually, any kind of mental insight comes from the unconscious, even if this seems to be an exaggeration, for sometimes you have the feeling that you have worked something out by your own effort, whereas at another time, an idea just comes to you, without any conscious effort. One must be naïve and honest and not be inflated and claim such good ideas for oneself; it was the wise old man, or the Divinity, speaking—if it is confirmed by your dreams. If someone dreams of a wise old man and has such an experience, it is an empirical demonstration. The fire ball will not provide the same experience, though in a way it is even more marvelous, for the person will be much more effected emotionally—he will be overwhelmed, gripped by the mystery, by the complete otherness of the Divine.

53 An experience of the divine is often of an overwhelming power beyond one's own comprehension. It is dangerous, but one has to adapt, just as one has to adapt to a manifestation in nature, such as the explosion of a volcano. It may be a beautiful sight, but one must not get too close; it is impossible to relate to it: One can only look at it. It is something you will never forget. Emotionally it does something to one, but it would need a poet to describe it. This would correspond to the manifestations of the archetype as natural phenomena. In human experience, nature has a numinous and divine aspect, and this explains why the human image of God has both aspects. In most religions there are personifications of God in both forms.

54 In the history of the development of the European mind, a strange kind of enantiodromia and opposition has developed since Grecian times. In the Homeric religion, the personified aspect was exaggerated. In the natural philosophy of pre-Socratic philosophers, the nature aspect was exaggerated. In Stoicism emphasis was laid more upon the nature aspect, while in Christianity there was at first a return to the more personified aspect, but from the 15th and 16th centuries onward, emphasis was again placed on the nature aspect. It seems as if in the development of the European mind, there began a certain balancing of the opposites, namely, of the difference or contrast between science and religion: Science versus religion became the great pseudoproblem of later modern times. I refer to it arbitrarily and derisively as a pseudoproblem because originally it was not a problem, and actually there is only one issue—the search for the ultimate truth. If one returns to that question and says that one's interest is in the truth and not in which faculty of the university it is to be found, then the problem collapses. But as long as some are caught in the projection of the archetype onto representations of nature powers, while others project it onto personified powers, the fight will continue.

55 Some might object, asking how natural scientists could also be caught by projections. To an analyst this is self-evident, but I want to speak briefly to those among you who have perhaps not given

much thought to these things. Whoever has read the history of the development of chemistry, and particularly of physics, will have seen that even such exact natural sciences could not, and still cannot, avoid basing their thought systems on certain hypotheses. In classical physics, up to the end of the 18th century, one of the working hypotheses—arrived at either unconsciously or half-consciously—was that space had three dimensions, an idea that was never questioned. This fact was always accepted, and perspective drawings of physical events, diagrams or experiments were always in accordance with that theory. Only when the theory was abandoned did one wonder how such a thing could ever have been believed! How did one come by such an idea? Why were we so caught that nobody ever doubted or even discussed the matter? It was accepted as a self-evident fact, but what was the root of it? Johannes Kepler, one of the fathers of modern classical physics, said that naturally space must have three dimensions because of the Trinity! So our readiness to believe that space has three dimensions is a more recent offspring of the Christian Trinitarian idea.

56 Further, until now the European scientific mind has been possessed by the idea of causality: that everything was causal—hitherto accepted without question. Scientific procedure demanded that investigations be made with that premise in mind, for there must be a rational cause for everything. If something appeared to be irrational, it was believed that its cause was not yet known. Why were we so dominated by that idea? One of the early fathers of natural science and a great protagonist of the absoluteness of the idea of causality was the French philosopher Descartes, and he based his belief on the *immutability of God.* This doctrine of the immutability of God is a tenet of Christianity: The Divinity is unchanging; there may be no internal contradictions in God, or in new ideas or conceptions. This is the basis of the idea of causality! From the time of Descartes onward this seemed so self-evident to all physicists that there was no question about it. It was indisputable: Science had merely to investigate the causes. We still believe this. If something falls down, one must find out why—the wind must have

blown it or something like that. Half the world is convinced that if you do not have a causal explanation for some circumstance, there must nevertheless be one, and if one does not yet know the cause, there *must* still be one! Our archetypal prejudices are so strong that we cannot defend ourselves against them: They just catch us.

57 Now the idea of causality as formulated by Descartes is responsible for enormous progress in the investigation of light, of biological phenomena, and so on. But the very thing that promotes knowledge later becomes its prison! The great discoveries in natural science have generally been due to the appearance of a new archetypal model through which reality can be described. This usually precedes big developments: A new model enables a much fuller explanation than was hitherto possible. Science has progressed in this way. Nonetheless, any model eventually becomes a cage, for if one comes across phenomena that are difficult to explain, one is often not able to adapt. Instead of admitting that the phenomena do not conform to the model and a new hypothesis must be found, one clings to one's hypotheses with a kind of emotional conviction and cannot be objective. Why shouldn't there be more than three dimensions? Why not investigate and see where we get? But people could not do this at that time.

58 The late physicist Wolfgang Pauli frequently demonstrated the extent to which modern physical sciences are, in a way, rooted in archetypal ideas. I remember a very good illustration given by one of Pauli's pupils. It is well known that the theory of ether played a great role in the 17th and 18th centuries when it was postulated that there was kind of a cosmic airlike pneuma in the cosmos in which light existed, etc. One day, when a physicist at a congress proved that the theory of ether was quite unnecessary, an old man with a white beard got up and said in a quavering voice, "If ether does not exist, then everything is gone!" This old man had unconsciously projected his idea of God into ether. Ether was his god, and if he did not have that, there was nothing left! This man was naïve enough to speak of his ideas, but all natural scientists have ultimate models of reality in which they believe, just like the Holy Ghost.

59 It is a question of belief, not of science, and therefore something that cannot be discussed. People get excited and fanatical if you present them with a fact that does not fit the frame. They are capable of saying that the whole experiment is false and photographs must be produced. It is practically impossible to get them to accept the fact. I knew a physicist whose dreams pointed to a new discovery that he himself had not yet made but which was in the air, so to speak. From his dreams we concluded that his belief in a symmetrical relationship between material things should be given up. The physicist said that such an idea would drive him crazy! But about three months later, exact experimental results were published proving that what he had dreamt was correct and that he would have to drop his former ideas about the cosmic order. This was a catastrophe for him![12]

60 So the archetype is the promoter of ideas, and it is also responsible for the emotional restrictions that prevent the renunciation of earlier theories. It is really only a specific aspect of what happens everywhere in life, for we could not recognize anything without projection, but it is also the main obstacle in arriving at the truth. If one meets an unknown woman, it is not possible to make contact without projecting something, without making a hypothesis, so to speak, which, of course, is done quite unconsciously, for example, "The woman is elderly and probably a kind of mother figure," or "she seems quite normal," etc. You make assumptions and then you have a bridge. When you know the person better, many earlier assumptions must be discarded, and you must admit that your conclusions were incorrect. One is hampered in the relationship until this is done.

61 At first, one has to project, or there is no contact, but then one should be able to correct the projection, and this applies not only to human beings but to everything else as well. The projection apparatus must of necessity work in us, for nothing can even be seen without the unconscious projection factor. That is why, according to

[12] Cf. Letter from Wolfgang Pauli of 5 August 1957 to C. G. Jung in: Wolfgang Pauli, C. A. Meier, and C. G. Jung, eds., *Wolfgang Pauli und C. G. Jung: Ein Briefwechsel 1932-1958* (Berlin/Springer, 1992), 162.

Indian philosophy, all of reality is a projection, which it is, in a subjective manner of speaking. For us, reality exists only when we have projections onto it.

62 ***Question***: *Can you relate without projections?*

63 I don't think so. Philosophically speaking, you cannot relate without projection. There is, however, a subjective feeling status in which you sometimes feel that your projection fits and there is no need to change it; and then, in a different situation, you feel uneasy and sense the need for it to be corrected. But a projection is never corrected without this feeling of uneasiness.

64 Let us assume that there is an unconscious liar within you and you meet someone who lies like a trooper. You can only recognize the liar in the other because you are a liar yourself, for otherwise you would not see through the other. A quality in another person can only be recognized if one has the same quality and knows what it feels like, for example, to tell a lie; only this makes it possible to recognize the same thing in the other person. Insofar as the other person really is a liar, you have made a true statement. Why, then, should you call this a projection that should be taken back? It forms the basis for relationship, for you then think to yourself: If X is a liar, whatever he tells me I must not believe entirely—I must question it. This is very reasonable and well-adapted to the circumstances. It would be very wrong to think it was only one's projection and that one should believe the other person. One would be a fool to do so. But if you take that philosophically, is it then a projection or a fact?

65 Philosophically, you cannot reach a conclusion, for you can only say that subjectively it seems to be correct. That is why Jung says—and this is a subtle point which is seldom understood when people think about projection—that we can only speak of projection, in the proper sense of the word, when a certain uneasiness already exists, when the feeling identity is disturbed and I have an uneasy feeling as to whether or not what I have said about X is true. But as long as everything happens autonomously within me, there is actually no projection.

66 The same thing applies to the natural sciences. For instance, the theory that matter consists of particles is based on the projection of an archetypal image, for a particle is an archetypal image. Energy is also an archetypal image—an intuitive concept with an archetypal background. It is not possible to investigate matter without a hypothesis, like, for example, that there exists something like energy, something like matter and something like particles.

67 But I may meet with phenomena that give me a feeling of uneasiness, for instance, the phenomenon of not being able to fixate particles, i.e., that I cannot say this electron or this meson is at a definite place in a given moment, although if there is such a thing as a particle, it must be at a certain place at a certain time—this seems to be archetypally self-evident. But now modern experiments show that this theory is untenable, that you cannot determine where certain electrons are at a particular moment, so we are confronted with a fact that calls into question our whole idea of the particle. Now we are uneasy and might recognize that when we speak of particles, we are partially projecting—it is a projection that hampers our view of reality. But before this uneasiness arises due to the fact that our projection does not fit—in certain experiments, the particle does not behave as we expect—our concept need not be doubted.

68 So in natural science, just as in interpersonal contacts, there is this same problem of projection: Even the most scientific and most modern and accurate forms of modern natural science are all based on projections. Progress in science is the replacement of a primitive projection by a more accurate one, so that we can say that natural science is concerned with the projections of models of reality into which phenomena seem to fit readily or not. If the phenomena apparently click with my model, all is well, but if not, I must revise my model.

69 How a model relates to reality is a great problem about which there was a famous quarrel between Max Planck and Einstein. Einstein claimed that the human mind was capable of inventing mathematical models of reality on paper. In this, he was generalizing his own experience because that is just what he used to

do. Einstein conceived his theories more or less completely on paper, and later experimental developments in physics proved that his models explained the phenomena very well. Thus, according to Einstein, the fact that a model constructed by the human mind in an introverted situation fits with outer facts is simply a miracle and must be taken as such. Planck did not agree and rather thought that we conceive a model that we check by experiment, after which we revise our model, so that there is a kind of dialectic friction between experiment and model by which we slowly arrive at an explanatory fact compounded of the two. This is Plato-Aristotle in a new form! But both have forgotten something—namely the unconscious! Today we know something that those two men did not yet know at that time, namely that when Einstein makes a new model of reality, he is helped by his unconscious. Without it, he would not have arrived at his theories.

70 But what role does the unconscious actually play? The unconscious seems to deliver models that one can arrive at directly from within, without looking at outer facts, which afterward seem to fit outer reality. Is this a miracle or not? There are two possible explanations: Either the unconscious knows about other realities, or what we call the unconscious is part of the same thing as outer reality. We do not know how the unconscious is linked to matter. If a wonderful idea occurs to me about, for example, how gravity can be explained, can I say that the nonmaterial unconscious gave me a wonderful idea about material reality, or should I say that the unconscious gave me such a marvelous idea of outer reality because it is itself linked with matter, because it is a phenomenon of matter and matter knows matter?

71 There we are at our wits' end and do not know how to proceed. We have to leave the question open and admit that the great unknown is that we do not know how the unconscious is linked to matter. At this point we are stuck and we do not know how we should proceed with our research. We can propose two hypotheses. Jung was inclined to think—though he never formulated the thought, or only very hypothetically, because we cannot do more

than to speculate or make a hypothesis—that probably the unconscious has a material aspect, which is why it knows about matter, because it is matter—matter that knows itself, as it were. If this were so, then there would be a dim or vague phenomenon of consciousness even in inorganic matter.

72 Here we are touching upon great mysteries, but I speak of them because it is too cheap to say that the old alchemist, i.e., the natural scientist of antiquity or the Middle Ages, projected unconscious images into matter, but nowadays we are enlightened and know what the unconscious and matter are, but those poor fellows just did not distinguish between the two, which explains why they were so backward and fanatical and unscientific! The psyche/matter problem has not yet been solved, which is why the basic riddle of alchemy is still not solved. The answer to the question the alchemists pursued we have also not discovered. We still have projections onto many things, just as the alchemists did onto matter, but we prefer to speak of their projections of the unconscious as naïve, for we have outgrown those models. We can still recognize them as phenomena of the unconscious, as dream material, but we no longer accept them as being scientific statements. For instance, if someone says that lead contains a demon, we can say that he is projecting the shadow and demonic human qualities into lead, but we can no longer claim that lead contains a demon, for there we have outgrown the projection. We now draw different conclusions about how and why lead is harmful to us.

73 Basically, however, alchemy is still an open problem to us, and when Jung came across it, he felt that he was touching upon something that would lead further but that he did not yet know where. I think this is also partly why people have such resistance to alchemy: It confronts us with something we cannot yet understand. But that is a good thing, for it throws us back upon ourselves and forces us to adopt the more modest attitude of having to describe phenomena in accordance with our present knowledge.

Lecture 2

74 In my introduction to date, I have tried to give you an idea of the importance of alchemical symbolism. A whole series of archetypal symbols that do not depict human forms, but rather symbolic images of matter, play a very special role. For man, these images—for example, water, fire and metal—are just as important symbolically as any personified representations of the unconscious. Moreover, in alchemy no distinction is made between the unconscious psyche and matter; religion, magic and the natural sciences are not yet divided. We are confronted with the original situation, where all the faculties and categories with which we observe outer and inner nature are not yet differentiated. Man as a whole looks at nature as a whole and makes certain working hypotheses in his search for the truth.

75 Furthermore, it has been pointed out that, as we have outgrown the early stages of natural science, we can now recognize much that was formerly said about the different materials and processes in matter as projections of the unconscious—even though no definite conclusions can be made about certain assertions. For instance, in a medieval document attributed to Albert the Great there is a theory about heavy water that looks like a completely intuitive anticipation of the heavy water we now know. Therefore, this symbolism also contains vague intuitions that anticipated later scientific discoveries and developments; nevertheless, we still do not know all that was anticipated, for we do not know what further discoveries will be made by natural scientists.

76 Ultimately, the question as to whether and how the unconscious is in some way connected with matter is, as I said, quite unanswered. We do not want to speculate and so refrain from making statements; we merely put forward a hypothesis that there is a psyche that

manifests in dreams and in involuntary psychological expressions that we can study, just as physicists say that there is something like matter, or energy, and study that. But we are beginning to see that certain results are so similar that it is as if we are tunneling from either side toward the center of the same mountain. Though we have not really met yet, it looks as though we are moving toward the same goal; there is, therefore, the possibility of meeting one day.

77 The most important point I stressed was, perhaps, that, in their experiments and also in their written descriptions of what they could observe, the alchemists worked without any conscious religious or scientific program. Their conclusions are thus spontaneous, uncorrected impressions of the unconscious with very little conscious interference. This is quite in contrast to other symbolic material that had always been revised. It is therefore very gratifying to discover that this spontaneous material is akin to certain products of the unconscious in modern people. With a natural kind of scientific attitude, a minimum of prejudice, and an attitude of inner withdrawal, and by only observing what comes up without drawing hasty speculative conclusions, one can see that the results are very similar. This approach of having no program is common to both alchemy and analytical psychology.

78 Before we discuss one of the oldest known alchemical texts, namely one from the prophetess Isis to her son Horus, in which the sign of the sickle moon appears behind the title, we should firstly consider how we came to be in possession of such texts at all.

79 As we know, all ancient alchemical reports disappeared in the Middle Ages and were then rediscovered. First, the critical sciences found them in large tomes. For instance, the history of philosophy and philology was collected in late antiquity into books that we would call encyclopedias, or into schoolbooks that had summaries like: Plato says…, Aristotle says…, the Stoic philosophers say…, and so on. Unfortunately, compared to our modern critical scientists, these people were rather muddled, and their theories were presented accordingly, making the whole thing resemble a stream of muddy water. What we have fallen heir to here are more ancient and more

recent writings and texts that can no longer be differentiated from the commentaries, for they have been copied and recopied, rearranged and abbreviated so often. In the uncritical Middle Ages, a selection was made of these texts that were again quoted. Chemistry met with a like fate.

80 Olympiodorus, for instance, of the fifth century, put together a volume containing a collection of older discourses. We have many different works of this kind, as well as separate writings. They were all reassembled and put into one huge Greek manuscript in Venice and accordingly received the title of the *Codex Marcianus* (Marciana being the library in Venice). Assembled in this *Codex Marcianus* is a whole conglomeration of old and more recent Greek and other source texts, and it is more or less as it was when the famous Marcellin Berthelot published it.[13] He published it without adding much textual criticism and, together with Charles Ruelle, added a rather superficial French translation; it could thus at last be printed and a discussion started. More versions and manuscripts have been collected since then, but it is still the most important edition and the definitive basic text.

81 To try and decide who was who, who wrote what, and the age of the different writings would be pure speculation—some speak of the first and others of the third century, differing by as much as three hundred years in their estimates—and very little order has been added to it. As with all natural sciences, there were firstly direct Greek traditions from Constantinople. From the 10th century onward, another stream of scientific tradition came to Europe from the Orient via Spain, Southern France and Sicily at a time when Europe had become connected to the Orient through the Crusades. The history of chemistry is completely identical with that of mathematics, geometry and astrology. Thus, some of it came via the Byzantine Empire, via Constantinople, and the rest came to Europe via the Orient and the Arabs.

---

[13] Marcellin Berthelot, *Collection des anciens alchimistes grecs*, vol. 1 (Paris: Steinheil, 1887); and Berthelot, *Collection des anciens alchimistes grecs: Text grec*, vol. 1 (Paris: Steinheil, 1888); and Berthelot, *Collection des alchimistes grecs: Traduction,* vol. 2 (Paris: Steinheil, 1888).

82 In general, the Arabs were very faithful translators and added very little; they simply translated from Greek into Arabic. Centers were established in the Orient, where these texts were translated, some of them in Persia, and we know of many famous Syrian translators. Today we have Greek and Arabic and later Latin texts, and where the original Greek text was lost, we still have the Arabic text from which we can conclude from the names, etc., that the original was in Greek. In these Arabic, Moslem centers were different sects that cultivated these traditions; for instance, the Shiites, a Persian sect, formed in 644 A.D. in opposition to the Sunnites, the orthodox Muslims; or, for example, the Druses, a half Christian and half Muslim people whose language was pure Arabic. Already in these Islamic centers some Arabs recognized that these alchemical texts were full of symbolism and that they were of a more religious rather than chemical nature. Occasionally they added a little from their own experience, but most often they were happy just to translate.

83 One of the most famous of the Arabs who developed the sciences on the chemical side was ar Razi, or Rasis in Latin. He was the famous man who introduced the necessity of weighing matter into chemistry. Formerly, it was simply said, "Put a little bit of sulphur into a little bit of lead, and then you have it." But Razi said, "A little bit can make all the difference! You must take so many parts, or so many ounces of each." Stipulating exact weights and division was an accomplishment that meant a great step forward for accurate natural science. Much merit is due to him in this respect, but none on the symbolic side for he was a pure technician.

84 Mohammed ibn Umail was a different story. In the Arabic world, he was called the Sheik, which in Latin was translated as Senior, "the old one," which would be the correct translation, so that he became Senior in the Latin tradition, and only later was it discovered that this Senior was Mohammed ibn Umail. About 100 writings of this most important mystic have been found in Hyderabad, but they have not yet been published. Though it is such promising material, so few people are interested in alchemy that nobody has bothered about

their translation or publication. There are gold mines in store and nobody to work on them![14]

85 A few small additions have been made to these original texts, and as already mentioned, there was a kind of return through the Crusades. One of the intellectual bridges to Europe was via the Templars, who were closely connected to the Druses, a more mystical and pagan sect within the Islamic world. They were the subjects of the "Old Man of the Mountains," the Imam and leader of the sect. They had a whole hierarchy of initiation, and the Templars became interested in the symbolism of their doctrine. It was probably in Jerusalem that these Druses got into close contact with certain High Templars and their so-called pagan practices, for which they were later persecuted. They were also influenced by the pagan teachings of Frederic II, the Holy Roman Emperor, at whose court in Sicily—to the great annoyance of the pope—were Jewish and Islamic astrologers and mathematicians and prophets.

86 It was in this way, as well as through the famous island of Rhodes where the Knights of St. John had a connection with the Orient and such places as Spain and southern France, that these writings came to Europe and were translated into Latin by Jewish and other translators. Thus, this natural scientific tradition began to spread throughout Europe. The Church, represented chiefly by Albert the Great and St. Thomas of Aquinas, but certain others as well, endeavored to eliminate this double tradition of Church and natural science, and to assimilate and integrate the whole into the Church doctrine. It was, however, only partly successful in its attempt.

87 This concludes my short resumé of the historical situation and the material we are going to be dealing with.

[14] Published since then: Theodor Abt, Wilfred Madelung, and Thomas Hofmeier, eds., *Book of the Explanation of the Symbols. Kitab Hall ar-Rumuz by Muhammad Ibn Umail,* vol. 1, CALA (Zurich: Living Human Heritage, 2003); and Marie-Louise von Franz, *Book of the Explanation of the Symbols Kitab Hall ar-Rumuz by Muhammad Ibn Umail. Psychological Commentary by Marie-Louise von Franz,* vol. 1A, CALA, ed. By Theodor Abt and Wilfred Madelung (Zurich: Living Human Heritage, 2006).

Part 1

Greek Alchemy

The Prophet Isis to Her Son

88 We shall now turn our attention to Greek alchemy and begin with an ancient Greek text from the *Codex Marcianus*.[1] It probably belongs to what we call the oldest writings and is entitled *The Prophetess Isis to Her Son*.[2] We know that her son is Horus, although the title does not say so. Behind the title is the sign of the sickle moon, but what that means nobody knows. I will present the material without speculation so that it can have a fresh impact, without paying attention to what has already been said about it. I am not using the French translation by Marcellin Berthelot, but rather my own.[3]

89 The document probably goes back to about the first century A.D., at least that is the *communis opinio* of the scientists, but it might be older. If you read what has been written about these books, you will find it said that they were most probably written in such and such a century and were certainly based on older texts, which implies some uncertainty. So let us just say that the text goes back to the Hellenistic period.

90 So, Isis is addressing her son—whose name now appears in the text. As a reader, you might recall the famous battle in which Seth blinded Horus and that Horus cut off Seth's testicles; and perhaps you recall that both were later healed by the moon god Toth and that they even cooperated in the resurrection of their father, Osiris. You might also recollect the famous battle of Horus, the sun god who restored order, with Seth, called the Hot One, who represented

---

[1] Berthelot, *Collection des anciens alchimistes grecs: Text grec*, vol. 1, 28-33; and Berthelot, *Collection des alchimistes grecs: Traduction*, vol. 2, 31-36.

[2] Cf. also the interpretations in: Marie-Louise von Franz, *On Dreams and Death: A Jungian Interpretation*, trans. Emmanuel Xipolitas Kennedy and Vernon Brooks (Boston: Shambhala, 1986), 11-23.

[3] Cf. also the translation of the text that Marie-Louise von Franz was also involved with in: Jung, *Alchemical Studies*, vol. 13, *CW* (Princeton, NJ: Princeton University Press, 1983), § 99; 107, 109.

chaotic passion, destruction, brutality, and so on, who was the enemy and murderer of Osiris. Thus, Isis begins,

91 Oh, my son, when you desired to go away to fight the treacherous Typhon [i.e., Seth][4] over your father's kingdom [the kingdom of Osiris], I went to Hormanouthi,[5] i.e., Hermoupolis, the town of Hermes, the town of the holy technique of Egypt, and stayed there for some time.

92 After the words "the town of Hermes," there is a little marginal note, written in the original hand that says, "She means that in a mystical sense." This means that the name of the town should be understood in a mystical sense. "The holy technique" —*hiera techne*—refers to alchemy.

93 After a certain passing of the kairoi and the necessary movement of the heavenly sphere, it happened that one of the angels who dwelt in the first firmament saw me from above and came towards me, desiring to unite with me sexually. He was in a great hurry for this to happen, but I did not submit to him, but rather resisted, for I wished to ask him about the preparation of gold and silver.

94 The *kairos* plays an enormous role in another very old alchemical text where the writer Zosimos, whom we know of through Jung's comments,[6] says that the whole of alchemy depends upon the *kairos*. He even calls the alchemical operation the *kairikai baphai,* the *kairos* coloring.[7] His theory is that chemical processes do not always happen of themselves, but only at the astrologically right moment. If I am working with silver, the moon, which is the planet of silver, must be in the right position, and if I am working with copper, Venus

---

[4] The squared brackets within a quotation include comments by Marie-Louise von Franz.

[5] The Horus temple at Edfu.

[6] Cf. Jung, "The Visions of Zosimos," in *Alchemical Studies,* vol. 13, *CW*, §§85-144; and Jung, "Zosimos and the Doctrine of the Anthropos," in: *Psychology and Alchemy*, vol. 12, *CW*, §§ 456-61.

[7] Cf. Zosime de Panopolis in Michèle Mertens, ed., *Les Alchimistes Grecs*, (Paris: Les Belles Lettres, 1995), 62.

has to be in a certain constellation, for otherwise these operations in silver and copper will not work. One cannot just take two metals and unite them but must also consider and wait for the astrological constellation and pray to the gods of those planets, and only when these things are also in order can the chemical operation work. Taking the astrological constellation into consideration is what is meant by this idea of *kairikai baphai.*

95 *Kairos* at the time and in this connection means the astrologically right time, the time when things can turn out successfully. The alchemist must not only know the technique but must always consider these constellations.

96 Therefore, Isis says that according to the passing of time,[8] (one moment follows the next and one has to choose the right moment) and according to the movement of the heavenly sphere (which means all the movements of the planets), it happened (the Greek word *synebe* is also a synchronistic happening of events) that one of the angels of the first firmament cast an eye upon her and wanted to unite with her sexually. She puts him off because she wants to get the alchemical secret out of him and she makes a bargain with him: She will only give herself to him if he first tells her all he knows about it.

97 When I put my question, he said he did not wish to answer me since it was such a great mystery [the superlatively great mystery – to give a freer translation – because this mystery is simply too overwhelming, too tremendous], but said he would return the next day and with him would be a greater angel, Amnael, who would be able to answer my question and solve my problem. And he told me about his sign [meaning probably how she should recognize the angel] that he would bear on his head, and show me: a ceramic vessel full of shining water. He [the other angel] wants to tell me the truth. This vessel is uncaulked: it has no pitch in it.

[8] Cf. von Franz, *Dreams and Death,* 12-13.

98 I am giving the text exactly as it is, and here in the margin of the text there is this sign {publisher: see sign in book p. 45}, and we know that this is a sign of the god Chnouphis. Sometimes the same sign is also used for the moon god Chons.

> 99 The next day, when the sun was in the middle of its course [at midday] there came down the angel who was greater than the other, and he was gripped by the same desire for me and made advances towards me. [He too wanted to rape Isis.] I, however, only wanted to ask him my question. [She again delays, thinking only of her question.] When he stayed with me, I did not give myself to him. I resisted him and overcame his desire till he showed me the sign on his head, and gave me the tradition of the mysteries without keeping anything back, but in full truth. [So she wins the battle and he tells her all he knows about the technique of alchemy.] He then again pointed to the sign, the vessel he carried on his head, and began to speak of the mysteries and the message. Then he first spoke the great oath and said, 'I adjure you, in the name of heaven and earth, of the light and darkness; I adjure you in the name of fire, of water, of air and of the earth [twice a quaternio]; I adjure you in the name of the height of heaven and the depth of the underworld; I adjure you, in the name of Hermes and Anubis, in the howling of Kerkoros and the guardian dragon; I adjure you, in the name of that boat and its ferryman, Acharontos, and I adjure you in the name of the three necessities and the whips and the sword.' After he had pronounced his oath, he made me promise under oath never to tell the mystery I was now to hear, except to my son, my child, and my closest friend, for then you are me, and I am you.

100 The text is rather short. It means that it is a tremendous mystery that Isis now gets from the angel, one that she may only tell to her son Horus and closest friend. Whether her son is her closest friend, or there are two people, is not clear from the grammar. Nor is it clear

whether "for then you are me, and I am you" means "you, my son, are me" or whether it is referring to the angel and Isis, but probably both apply. It simply means that the person who imparts that mystery to the other person simultaneously fulfills the mystical union, the sacred marriage, between mother and son, Isis and Horus, or the union between the angel and Isis, because each time the mystery is told, the two also become one. That is probably the meaning.

101 Now you go and watch and ask Archeron the peasant. [One variation calls him Acharontos. There is no transition here in the text, but probably from now on we are hearing the mystery. Unfortunately, in those days they had no punctuation, no way to indicate quotations. One never knows where the quotes should be, but I think it is obvious that it begins here. It means that now the mystery will be imparted and one should listen closely.] Come and look, and ask the peasant Acharontos, and learn from him who is the sower and who is the harvester, and learn that he who sows barley will harvest barley and he who sows wheat will harvest wheat. Now my child, or my son, you have heard that as an introduction, and now realize from that, this is the whole of creation and the whole process of coming into being, and know that a man is only able to produce a man, and a lion a lion, and a dog a dog, and if something happens contrary to nature [probably meaning contrary to this law], then it is miraculous and cannot continue to exist because nature enjoys nature, and nature overcomes nature. [This is the famous saying that appears in many other texts, but usually as, 'Nature enjoys nature, nature *impregnates* nature, and nature overcomes nature.'[9]] Having part of the divine power and being happy about its divine presence, I will now

[9] Cf. Jung, *Aion: Research into the Phenomenology of the Self*, 2nd ed., vol. 9/II, *CW* (Princeton, NJ: Princeton University Press, 1978), § 244.

> also answer their questions about sands,[10] which one does not prepare from other substances, for one must stay with existing nature and with the matter one has in hand in order to prepare things. Just as I said before, wheat creates wheat, and a man begets a man, and thus gold, too, will harvest gold, like produces like. Now I have manifested the mystery to you.

102 At the beginning of the next section, it is strangely in the plura—"we will prepare" and so on. This plural form possibly means that Isis and Horus are already together. Then comes a classical beginning that was common for ancient recipes. In German, it begins, "Man nehme...," and in Greek with *"labon."* Here it begins,

103 Take quicksilver, fix it in lumps of earth or by magnesium or sulphur and retain it. [This is a fixation through warmth, the mixture of ingredients.] Take one part of lead and of the preparation fixed through warmth, and two parts of the white stone, and from the same stone one part, and one part of yellow Realgar [that means red sulphur of arsenic] and one part of the green stone [one does not know what that is]. Mix the whole with lead, and when it has disintegrated, reduce it three times to a liquid [i.e., melt it three times].

104 Take quicksilver that has become white through copper, and take from it another one part and from dominant magnesia, with one part of water, and from what remained at the bottom of the vessel that has been treated with lemon juice, use one part, and from arsenic which has been catalyzed with the urine of a not yet corrupted boy, one part, and then from Cadmeia [cadmia, calamine in English, which simply implies a mineral which engenders fire] one part and one part from pyrite [also a mineral that engenders fire] one part, and one

[10] Berthelot, *Collection des alchimistes grecs: Traduction,* vol. 2, 33. Translates "certains minéras mételliques." Vol. III, p. 33 translates "certains minéras mételliques."

> part from sand cooked with sulphur, and from lead monoxide with asbestos two parts, and from the ashes of Kobathia [that is probably also an arsenic sulphite] one part, and liquefy the whole with a very sharp acid, a white acid, and dry it, and then you have the great white remedy.

105 This continues for two more pages; I will take the liberty of shortening it, although I want to give a sense of what such recipes were like for up till now, we have not known what these words mean. Naturally chemists have made a profound study of the texts and with a certain probability have been able to make out which Greek words might mean which substance, since in some cases there is a little description showing that they have such and such an effect, from which the chemist could deduce that a certain definite substance was indicated. But in the case of a number of other words, for instance Kobathia that I have translated as "the green stone," and the word that I did not translate but left as "magnesia," though it was not what we now mean by magnesia, we really do not know what they mean. We are fairly sure they referred to some cooked chemical substances, but they are so paradoxically described in the different texts that we cannot be certain.

106 Then there is a quite different material, namely the urine of an uncorrupted boy. Naturally, urine also contains important and corrosive substances and was used a lot, but the fact that it must be of an uncorrupted boy, one who has not yet reached the age of puberty, also shows what a large part magical representations played. It is a general prejudice, or an ancient superstition, that the urine of uncorrupted boys is particularly efficient, not only in chemical operations but also in love charms, etc., where it is more efficacious than ordinary urine. It has something magical in it.

107 I am singling this out because here we know something more from other fields. For instance, we know that it was an African and also particularly an Egyptian tradition to use the urine of an uncorrupted boy for magical purposes. Shortly before puberty, boys are more gifted mediums, a faculty they lose later on. Magicians who

Figure 1
Boy urinating

practiced hypnotism very often used other people as mediums, putting them to sleep so they would reveal the truth. In ancient times, children—sometimes girls, but more often boys—who had not reached the age of puberty were preferred for such very widespread magical experiments. Uncorrupted boys were regarded as being purer vessels of the unconscious through which ghosts and gods could speak. There are innumerable magic recipes where, for instance, it is said, "If you wish to find something that has been stolen, put an uncorrupted boy to sleep: cook such and such a thing and give it to him to eat, and when he is asleep, ask him where the lost object is." While in a trance, he will tell you. That was the role of the uncorrupted boy in another context and therefore probably the urine of an uncorrupted boy has the same connotation here, where it is also regarded as the magical substance, since they have the same associations in mind.

108 ***Remark***: *A parallel to Isis having the alchemical mysteries revealed to her by the angel would be the fallen angel, Azazel, giving the Jews knowledge of the blacksmith's art. The professor at the E.T.H. who lectured on alchemy at an Eranos meeting said that the idea that the smith was connected with alchemy originated in Tobalki.*[11]

109 Yes. In the book of Enoch, there is a whole description of all the techniques delivered by the angels. Originally, the art of the smith at the forge and that of the alchemist were regarded as being the same, though I think the Tobalki idea is rather arbitrary. But it is a tradition. In the Old Testament it is said that the daughters of men got the art of the forge and alchemy either from the angels or from the fallen angels, either through whoredom, or, as in this case, its opposite, for Isis at least puts him off until she has got out of him what she wants to know. So there are different versions. Sometimes it is said that the daughters of men had relationships not with angels but with giants, so angels are sometimes replaced by giants.

110 The text continues for over a page with these recipes and then turns to operations. I will cite a little to give the feel of it.

> 111 If you want to make something white of the bodies [i.e., the material], mix it with quicksilver and drops of asbestos and urine and goat's milk and natron, and then you can make everything work, and if you want to know how to double a substance, or how to colour the material, and what all the dispositions are, then [and this is important] know that everything has the same meaning, that everything tends to have the same meaning [i.e., the meaning is likely to always be the same for the same operation]. Now realize the mystery, my son, the remedy, the elixir of the widow.

112 Isis is frequently referred to as the widow in the text and the mystery—the *lapis philosophorum*—in alchemy is, from the beginning, referred to as the mystery of the widow, the stone of the

[11] Here it is misunderstood, cf. Rudolf Bernoulli, "Seelische Entwicklung im Spiegel der Alchemie und verwandter Disziplinen, " in *Westöstliche Seelenführung*, Eranos-Jahrbuch 1935, ed. Olga Fröbe-Kapteyn, vol. 3. (Zurich: Rhein-Verlag, 1936), 236.

widow, or the orphan's stone. There was a connection between the widow and the orphan, but it all points to Isis. The text ends with another recipe:

113 Take arsenic, cook it in water, mix it with olive oil, and then leave it in a bottle and put coals on it until it steams and the same thing can be done with Realgar...

114 Here the text breaks off and is then repeated all over again. Here we see what we are up against! Sometimes a formula varies a little: A man may not be called Acharontos, but Acharos, and so on, but otherwise it is exactly the same. (Acharontos is quite a problem that will be gone into later.)

115 I would now like to discuss the text further and to amplify it bit by bit in order to find out what it could mean. A general amplification for the first part, or rather for the whole structure of the tale, has already been mentioned, namely that it is a parallel to the book of *Enoch*. There it is said that all arts and crafts, as well as cosmic tricks, and so on, were stolen from the angels or, according to other versions, from giants. In other words, at first the angels, or the giants, had them, and then the women were given them by them. In our text it is not the women but Isis who is given the knowledge by the angel and who then imparts it to Horus.

116 What does this myth mean psychologically? All evil comes from women, as we know from *Genesis* and the story of Eve, who was also closer to the problem of how to get knowledge from God. In that story she got it from the snake and then imparted it to Adam. This was also theft, for God wanted to keep knowledge of Himself to Himself, and afterward man was able to differentiate between good and evil, as God did. Thus, in *Genesis*, God's secret is stolen, and once again by a woman. This theft is looked upon as being pure evil, and in the book of *Enoch*, the theft of the technique by women is colored in the same way, namely, that the theft of these secrets has played a part in the corruption of our world and to the loss of the world's original innocence. But in our text the feeling is quite

changed, for when Isis succeeds in getting the secret from those angels, it is seen as a great achievement. So here we have a switch in the feeling judgment, even though the event itself seems to be a very close parallel: The female element, the feminine principle, receives knowledge from deeper layers and is then the mediator who hands it on to mankind.

117 In the story of Eve, we can recognize the symbolism of the anima for the story is even truer for the anima than just for women, and in our text this same idea is expressed symbolically from the unconscious. The goddess Isis has the sign of the moon beside her. In these late times, Isis was identified with Hathor, the cow goddess, with the moon goddess, and with the sky goddess, Nut. In late Egyptian religion she is a kind of cosmic feminine goddess who embraces all the other goddesses of ancient Egypt and who is, so to speak, the great carrier of the mystery of nature. She embraces all of nature. In the novel *The Golden Ass* by Apuleius, Isis is addressed as "*Domina rerum,*" ruler of all cosmic nature, for in those late times she was worshipped as the personification of cosmic nature.[12] In our text she does not appear directly as a goddess, but rather as a prophetess—"Isis prophetis." That she is also a prophetess is naturally stressed because she anticipates future developments. She tells the truth, which then comes to pass; she imparts the truth that was previously hidden.

118 ***Question****: I am still vague as to the relevance of this to the total motive or purpose of Jungian psychology. I see that you have spent some energy and effort on this text. Now do I hear you say that this is relevant in terms of the interpretation of the symbolism of one's dreams?*

119 Yes, certainly. If you have a man in analysis who dreams that a mysterious woman comes toward him—I remember such a dream that was the initial dream of a man who had a sex problem, although I do not know exactly what, for he was not my analysand. In his dream a wonderful woman who made a great impression on him

---

[12] Cf. Jung, *The Structure and Dynamics of the Psyche*, 2nd ed., vol. 8, *CW* (Princeton, NJ: Princeton University Press, 1981), § 414.

told him that the whole secret consisted in drying the powder within the apple.

120 ***Question***: *So the point would be the relevance this had to the person's life?*

121 Yes. Suppose a man comes to analysis with a sexual problem—he is impotent or a Don Juan. We may say that we will see what the unconscious says about it. Colleagues have told him long ago what can be said consciously, but he tells you that it has not helped him and he is at the end of his tether. He says he knows that he has a mother complex, but nothing has changed! Apparently that does not help! So one says, "Let's look at the dreams!" And then in a dream a marvelous woman appears and tells him that it is all the problem of drying the white powder in the apple. He thinks that is rubbish, but one has to be able to say something to him about it. He will not give any associations, for most often people cannot give associations to their archetypal dreams. White powder in an apple does not suggest anything to the man; he might at best say that he likes apples. When one gets nothing out of an analysand, one has to know mankind's associations. If one can get the analysand's associations, so much the better, but such motifs in a dream generally draw a blank and one has to point out, for instance, that mankind has always believed that the apple contains the knowledge of God, of good and evil. One recalls the Bible, and that people always said that the apple renewed the secrets. One tells the analysand in question a few relevant myths about it, and then he begins to get impatient and says, "Yes, but what does that mean for me?" Comparing the myths shows that there are other valuations than in the Bible where eating an apple, that is, acquiring knowledge, is taken to be an accident and the Fall of Man. Only in later Catholic interpretation is there the *felix culpa* that says, "Thank God Adam and Eve sinned for otherwise Christ could not have redeemed us." But originally the feeling tone was that Adam was corrupted through Eve and everything then went wrong. Even the Church always said that Mary put everything right and Eve everything wrong. Eve is only tolerable because things were put right later, but the feeling in the Old Testament is that the origin of all evil

is Eve's sin, and that it was very unfortunate that Adam and Eve ate that apple. In our text, however, it is an achievement for now Isis has been given the marvelous secret by the angel and she is going to tell her son about it. The text tells us that a lion generates a lion, and this is what Isis tells as the secret.

122 As already indicated, this story is analogous to the biblical story, but with a completely different feeling judgment. In the Bible, obtaining the secret from the angels is seen as a corrupting accident, while here it is described as a wonderful achievement and nothing is said about everything now going wrong with the world because the secret has been revealed, but rather it is so marvelous that Isis will only tell her son and her best friend about it.

123 If one wanted to give a psychological interpretation, what would this difference mean? Mankind is quite divided on the question of how to evaluate the origin of science and technology, the origin of chemistry and of the natural sciences, and of having knowledge *per se*. Does knowledge corrupt, or does it help?

124 ***Remark**: It seems to me that the Bible says that knowledge—which is what the apple represents—is corruptive in itself.*

125 Yes, through the apple of knowledge we got thrown out of Paradise.

126 ***Question**: Are you looking at knowledge as belonging to God?*

127 Yes, it is identification with God, which is why taking on this knowledge constitutes an act of inflation. The ego seized something that did not belong to it, became inflated and lost its balance, and everything went wrong. But here, in the Isis story, the evaluation is entirely opposite, for *we* have made great progress, *we* have got the secret out of the angels. This is something so immense that I will only tell my son and my friend about it. There is no mention of inflation or bad luck.

128 In this text there is the opposite of the religious tradition and natural sciences *in nuce*. Have the techniques and natural sciences we have attained brought us misfortune? Have they only corrupted man's original state, or are they an indication of progress? It is something much deeper, for it concerns an increase of conscious-

ness, a development of human consciousness. Is that advantageous to us or not? Are we getting worse and worse by becoming more conscious, becoming increasingly estranged from nature and losing our balance, or is it the one thing that we must do? If we try to become conscious, do we fulfill the will of God, or go contrary to it? That is the real question. We are dealing with a religious projection and, if we put it more humbly and psychologically, with a discussion as to whether or not an increase of consciousness is progress.

129 Some analysands—both men and women—often think that it might be better to let sleeping dogs lie. Why should one dig up problems about which the more you think, the more muddled you become? Leave it to nature, and the problems will right themselves somehow. For example, a young man who had a mother fixation and who did not want to leave home came for analysis. From his dreams, I showed him that obviously he should pull away from his mother. A short while later, she came storming in, asking why we dig up such things and destroy the family's harmony, why we say such things to her son and destroy their good contact—the whole family was upset, and the boy was no better!

130 So, is an increase of consciousness a good thing or a bad thing? We therapists need to ask ourselves that question every time! This is necessary even in everyday life, for example, when someone speaks to you in the train and asks you what you do professionally, and if you say you are a psychoanalyst, they say that is very interesting and that they have had a dream and will tell it to you. Perhaps they think dreams mean nothing, but the dream shows the man's problem, and you wonder whether you should give him a drop of the poison of knowledge by giving him an idea as to what it really means, or whether one should just make it clear that it is not a consultation.

131 Knowledge is either poisonous or healing—either one or the other—and that is why some myths say that knowledge brings out the corruption of the world and others that knowledge is healing. According to the Bible, it firstly brings corruption, but later, thank God, it turns into healing. In the Old Testament it meant corruption,

but Christ made something out of it that turned it into healing. As a result, a double attitude imposed itself: the teaching of the *felix culpa*.

132 In an actual situation, however, you cannot assume a double attitude but must face the terrible problem every time: Shall I tell them, or not? You carry the whole ethical responsibility, and each time you do not know whether you have done the right or the wrong thing. It is the problem of consciousness! What should man do with his consciousness? How should he handle it? If I am conscious of what a dream means, how should I handle it? Shall I use it as poison or as a healing factor? Consciousness, or knowledge, is a terrific problem that we have to take very seriously, one that we have not at all solved yet.

133 ***Remark:*** *We never will solve it, for it is a problem we have to learn to live with.*

134 Yes, that's true, but formulated like that, it is just a generalization. One must go into it more deeply and adopt a more specific attitude, for otherwise one can be sloppy about it and say that it is a problem one will always have since one is a psychotherapist, but it is a problem of relationship. It *is* a problem and one that we have to take seriously and not just dismiss. In general terms, you can say that it is the problem of mankind, for man is that strange invention of nature that carries a new form of consciousness. Anthropologists say that man is distinguished by the phenomenon of consciousness, but that we do not quite know how to evaluate this quality. Is one to experience it as a curse or as a blessing?

135 Our text, with which we are at the beginning of the natural sciences in the European tradition, gives an entirely positive answer to this question. It comes from pagan sources without any Judaeo-Christian influence, but with Egyptian and Greek influence, and there is an entirely positive evaluation. When you analyze modern man, for instance, modern physicists, you are repeatedly confronted with a type of man who has this same attitude. He believes in science and that he will help mankind by his additional discoveries. So here we have the same attitude and situation. Therefore, it is interesting

to study the unconscious symbolism of such a trend for it is again present in our time and is much discussed.

136 I am very pleased to be asked such questions because these things have to be brought into reality. You may ask why dig up these heavy old texts with all their complications. But we need to realize that here are the roots of both the good ideas and the prejudices of our culture! If we do not discuss the basic prejudices of our civilization, we shall never come to understand other points of view. We must know what prejudices we have, though we may still choose to keep them, saying that we like them, but we should be aware that one can think differently, that opinions do differ! Such broadness of mind is necessary if one wishes to analyze people objectively and not be the propagandist of one trend; an analyst should be broad-minded and see what the inner nature of the analysand constellates as a healing process, wherever it leads. This at least is our conviction.

137 ***Question****: How does this attitude toward knowledge compare with an ancient Promethean attitude?*

138 That is a very good question. The Greek myth of Prometheus mirrors the typical Greek attitude and, unlike the Bible, does not primarily make it an ethical problem of good or evil. In it, too, there is a theft from the gods. Fire is stolen, something that the gods wanted to keep to themselves. According to the myth, Prometheus, who was the robber, must be punished. Certainly, he gets into great difficulties, and things do not go well for him, but there is no moral evaluation. This is a different nuance. The Greek mind just states that stealing knowledge from the unconscious must be paid for, but you can still have the right attitude! You can say, never mind, I will pay, but I want it! The myth does not recommend doing or not doing it, but you must know that there is always a price to be paid. In this respect, the Greek mind is very different from the Judaeo-Christian attitudes, for they make it a moral problem. That is something we do know, and it is a very basic archetypal truth. Knowledge is part of the development of consciousness; there are other aspects, but that is one, and it must be paid for. It is costly, but it is up to oneself to choose if one is willing to pay the price or not. In the Judaeo-

Christian tradition the stress is on the ethical aspect, while the Greek approach is more dispassionate and more a statement of facts. But in our text there is yet another nuance, and the evaluation of knowledge is highly positive for it means divine progress.

139 ***Remark**: You spoke twice of the angel's desire for sexual relations with Isis, and the second time you used the word "rape," but that would make a difference in terms of paying for it, for the one is forced while the other is voluntary.*

140 Literally, the text simply says that the angel wants to unite sexually with Isis, but that she does not want it. I just shortened that to the word "rape." She simply made a bargain, as a woman typically does. She says he should not be in such a hurry but should first tell her the secret, and then, in a typically feminine way, she does not say afterward whether she paid the price or not. Isis was a woman! The Greek actually says that he rushed into what he wanted, "but I, Isis, had in mind what *I* wanted." What would an angel's sexual attack on Isis mean psychologically, and her delay in order to attain knowledge? How does this compare psychologically to the psychological situation in which we always find ourselves?

141 ***Remark**: It is the irruption of collective contents, for which she demands an explanation.*

142 In our terms the angel would represent a content of the collective unconscious that irrupts into one's psychological system with a demand, in this case a sexual one. What is the parallel to our experience? Alchemy was born through Isis's resistance and the fact that she did not cede quickly, or even stop it altogether. We do not know what she did in the end; she very discreetly will not even tell her own son. But what does that mean?

143 If Isis were a human woman, the angel's attack would be an animus invasion. But I would rather formulate it much more generally because that would only apply to a single case, and this is not case material. It means that very often contents of the collective unconscious irrupt in an instinctive form, in the form of some kind of instinctive urge, be it power or sex, or something of the kind. This means the libido irruption of the unconscious firstly presents itself

on a relatively animal or low level. This is something we experience again and again. A development of further consciousness often manifests initially in this form. It was one of the great problems in psychological research to recognize this. If such an irruption takes place, it means one is flooded by a sexual impulse, be it in the form of fantasies or a concrete physical impulse. We then have to decide whether it is a genuine sexual impulse or a disguised unconscious impulse that really intends knowledge or a progress of consciousness that appears initially in this form.

144 As an unprejudiced person, one would initially want to try it out, but it has often been proven that to delay is wise. Let us say that a man has a tremendous anima projection onto a woman and the experience comes as a very strong urge for sexual union. Let us assume that she falls for it, and afterward the whole thing disappears! With the Don Juan type this often happens—*après le coup,* it means nothing more to him! He leaves her and thinks, "Oh, dammit, that was not what I wanted." One could say that from the very beginning it was not really that: It was only veiled in that way. Certainly, the impulse did not reach its goal and meaning, and no progress of consciousness was achieved. The urge might just as well have been resisted and an effort made to firstly find out what it was really driving at because, as we frequently see, impulses of something you want to do appear initially in the form of physical reactions because they cannot reach consciousness directly.

145 For example, if you are faced with an analytical situation where you just do not know what to do, it can happen that while sitting opposite each other; you have a sudden sexual reaction, to which it is *not* advisable to accede—quite apart from the conventions, but we are not discussing the conventions here and can speak openly. Experience has shown that it is wiser to stop and ask why this happened at this particular moment of the analysis. What was the discussion about when the urge suddenly welled up, which dream was being discussed? You can be absolutely sure that you have touched on a point that both you and your analysand should become conscious of; something is pushing toward consciousness and is so

far from what you can conceive of, it can only manifest in a physical way. It is a kind of below-stairs explosion because it cannot come up by the staircase. It is as though you try to push an animal up the stairs and it jumps out of the window instead. Something wants to come up from the unconscious, but there is a short circuit, and it appears as a sexual urge because there is some sort of difficulty in getting further.

146 But sometimes it is a genuine sexual urge. You cannot always say that it is not exactly what it appears to be, because, after all, we are warm-blooded animals and have our normal physical reactions. But for a start, it can happen that in such a situation we do not know what is what, and then Isis's technique is pure wisdom, namely to delay and to firstly ask the thing that rushes in for all its secrets. There is still time afterward to make up your mind to have a little affair or not. Isis does not reveal what her final decision was—she is very discreet! She does not say if she did or didn't. That is a free ethical decision among human beings—or here, among gods—and that is on another level. But as long as it is such a forceful urge, you are not free to decide. Only after you have delayed in this way and asked what is behind it are you able to find out what you are really confronted with.

147 A sexual urge can even take place when you are confronted with a dying person. How misplaced that seems! In such a case it would be very plausible to think that this was not your natural sexual instinct wanting to copulate with a dying person such a thing would be impossible. You know from the very start that this is not what it means; it is, however, a typical situation and something with which I have frequently met. Behind it is a wholly archetypal symbolic problem. Why is the sexual urge so tremendously important at this moment that it falls on the dying person and those in the surroundings? That is just one example among many others. Here, you have to delay the angel and say that he should first tell his secret for you want to become conscious of what is behind the urge. A strange connection between instinct and archetype is taking place here.

148

INSTINCTS		ARCHETYPES
	experience	
Infrared		Ultraviolet
Physiological:		**Psychological:**
body symptoms, instinctual perceptions, etc.		ideas, concepts, dreams, images, fantasies, etc.

149 Sometimes in his writings, Jung refers to instinct as if it were the same thing as the archetype, and sometimes as if it were different. What he means is that the archetype, if we look at it as opposite to instinct, would be an inherited and instinctive way of having emotions, ideas, and representations with symbols, and instinct would be the inherited way of acting physically, a certain kind of physical action. Naturally, the two are connected.[13]

150 For example, suppose when walking in a field, you suddenly begin to run for no apparent reason and jump over a hedge, and on looking back, you see that a bull was chasing you! The person concerned would say that was a miracle, for without knowing why, they suddenly felt the need to run. They had not realized what was happening, but their instinct saved them. This sort of thing happens frequently. One crosses over the street, not knowing why, and then something falls from the roof! It is very important for us to learn to trust such impulses.

151 If I begin to run without even noticing any danger, but thank God, my body is cleverer than I am, that is something that happens physically. But I might instead hear a voice or have a hallucination that tells me to run. In one case the warning comes as a physical reaction, and in the other as a thought; this is the difference between instinct and archetype. The voice would be a manifestation of the archetype and the physical movement a manifestation of instinct, but in reality, they are two aspects of the same thing. Actual physical behavior according to pattern would be instinct, and the concomitant inner representations—emotions, auditions, visions—

[13] Cf. Jung, *The Structure and Dynamics of the Psyche*, 2nd ed., vol. 8, *CW* (Princeton, NJ: Princeton University Press, 1981), § 414.

would be manifestations of the archetype. Man has an inherited structure within him that makes him act and think in a certain way. This is why we are sometimes not clear about the two. Since these contents of the unconscious have a kind of physical aspect, and also a somatic and psychological aspect, sometimes something that should go through the psychological aspect switches over into the physical, or the physical aspect switches into the psychological for they are like communicating pipes: If there is a blockage in one, water flows out from the other.

152 It often happens that people who have great psychological problems, the cause of which they consider to be psychological, experience something on the physical side, and the whole problem collapses. They had blocked an instinct; let us say a sexual urge, which then manifested in their minds as a philosophical problem about God. This is what Freud generalized! He saw that this often happened and thought that you could explain everything on that level. But that is not so: You might just as well block the other end, and then it goes through the other way around. This is one of the eternal conflicts: Shall I live a thing concretely, or shall I take it symbolically? Is this meant as a realization, or must it be simply lived, without thinking about it too much? This is one of our great problems. Our text tells us that by blocking or delaying a physical urge, a progress in consciousness takes place.

153 ***Question**: This was not the first bargain struck on behalf of knowledge, for Isis undertook to cure the sun god Ra of the bite of the poisonous worm, provided he would tell her his sacred name. How do you explain this parallel?*

154 Yes, it is certainly a parallel. When Ra became old and senile and was unable to carry on properly any longer, Isis put a poisonous serpent in his path, and it bit and poisoned him so that he became very ill. At that time it was believed that a man's power rested in his secret name, which was his soul, or mana—his life power. When Ra lay on his sick bed, Isis came to her own father and offered to cure him if he would first tell her his secret name. Faced with this blackmail, Ra broke down and told her his name, and from then on,

she had the power of the sun god. But what does it mean? We cannot discuss this on the same level as the other motif that would be the level of a physical urge behind which we believe something archetypal to be hidden. To answer your question, we would need to go briefly into the development of consciousness in the Egyptian civilization.

155 In Egypt, the cult of the sun god and the sun god's son was, in general, in terms of the social and political structure, a patriarchal order. In about the years 3000 to 2800 B.C.E. sun worship gradually exceeded that of the moon and bull worship; the king was represented as the sun god and was no longer closely linked with the moon and the bull, although there was a slight difference. Along with this development and increase in the sun cult came a development in law, science, geometry, the planning of fields, of building, and so on. There was enormous progress in rational civilization, in both organization and war. It was a development of the masculine world, the world of the mind and the world of order that went hand in hand with the sun cult.

156 To a certain extent it may be compared with the early development of the Christian civilization where the same thing took place—belief in law, in dogma, in order, and in knowledge, and then, because these things come to an end, to an enantiodromia, the masculine mode of consciousness tires. That is a typical archetypal event, and then the feminine, or the unconscious and nature, the chaotic, have to take back the light. This first great myth is the myth of the enantiodromia, where the masculine, the male sun god, hands over all of his power to the feminine order.

157 Nowadays, our official organizations believe more and more in red tape, in more and more congresses, more regulations, and more religions to save the world! They are intent upon bringing order, thinking that it will solve the problem, and that those other tendencies that we find in the dreams of our patients will not succeed. But the world has once more tired—which is why the Pope declares the Assumption of the Virgin Mary,[14] and we can observe a

[14] Cf. Jung, *Psychology and Religion: West and East*, 2nd ed., vol. 11, *CW* (Princeton, NJ: Princeton

reevaluation of the feminine in the dreams of people today. To give one example: Revolted by the slaughter now taking place in Tibet[15], the other day a man wrote a fierce article to the effect that we, the Swiss, who are also a mountain people threatened by surrounding big powers, should show more sympathy and feeling for these other little mountain people who are fighting for their freedom. It is not enough to just read the papers and express sympathy, for tomorrow the same thing could happen to us with a Russian invasion. We should do something about it and stop trading with China. But then he dreamt that the world was coming to an end and that in a glacier in the mountains, a few people dug up an old ship in which sat a beautiful woman. The ship was like Noah's Ark, moving toward the sea. And it was said that only those who went in the old ship with the woman would be saved!

158 The unconscious tells us that what we see with our masculine, political, thinking mind is only a small aspect of what is really happening. We are now confronted with the deluge. Our real problem at the present time is that of overpopulation and not the tension between the Arabs or the Russians. We are confronted with a hopeless situation. The saving principle is the feminine principle, and this time it will not be Noah sitting in the Ark, but a woman, that is, a goddess. What does this mean? This is what the dreams we are sometimes confronted with look like! You cannot evaluate this woman simply as a woman. The dreamer's relationship to women was in order—there was nothing wrong on that level. So what does the woman in the ark and those few people who were with her represent? That is not easy to interpret. At the end of the Egyptian civilization there was a similar enantiodromia. Suddenly, Isis got everything into her hands and the male gods faded, and it is interesting that this was at the end of the age of Aries. And today, at the end of the age of Pisces, it is again a woman who is gathering the harvest, and the men are a bit tired.

University Press, 1989), § 743, § 748.

[15] 1959.

159 ***Question***: *But the angel did not lose anything when he gave his secret to the goddess. He still understood it himself, did he not?*

160 Yes, but whereas the angel made no use of his knowledge, Isis founded alchemy. She did something with it, whereas he just kept it to himself.

Lecture 3

161 We have discussed the possible meaning of the handing over of the secret of alchemy by the angel Amnael to the goddess Isis. We used amplifications from ancient legends that say that all natural scientific knowledge, from mathematics to the making of women's cosmetics, was taught to human beings by angels or giants. We also discussed the strange fact that very often at the end of the patriarchal civilization there comes an enantiodromia, and the power is handed over to a feminine figure, as it happened, for instance, toward the end of the Egyptian civilization, when the cult of Isis became predominant, and Isis increasingly took over the role of all other gods. There are even late Egyptian prayers in which Isis is invoked as the one who is all other gods in a feminine form. We compared this with what is taking place in Christianity today, at least the Catholic part of it, in which the Virgin Mary has suddenly been raised to a more dominant role than hitherto.

162 We should not forget, however, that these mother goddesses are also connected with matter and our concept of it, for not only is the word "matter" itself connected with the word "mother," but the whole projection of matter, and the model archetypal idea at the back of the minds of natural scientists, is drawn from the mother archetype. Plato, for instance, said[16] that space is like a wet nurse to the whole cosmic order, thereby regarding space as a feminine container.

163 The idea of matter is always secretly connected with the mother archetype. So, if the Pope shifts emphasis in the Christian cult to the Virgin Mary, this is, consciously or unconsciously, a blow struck against communistic materialism. It is a gesture and an attempt to

[16] Platon, "*Timaios,*" in *Hauptwerke,* ed. Wilhelm Nestle (Leipzig: Kröner, 1931), 275-285.

get at its materialistic aspect by placing emphasis on matter in a different form. Interest in matter therefore springs from a resurgence of this archetype.

164 When young natural scientists choose their profession, frequently Mother Nature appears to them in dreams in the form of an old woman, or such a figure, and shows them the way. I have seen several dreams like this from young people who were uncertain whether to study natural science—medicine, for instance—or something else. One can indeed actually prove by the dream material of modern people that a strong interest in the material aspect of outer nature very often springs from the constellation of this archetype, for it is the dynamic factor behind natural science. If the biblical story evaluates this imparting of knowledge to man as a catastrophe, or as unlucky, it can certainly be compared to the fact that natural science, including mathematics, has, from the very beginning, tended to possess people in an autonomous way, to possess their interest to such an extent as to give them a demonic drive, upsetting not only their personal balance but also, to some extent, the balance of civilization.

165 This excessive drive of natural science and its destructive aspect is nowadays such a banality that I do not need to enlarge upon it, but it springs from the fact that one archetype is, as it were, moving out of the general instinctual order. Therefore, one can say that the myth of the origin of natural science is partly the myth of instinctual dissociation; *homo faber* is already dissociated, or more precisely, is estranged from his natural instinctive roots in a dangerous way. This is what the biblical myth says, while this Isis myth, on the contrary, lauds the same event as enormous progress. If there are two myths, one of which is more or less the opposite of the other, or the same thing with a different evaluation, we can only conclude that there is a basic uncertainty within the human being, even in his unconscious; the problem is real and not invented, and we have to look at it from both angles.

166 The angel bears a vessel on his head that has not been caulked with pitch, and it contains shining water. This absolutely transparent

or clean water, the Greek text says, is the symbol of the mysterious basic matter *par excellence* in alchemy. The idea of the eternal water is, as Jung's innumerable amplifications and associations with other texts show, one of the very greatest alchemical symbols. It is the divine water that is not, of course, H2O, but is actually a symbol for the most basic matter of the world, for the *prima materia.* So this image tells us that the angel bears the mystery of the basic material—we would say of the cosmos—and this is exactly what these alchemists, just like modern physicists, had in mind: that all material phenomena possibly go back to one basic material. The search for this was their great *fascinosum*, for connected to it was the feeling that if this basic material could be discovered, one would, in a way, be looking into the divine fabric of the cosmos.

167 Isis insists on getting the secret. The text then continues with the oath that obliges Horus not to disclose it. This accords with the general style of mystery initiations in ancient religious times. In the Hellenistic world, its emphasis shows that the great thing has now been imparted. This being so, Isis's son, Horus, must realize that the secret is for him only and for nobody else, and that he may never speak of it.

168 We have in this oldest text something that we shall meet again and again throughout the history of alchemy, namely, the motif of the great secret that cannot be told just scientifically and imparted from one individual to another. In the history of alchemy and chemistry this has always been regarded as a trick to make the whole thing appear more important and mysterious, and to veil certain secrets. Naturally, there is a certain amount of truth to this because alchemy at this time was also chemistry, and therefore knowledge as to how to make alloys, etc., was a trade secret that needed to be kept, for the very banal financial reason of keeping the upper hand. The same thing goes on in our modern industries; there is even a system for spying out the secrets of industrial management and metallurgy, for such knowledge means power and money, just as it did in olden times. If, for instance, you could make an alloy that looked like gold, thanks to the very indifferent police control at the

time, false money could be made and a fortune quickly acquired, so naturally the secret would only be imparted to one's best friend.

169 But this banal aspect does not explain the whole phenomenon. Consider what happens in an analytical situation! Perhaps we have all experienced that certain things can only be said, or explained, or done, with one other person, and generally, if an analysis goes deep enough, there comes a point where analyst and analysand share the secret that they both know could not be shared with anybody else, and which therefore establishes a unique relationship.

170 People in the surroundings experience this in exactly the same way as it was felt about in alchemy, namely that there must be something dirty about it, for otherwise it could be spoken of straight out. But it is quite impossible to say and do certain things except with one person; that is the uniqueness and exclusiveness of every real human relationship, and of every real meeting with the unconscious. This is why it is so difficult, and in a way misleading, to report on case material, for certain things come up which cannot be told, not for reasons of discretion or because they have to do with sex, or concern a divorce, or marriage, or have something to do with finances, or some kind of indiscreet dirt—which people always think is the case—but because the thing is *ineffable.*

171 Sometimes the relationship or analysis goes on in half-said words which are understood in a specific way by the other person, but which you cannot repeat when speaking of the case. You can tell the dreams and repeat what you told the analysand about their meaning, but you know perfectly well that you are telling only half the story. There are also things that cannot be told because they happen without your knowing. Somebody may say later, "I don't remember what you said to me at the time, but you laughed in a certain way which suggested something to me." That can happen without either party noticing at the time. Effects like this cannot be helped and cannot be spoken of, though in actual fact they may form the basis of the analytical and therapeutic process.

172 There is also the sympathy between two people, the *sympathia*, that actually means they suffer together, that both are impressed by

something. This condition of "togetherness," which comes from participating in the same experience, cannot be explained—not because one wants to make a secret of it, but because it is inexplicable and irrational and very complex. So one can say that in every process of analysis there is a secret; this is why one generally cannot talk about it. If, therefore, you are reporting a case, you are firstly only reporting it in part, and secondly, you are speaking of a unique thing. Nevertheless, people go home after such a report and think that they now know how the process of individuation works. They will later be completely thrown off the track because their process of individuation is guaranteed to unfold quite differently. *Per definitionem,* it is an individuation, which means something unique.

173 For this reason it can even be misleading to recount a unique case for, involuntarily, people generalize about it, and as soon as they think that they now understand how therapy is conducted, they are already barking up the wrong tree. There is always a real secret involved, and as soon as you touch the uniqueness of the process, or of the individual, it cannot be talked about anymore. When I am asked to speak on case material and I look through my cases, I often feel it would be wrong to choose any of them. Generally, one can only speak of mild cases, or of those that have gone wrong—which is humiliating to one's vanity, but at least such a case can be talked about.

174 ***Question****: Isn't Isis referring to something like that when she says, "You are me and I am you," after which there is nothing more to be said?*

175 Yes, exactly! That is what I'm driving at. There is this "I am you and you are me," in it, and that is the element that cannot be talked about. That is the *unio mystica*, that ineffable, deep thing that happens beneath what we try to push away with the word "transference," thus making it a technical thing. But it is a real mystery, a mystical experience, and one that can therefore never be imparted or shared with another person.

176 Isis swears first in the name of Hermes, which is probably the Greek translation for Thoth, the moon god and ape god, then in the name of Anubis, which has not been translated and therefore is recognizable in its Egyptian form, and also in the name of Kerkoros—the howling of Kerkoros, whereby the word "howling" is alluding to the howling of the dog Kerberos. In the parallel text the name is Kerkouroboros. Ouroboros is the snake that eats its own tail. So it must refer to a doglike demon that has been confused with this snake and is here described as a snake and the guardian of the underworld. This is a mixture of the figure of Kerberos—therefore "Ker" in the first syllable—with certain guardian figures of the Egyptian underworld, among which we very often find the snake which eats its own tail. This tail-eating snake is depicted on certain Egyptian tombs.

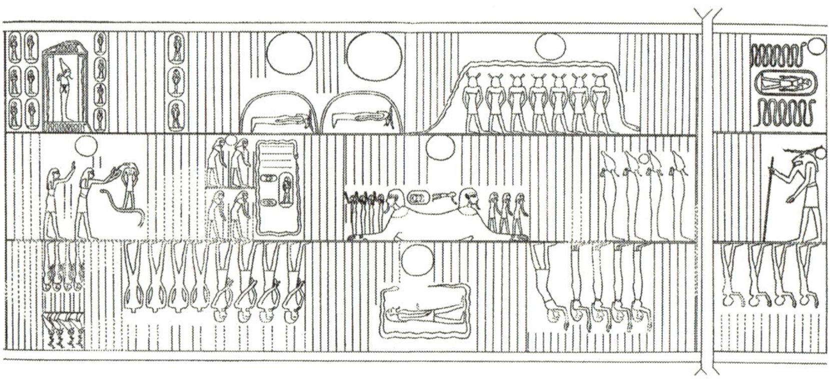

Figure 2
Double Sphinx

177 In the tomb of Ramses VI, for instance, there is a drawing of a house with two sphinxes, a schematic representation of the underworld where the resurrection of the sun god takes place. Just before his resurrection the sun god is represented as an ithyphallic man lying on his back with an erect phallus, and around him is the snake that eats its own tail. An inscription merely says, "This is the corpse." Evidently, in the underworld when the sun god has reached the moment when death and resurrection meet, when he is in his tomb in the depths of the underworld, he is represented as being surrounded by this snake. According to the Egyptian text, the snake that eats its own tail is considered to be the guardian of

the underworld, and it is probably this snake that is invoked in our text.

178 The text continues, "I adjure you also in the name of the ferryman Acheron." And later, "Go to the peasant Acherontos and he will tell you the whole secret." Naturally, one thinks firstly of the Greek underworld stream, Acheron, but since the translation obviously represents Egyptian ideas and images, we have to consider what underworld godhead or figure might have given rise to such a name.

179 In this connection I have found some very interesting amplifications.[17] There is an Egyptian god, or concept, called Aker, or sometimes Akerou, the plural form. This god is represented by two lions sitting back to back, sometimes with the disc of the sun between their two backs. This figure is also called Ruti (or Rwti), the double lion, and that is how the god, or the word Aker, is represented.

180 The figure is shown as the double lion, or the double dog, or as Yesterday and Tomorrow, because in Egyptian mythology this whole picture represents the moment of resurrection of the sun god. Yesterday he was dead; tomorrow he will be alive again. Midnight, when the sun is at its lowest point and begins to rise again, is the turning point from death to life, from yesterday to the new day. This lowest moment of the enantiodromia and of the resurrection is Aker, for Aker means "that moment."

181 Aker, however, not only means the moment, but also the place and the situation, the situation of death and resurrection, of yesterday and tomorrow, of the resurrection and regeneration of the sun god. Sometimes Aker is not represented as this deepest point of the underworld, but as the door to the Beyond whose doorkeepers are the double lions. So there is an admixture of two ideas: He is the entrance into the Beyond, the *limen*, or he is the deepest point in the underworld itself. In the tombs of Tuthmosis III and Amenophis II there is the same scene.[18]

---

[17] Cf. also the comments by von Franz, *Dreams and Death,* 15-16.

[18] Aker as the double sphinx and guardian of Sokar, of the underworld, represented by the oval shape, in the fifth hour of the *Amduat*, the lowest register; cf. Erik Hornung, ed. and trans., *Die Unterweltsbücher der* Ägypter (Zurich: Artemis, 1992), 102-103.

Figure 3
Aker

182 I would like to cite some of the invocations here. In one of the many variations of the Egyptian books of the dead, the Book of the Caverns,[19] the sun God, upon arriving in the underworld, says,[20]

183 Oh Aker, I went your way! You, whose forms are mysterious, open thy arms before me. Here I am, those who are within you call to me.

184 When he says, "those who are within you call to me," Aker is simply the whole underworld, the space in the underworld, and those who are in the underworld are the spirits of the dead and the god of the dead, and the spirits call the sun god when he plunges into the underworld. The text continues,

185 I have seen thy mysteries, my sun disc and Geb, the earth god, are those whom I carry on my back. Khepri is now inside his envelope. Open thy arms, receive me. Here I am, I will chase away your darkness!

---

[19] Hornung, "Hoehlenbuch," in *Unterweltsbücher der* Ägypter, 3.2.2 References are given in act, register and scene.
[20] Marie-Louise von Franz is translating from Constant de Witt, *Le rôle et le sens du lion dans l'Egypte ancienne* (Leiden: Brill, 1951). We are quoting from Hornung, *Unterweltsbücher der Ägypter.*

186 Khepri is the resurrected form of the sun god. He is now in the egg, so to speak, in the envelope, his sarcophagus, and he will appear over the horizon in the next moment.

187 In the tomb of Ramesses VI, Aker is depicted as two lions (Ruti), and beneath them are the words, "See what this God looks like. Geb and Khepri watch over the images that are within him."[21]

188 So, Aker is the space that contains the dead, or the images of everything that exists. He is not only the double lion, or the door to the Beyond, but that mysterious space in the underworld in which there are the dead people and the images. He watches them and has them in his arms. This great God stays below in the underworld and speaks with the great image that carries his corpse. As can be seen in the drawing, Aker is the great image that carries the corpse or body of the sun god. The sun god sheds light on everything lying in the arms of Aker, and he (it is not clear if "he" refers to the sun god or to Aker, but other texts make clear that it refers to Aker) brings about the reunion of the bones—he collects the scattered bones of the corpse.[22] One of the great motifs of the Egyptian Book of the Dead is that the dead are dismembered, as was Osiris, and must therefore be reassembled before they can resurrect. They must be put together again to be able to rise from the underworld. It is Aker who collects the bones and limbs of the god.

189 Another representation found in the tomb of Ramesses VI is of the double lion standing between the primordial waters, underneath which is the inscription "Aker" and then an ellipse that, in this connection, symbolizes the underworld, or the world of the dead. The inscription indicates that Aker and Shu, the air god, are the two creators of the world.[23] Aker, therefore, is not only the agent in the resurrection of the sun god and the whole underworld, but he is also

---

[21] The text of the scarabus in the oval: "Thus, this god is created in his sarcophagus on the back of Akers. Khepri from the body of Akers watches over the secret that is in the Dat." (translated from Hornung, *Unterweltsbücher der Ägypter*, 348.)

[22] "Represented is the corpse of Osiris with an erect penis, indicating the constant potency of the god. Wound around the corpse is a protective snake, and crowning the scene is a sun disk, that is missing in the other scenes of this register, for the represented "enemies" may not participate in the presence of the sun god. It is intentional that this central image of the lower register is placed exactly under the double sphinx (Aker) of the middle register, for together both images make a whole." (translated from Hornung, *Unterweltsbücher der Ägypter*, 352.)

[23] de Wit, *Lion dans l'Egypte ancienne*, 101.

one of the agencies in the creation of the world. As I mentioned earlier, sometimes the double lions are replaced by two of Anubis's jackals, two doglike animals, and then the inscription below is, "These are the openers of the way, the agents of resurrection."[24]

190 I think, therefore, it would not be too far-fetched to conjecture that Acheron, or Acherontos, alludes to this Egyptian god. And as we know, the main content of the great secret imparted by Isis to Horus is that a lion generates a lion, barley generates barley, wheat generates wheat, and so on; therefore, a man is only generated in the same way, and, it is also specifically said, a dog a dog. So what at first seems a completely banal statement of nature, namely the secret of sexual generation, and of the germs, and plant generation, reveals itself as having, in the late antique Greek and Egyptian of that time, a completely other net of associations. These images were all connected to the idea of the resurrection of the dead, of the recreation of the sun god, and of the recreation of the world, and our text makes a hidden allusion to this.

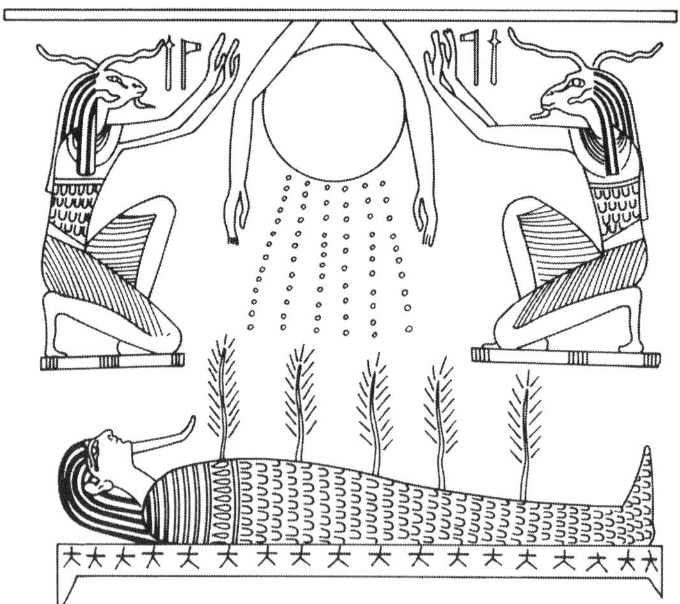

Figure 4
Osiris, Corn Mummy

[24] Ibid., 165.

191 It is well known that the resurrection of Osiris was often represented by the simile—though it is more than a simile—of the resurrection of the corn. In late antiquity, for instance, in many Egyptian towns there were rituals during which a pine tree was cut down and hollowed out, representing the body of Isis, or the coffin—for the coffin *is* the mother Goddess.[25] Wheat or barley was then put into it and watered, and when the grain was put into the sun, it sprouted—this was a spring ritual of resurrection. One can still see these corn mummies in the museum in Cairo. Corn was sown into a kind of flat box with sand in it in the form of the mummified Osiris. It was sprinkled with water, after which it sprouted and then withered. Such containers representing the resurrection of the dead were known as Osiris Gardens. The process was repeated at every classical Egyptian funeral: Corn was placed inside the bandages of the mummified corpse and sprinkled with water, and when the corn began to sprout, it was a sign that the dead had now resurrected. All these rituals were performed in this typically primitive and magical form quite literally on the mummified corpse. The process of the corn dying in the earth, followed by its resurrection as wheat or barley, was closely connected in the minds of the people to the idea of the resurrection of the god Osiris, and later, of every human being.

192 Now what on earth has this to do with alchemy? Clearly it seems to refer to certain late antique mysteries of the dead in the Hellenistic Egyptian world, and we can recognize the connection with the archetypal mystery of death and the resurrection of the young spring god. But why should this prove itself to be the essential explanation of the whole alchemical mystery when, in the text I cited earlier, it is followed by such completely banal recipes? In order to understand what these people had in mind, I believe one must first of all be extremely naïve and follow a naïve train of thought.

193 Let us consider how we imagine our own resurrection, if we indeed hope for one. Even if we do not believe in it, the first thing that occurs to us is naturally our corpse, and what happens to it. The

[25] See "Kornmummien" (corn mummies) in Hans Bonnet, *Reallexion der ägyptischen Religionsgeschichte*, 2nd ed. (Berlin: Gruyter, 1971).

worms eat it, or it is burned to ashes in the crematorium! If we are both naïve and honest, we must admit that we cannot free our minds of the immediate sight of what remains of us after our death. Therefore, in all human civilizations, the corpse is treated with great care and undergoes all kinds of rituals because it represents a mystery. The form of the human being who lived is still there, but something is lacking or has changed. Naïve feeling still takes what lies before us as our father, or our friend, or whoever it may be. If not, what is it? If we hope for such a thing as resurrection, then the body that has disintegrated must somehow be put together again. If we continue to naively follow this thought, we will think that if one knew the basic matter from which the whole complex phenomenon of the body is built up, it could be remade.

194 I am not preaching this as something true! I only want to show that it would be an idea likely to occur to a naïve mind, and when I discussed the problem of resurrection with people, I have often seen that they do think along these lines. They speak of the glorified body—but there might be a basic matter, or substance. As we do not know what matter is, why should God not remake the whole body from this basic matter that we do not know and that is God's own secret? This is a common belief among many Christians who have not thought too deeply, but who, in an effort to understand, have a general idea of the resurrection of the body. I think that similar naïve thoughts were behind these texts, namely that the problem of resurrection is somehow linked with the problem of what matter is, and that if it has a basic form, it can be transformed.[26]

195 Now if there is a basic matter that can be transformed into something else, then that basic matter is immortal and can never be dissolved. There we have the idea of the atom—that cannot be further split, as the word itself means—that is, the most basic particle. It also means the individual, the last unit. It cannot be split or disintegrate and is therefore immortal and eternal. Here one touches on an eternal thing and if one gets to the bottom of that, one

[26] See also von Franz, *Dreams and Death*, X-XVI.

has the secret of resurrection and of immortality, and of how God made the world.

196 That was the trend of thought and the reflection behind the ideas contained in this text. It accounts for why the investigation into the basic composition of cosmic matter was so important. That the problem of the resurrection of the dead was for these people bound up with such thoughts shows that the hope for immortality, the whole tremendous emotional drive man feels in his longing for immortality, was poured into alchemy at that time. This explains how the imagery of the process of individuation got projected into this problem.

197 So far, these are only assertions that I have amplified with a few Egyptian texts, but in the next chapter I shall present a completely different fifth-century text from which we can see that such thoughts really existed. Until now, they have only been alluded to, so that we have had to reconstruct from other texts.

198 After the allusion to the statement made earlier that a lion generates a lion and a dog a dog, the text continues,

199 Having been fortunate in participating in the divine power, we can now proceed with the preparation of other things. Therefore take quicksilver … and so on.

200 Recipes then follow that I cannot interpret because I simply do not know what they mean. Some, like the urine of an uncorrupted boy, can be amplified for we know that this played a role in the magic of late antiquity. What other substances refer to we do not know, and historians of chemistry conjecture and quarrel as to their probable meaning, which, in most cases, has not been definitely established. We only know that they are mixtures of metals, etc., principally used in the manufacture of alloys, and that there were certain procedures of melting or of slow corrosion by acids. While still reciting such recipes, Isis says, "Now, my child, you know the mystery which is the elixir of the widow." This sentence shows that some of the recipes referred to healing elixirs, to some powerful medicine, in the African

sense of the word, rather than to the production of some kind of metal. How does that link up, if you think of it naïvely?

201 The following experience from my childhood might elucidate this. When I was about 10 years old, I frequently had to stay home from school because of illness. I went to school only in the mornings, and in the afternoons, when my sister was at school, I was alone and very bored, as I had no one to play with. At the back of the henhouse I established what I called my laboratory. I had once read that amber was formed by resin falling into seawater and solidifying after many years. So I thought I would make amber. Promptly, in my fantasy, amber became a yellow pearl, and I thought I would make a round yellow pearl of amber.

202 After endlessly climbing up and falling from fir trees, I had finally collected a quantity of resin; then I had to produce seawater. From the dictionary I discovered what seawater consisted of, and I stole salt and iodine from the bathroom and mixed together, as best as I could at that age, something that I called seawater. Thinking that the amber had to be purified before the yellow pearl could be produced, I started to melt and cook it to get rid of the dead ants and such things in it. While doing this and watching the amber heating up and melting, in my loneliness, I started to feel pity for it, thinking that I had to make some kind of propitiation to it for having burnt it. So I started talking to the resin, saying that it should not be unhappy if I burnt it for in the end it was to become a wonderful yellow pearl, and it must just bear being tortured with the fire now.

203 In this way, I got into a whole fantasy about producing this yellow pearl. Seen rationally, I had gotten the idea from something I had read. But in the loneliness of the task, the thing became amplified into a complete alchemical opus, including prayers for its success. I prayed to the amber, begging it not to be angry with me for cooking it, and promising to make it into a pearl, and so on. That is a primitive or infantile mentality, and we must suppose that the alchemists had a similar attitude. It must be remembered that at that time it was very dangerous to make chemical experiments because you were then seen as a witch doctor—with all the consequences

that that entailed. You were respected, but you were also hated and feared, and therefore such things had to be done secretly and in loneliness, which always brings up the unconscious.

204 You could describe this childhood occupation, that lasted for over a year, as play or something like an active imagination with chemical substances—which is, to a great extent, what alchemy is. An active imagination can be done, for instance, with colors—nowadays we do it chiefly by painting, or by writing stories—but it can also be done by collecting substances and mixing them. That is what alchemists did at the time, and instead of producing a purely chemical experiment, they went off the track a little bit into a process in which their fantasies were predominant, just as it happened to me when, while wanting to make amber, I fell into the fantasy of producing a yellow pearl.

205 Synchronistic events often happen in connection with experiences like this; they are experienced as miracles and naturally confirm such fantasies. I heard the story of a scientist that shows that such things still happen in modern chemistry laboratories.[27] He wanted to produce a certain vitamin in chemical form and he had everything figured out, and he knew that it should work, but the product did not seem to want to crystallize. *When* a thing crystallizes depends upon very irrational factors. Of course, the weight and heat and form of the mixture all play a part, but even today, there are factors that cannot be overlooked in the manufacturing of chemicals, and one does not know upon what they depend. So, contrary to all expectations, the wretched thing just did not want to crystallize! He watched it day and night, saying it ought to crystallize, but it just remained liquid. The scientist grew tired of watching it and got a helper to carry on and to keep the heat at a certain temperature. Meanwhile, he went home and fell asleep and had the most amazing alchemical dream in which a voice said, "Now go, and you will see that it has crystallized!" He got up and telephoned, and it was true: it had crystallized! This man's unconscious was actually connected to, and informed about, the chemical process going on in the retort.

[27] It may be Tadeusz Reichstein who succeeded in the synthesis of vitamin C in 1932.

206 You can label that synchronicity, but in doing so you have not explained anything. It is simply a fact. And it shows that we do not know *how* the unconscious is connected with matter, but only that it *is*, and that it has a knowledge of such things; *how*, we do not know for our scientific knowledge in this respect has come to an end, for the time being. Apparently, chemistry, even in our modern times, still has a connection with the unconscious of the person performing the experiment, even to the extent of such things happening as I have described. Here again, we are touching upon a secret. An experience of this kind was generally behind the experiments of the alchemists, though on a more primitive and cruder basis.

On the Sacred Art

207 If we sum up the text we have just discussed in the preceding chapter, not from a psychological but from a historical standpoint, we see that there are religious ideas and concepts in alchemy that lead back to Hellenized Egypt, with its early admixture of Greek and late Egyptian religions. I cannot present all the texts here, but in others there are traces of Jewish and Gnostic symbolism and many other religions of that time.

208 The other element that is connected with this manner of thinking, though not with the texts, is that of the recipes that are obviously remnants of secret craft traditions of African medicine men, and those that were concerned with the making of love charms, with medicines to ensure beauty, with the making of alloys, and so on. All such recipes were the secrets of the smith craftsmen and medicine men. During the Egyptian civilization they were probably handed down by certain classes of priests who had monopolies on the manufacture of their particular alloys or medicines, which they obtained through the ruling Pharaoh and probably kept in secret books stored in the temples. This is how it is described in a rediscovered papyrus, now in a museum in Cairo, that contains all the recipes for the embalming of corpses.[28] The instructions for this

[28] Papyrus Boulaq III and Papyrus Louvre 5158, from the first century A.D.; cf. Günther Roeder,

very complicated procedure are given in a purely technical and chemical language. It concerns the secret of the class of Anubis priests, whose knowledge was imparted only to priests who had been initiated. This probably goes back to the oldest kind of tradition of primitive African medicine men that can still be unearthed in Africa today in a simpler form, though the psychological attitude and the secret behind such procedures are unchanged.

209 The Greek text that we shall be looking at next introduces a third element into these early chemical writings, namely Greek natural philosophy. Perhaps one of the greatest historical events of late antiquity was that in Greek natural philosophy, in the pre-Socratic philosophy with men like Democritus, Heraclitus, and Thales of Miletus, Anazimenes, and Anaximander, there was speculation about the established theories on nature out of which such technical terms as time, space, atom, matter and energy were created.

210 As we know, all the basic concepts of modern physics go back to Greek philosophy, for the Greeks were the creators of these concepts in their specific, natural scientific meaning, though they did not experiment with matter to a great extent. They had few or no laboratories, and most of their theories about nature came from speculative intuition, though sometimes they used practical examples to explain what they meant. For instance, if Democritus says that the atom has different forms, something like a little pyramid, with corners like hooks by which they are connected, he is creating, so to speak, a materialistic model of his idea of the atom. The soul—according to Democritus's model of reality—was made up of round atoms, the same atoms as those of fire, that roll through the spaces of the atom.

211 The Greeks never thought of proving or demonstrating such things by experiment, as is common scientific procedure nowadays. If someone has a speculative model today, he tries to prove whether it fits the facts or not through practical experiment. The Greeks did

---

Urkunden zur Religion des alten Ägypten, 2nd ed., Religiöse Stimmen der Völker, ed. Walter Otto, vol. 4 (Jena: Eugen Diederichs, 1923).

not do this. But then Greek thought met the Egyptian secret sciences—though regrettably in a very late watered-down phase—that consisted entirely of an age-old practical craft tradition about the behavior of matter. The Egyptians knew a great deal from the practical angle. They knew how to make enamel and invisible ink and all sorts of complicated alloys. When these two worlds met in the Ptolemaic dynasty in Egypt, it was enormously fertile for both parties, for the knowledge of recipes and the religious body of thought of the Egyptians came into contact with the accurate scientific thought of the Greeks. We could call this moment when the thought models of Greek philosophy met with the experimental practices of Egyptian traditions the birth of alchemy.

212 To give a little more insight on this point, I would like to read a brief outline of a very long text by a later alchemist, Olympiodorus. One comes across his name often in C. G. Jung's writings.[29]

213 Olympiodorus was a minister and official at the Byzantine Court in the fifth century A.D.[30] He was a member of the delegation that journeyed to Attila, King of the Huns, and he wrote a rather famous history of his time that he published in 425 A.D. Some of his biographers say that during the time he was at the Byzantine court he was known as a great magician and medicine man who was, according to the texts, very occupied with alchemical experiments. In histories of alchemy, however, this is refuted for he did not possess much practical knowledge, and even if he did perform such experiments, it is certain that he was more interested in the theoretical or symbolic aspects of alchemy.

214 He claimed that the aims of alchemy could not be achieved in a rational way, that you could follow the recipes as much as you liked, but you would never get anywhere without the help of magic and

---

[29] Especially see Jung, *Alchemical Studies*, vol. 13, *CW*; and Jung, *Psychology and Alchemy*, vol. 12, *CW*; and Jung, *Mysterium Coniunctionis: An Inquiry into the Separation and Synthesis of Psychic Opposites in Alchemy*, 2nd ed., vol. 14, *CW* (Princeton, NJ: Princeton University Press, 1989); and Marie-Louise von Franz, ed., with a Commentary, *Aurora Consurgens: A Document Attributed to Thomas Aquinas on the Problem of the Opposites in Alchemy. A Companion Work to C. G. Jung's Mysterium Coniunctionis*, trans. R. F. C. Hull and A. S. B. Glover (Toronto: Inner City Books, 2000).

[30] Marie-Louise von Franz believes it to be possible that the alchemist Olympiodorus is probably identical with Olympiodorus the historian, cf. von Franz, *Dreams and Death*, 16.

magical powers. So he began to have a double attitude about what could be called serious or practical science on the one hand, and magic on the other, a split we have not met in earlier texts. The reason for this was that Olympiodorus had had a Greek philosophical education that he tried to apply to his alchemical knowledge.

215 I would like to present this text as I did that of Isis, namely in its strange literal confusion so that one forms one's own impression of it. I will take a section from paragraph 40 of the text *Über die heilige Kunst* (On the Sacred Art) followed by paragraph 41, that gives, as it were, the essence, or what is typical, of his writings.[31]

216 Olympiodorus speaks of lead and quotes the Prophetess Maria, who is reported to have said that black lead must be considered as the basis of the work. And now he comments upon this and continues the theme in paragraph 41:

> 217 Now see how black lead is prepared. As I said before, common lead is black from the very beginning, but *our* lead becomes black, which at the beginning it was not.[32]

> 218 Experiments will teach you, and by them you will discover the real demonstration and proof, that opinions worthy of credence are unanimous on this matter. I will now try to approach our goal. If the Asem [an alloy like silver, though exactly what is not known] does not become gold, or could not become gold though it is a work, one should not despise what the old people said, namely that the letter kills but the Spirit brings to life. ['... For the letter killeth, but the spirit giveth life.' II *Cor.* 3:6.] Now this is in complete harmony with everything said by the old philosophers and points to the same end, to the saying of the Lord. [Olympiodorus was a Christian and quoted the Bible, pointing out that one must not take alchemical texts and recipes literally, for that killed,

[31] Cf. Berthelot, *Collection des alchimistes grec: Traduction, vol. 2, 101-104.* Olympiodor, philosophe d'Alexandrie – Sur l'art sacré.
[32] Ibid., 102, § 40.

but one must understand the spirit of the text and what *that* meant.]

219 The oracles of Apollo are also in harmony with what we mean for they mention the tomb of Osiris. [This amplifies our other text.] But what is the tomb of Osiris? There is a corpse, swathed in linen mummy bands, with only the naked face visible, and, interpreting Osiris, the oracle says, 'Osiris is the suffocated coffin in which are hidden his limbs and whose face only is visible to mortal beings. Hiding the bodies, nature is astonished. He, Osiris, is the original principal of all moist substances. He is kept down as a prisoner by the sphere of the fire. He, therefore, has suffocated all the lead, [and so on.][33]

220 Another oracle by the same author says,

> Take some gold which is called the male of the Chrysokolla [whatever that substance is] and a man who has been kneaded together. The gold of the Ethiopian earth produces this from its drops. A certain species of ant brings the gold to the surface of the earth and enjoys it. Put him together with his wife of vapour, till the divine bitter water comes out. When it has thickened, or is coloured red [red copper] with the juice of the Golden Vine of Egypt, then smear over it the leaflets of the light-bringing goddess [that must be the moon] and also of the red copper or of the red Venus ['cypris' can stand for either copper or Venus - probably Venus is meant] and then thicken it until it coagulates into gold.[34]

221 Now the philosopher Petasios, who speaks about the beginning of the alchemical world, is in complete harmony with this, and he also means our lead when he says that the sphere of the fire holds down and suffocates through the lead.

[33] Ibid., 103, § 42.

[34] Ibid., 103-104, §43.

Then, interpreting his own sayings, he says, 'All of this comes from the male – or the arsenic water.'[35]

222 The word "arsenic" means male; it is not referring to the arsenic we know, but refers to all substances that have a dynamic drive in them that affects other substances.[36] Everything that seems to affect another substance was male because it was active. So it is not to be confused with what we call arsenic. When he speaks of arsenic here, he is referring to the sphere of the fire.

223 The lead is so possessed by devils and is so shameless that those who want to learn about it fall into madness, on account of their unconsciousness. [Jung often quotes this idea.[37]]

224 Now I will explain about the chemical elements and then this will become clear. They call lead the egg – I mean the egg of the four elements – that is what Zosimos says, and by that he really always means lead. If they explain its shape, they really in secret allude to the whole thing, because, as Maria says, the four elements are one. When you hear the word 'sands'[38] you must understand that that means 'shapes' or ideas [in Greek *eide* can mean either one or the other]. If you hear 'eide' [shapes, forms, ideas], that really means 'the sands' – the type of sand – because the four bodies, or the four elements, are also the four 'bodiness' [this is an invented word, also in the Greek].

225 Zosimos explains the four-bodyness in the following way: now the poor [in Greek the adjective is feminine] feminine thing falls into the four-body in which it is chained, and at once changes from one colour to another, all the colours into which the technique wishes to bind it: white, yellow, or even

[35] Ibid., § 43.
[36] Cf. Jung, *Mysterium Coniunctionis*, vol. 14, *CW*, § 195.
[37] Cf. ibid, § 493.
[38] Cf. also note 24 above.

Figure 5
Mary Prophetess, pointing to the union of the Upper and Lower

black, or firstly black, then white, and then yellow, and when this feminine thing has evidenced all these colours, and has rejuvenated itself, it continues into old age and then dies in the four-body, which means iron, tin, bronze and lead, with each of which she dies in the *rubedo* – this state of becoming red — and so is completely destroyed so that she cannot run away, [a fact that is very satisfactory to the alchemists, for now she cannot escape]. And then one repeats the whole thing, by which her persecutor is also chained [the one who persecutes this woman is also chained], all of which takes place outside the round vessel. What is the round vessel? Either the fire or the round form of the vessel prevents her from running away. Just as though, in an illness, the blood had been destroyed and was not renewed, so in her silver state she is seen to have red blood, and that is the gold."[39]

[39] Berthelot, *Collection des alchimistes grecs: Traduction*, vol. 2, 104-105, § 43, § 44.

226 This is a long literal passage of real alchemy from which one can see how charitable Jung has been in selecting passages and publishing them together in chapters, because if one reads the original text, one might also fall into the madness of the lead! When you read Jung's books, you think it is impossible to understand a thing—it is all so complicated—but in fact he has simplified it enormously and has made a tremendous effort to get the pearls out of the dunghill and bring some form into it, for the original material was like the above. Once you have accustomed yourself to follow this line of thought, you will find the whole thing is completely logical: It has the same logic as a dream and can be taken as such. The first time you hear a dream, too, you could think it is completely crazy, but if you read this material as you would a dream, you will get into its meaning.

227 For example, Olympiodorus speaks of the black lead, and it is clear that this is the original substance and is therefore the mystery of which we have already spoken—the *prima materia*—the basic substance of the world within which lies God's secret of life and death. He speaks of it as "our lead," which is not black in the beginning, and compares it to common lead, by which he means the material that ordinary craftsmen call lead (as was used, for example, to manufacture water pipes during the time of the Roman Empire) which is not what they—the alchemists—are referring to when they speak of lead. When they speak of lead, they are referring to a more basic substance. It is a different kind of lead, he says, with which you must experiment in order to discover what earlier writers had meant by it.

228 He then quotes the Bible, saying that the text must not be taken literally, which is also understandable, and says that the transformation of the lead is a secret. Then he quotes an oracle of Apollo, which must be in an older writing that has been lost, and says that this is Osiris's coffin.

229 To understand this you must know the legend in which Seth kills Osiris. Seth made a lead coffin which, at a party, he encouraged the inebriated guests to get into under the pretext of finding out who could fit into it. After several guests had joined in the experiment,

Osiris, too, tried the coffin. Seth promptly put the lid on, sealed it with lead, and threw it into the sea. Therefore, it could be said that Osiris was suffocated in lead, so one can think of the tomb of Osiris as a lead coffin, or a coffin sealed up with lead, within which lies a dead God, or the divine spirit, in the form assumed in death. This is the meaning that Olympiodorus is trying to convey.

230 Osiris lies as a mummy in the coffin, with only his face visible. We know of mummies swathed in linen bands, wearing a mask depicting the face. The meaning of this is not clear, but one could say that there was something human and something inhuman in it. If you were to interpret it symbolically, as a dream, you would say that it must refer to a semihuman being for, if the face were human, then it can be partially understood from the human aspect, but the rest one cannot understand.

231 Olympiodorus continues by saying that Osiris himself is the suffocated coffin (or the tomb) that conceals his limbs and shows only his face to human beings. *Brotois* is a name for human beings and means "the mortals." Osiris is immortal, or the mortal immortal one, who shows only his human face to mortals while the rest of his body is a secret. "Hiding the bodies, nature marveled." I cannot entirely understand this, except that it must mean it is partly understandable because there is a human face, and partly a mystery, about which even nature marvels. I cannot give any further explanation. "That is the beginning [*arche*, origin, original matter] of all moist substances", i.e., basic matter, primordial matter, the starting point. The moist substance stands for the basic material of the cosmos that is caught in the sphere of the fire.

232 From what takes place later, it can be seen that there was the following connection: Matter was put into a bottle which was then securely sealed and cooked, and it had to hold its own within it. This is an exact parallel of the divine spirit, Osiris, the god man, lying dead in his lead coffin, for the matter in the bottle is in exactly the same state.

233 This was precisely what I felt when I tortured the resin in my early childhood, for I felt it was being tortured by fire in its bottle,

so to speak; it could not run away, i.e., it could not evaporate for I also had sealed my bottle. It was caught, and I had it in hand and was doing something to it. The analogy is Seth catching Osiris, and because he was caught by Seth, by the powerful principle of evil, he is transformed and resurrected. This was probably their association.

234 So he has suffocated all the lead. I do not understand this exactly, but it seems that this imprisonment in a coffin, or in an alchemical vessel, represents a process of suffocation, the death of the *prima materia* by suffocation.[40] Obviously there is an analogy here to what we do when we stop a human being from naïvely projecting and force that person to look only at him or herself. That would be like suffocation, for one wants to go to one's analyst and say, "That is how my mother brought me up." When, however, the analyst replies that one should see the part played by one's own complex, one has to then accept everything for which one had previously blamed God and fate, parents and husband. That has all to be taken back, and it is like suffocation, a kind of death, for the drive to project everything onto the outside world is stopped.

235 The vessel is a symbol for the attitude that prevents anything from escaping to the outside; it is a basic attitude of introversion that, in principle, does not let anything escape into the outside world. The illusion that the whole trouble lies outside oneself has to come to an end and things have to be looked at from within. In a certain sense we "suffocate" the *mysterium* of the unconscious. We do not know what the unconscious is, but we "suffocate" it through this concentrated treatment by which all projection is stopped. The psychological process becomes concentrated, and its intensity increases. It is also torture by fire because when the flow of intensity of the psychological process becomes concentrated, one is roasted—roasted in what one is. Therefore the person in the tomb and the tomb itself are the same thing, for you roast in what you yourself are and in nothing else; or one could say that one is cooked in one's own juice and is therefore the tomb and the coffin in the tomb, the one

[40] Cf. Jung, "The Psychological Meaning of Sacrifice, " in *Psychology and Religion*, vol. 11, *CW*, §§ 381-413.

being suffocated and the one doing the suffocating, the coffin and the dead god in it.

236 The one within is naturally not the ego, but one's whole being, for one is looking at one's whole being and not simply one's ego that would run away. This is so painful that we all try to escape. I think I have not analyzed anyone for years and years who has not, from time to time, flirted with the idea of dropping it all and returning to so-called "normal" life. Therefore, I think it is very understandable that the text, after a time, speaks of the woman who always tries to escape and who has to be bound into the fourfold body, or the four-body. I am preempting here what will follow, but for now let us go back to the text.

237 Take some substance, the golden stone, that is called the male part of the Chrysokolla [he probably had some specific concrete material in mind] and a moulded man.

238 Now who is the molded man, or the man who has been kneaded into shape? Olympiodorus is a Christian. It is, therefore, a definition of Adam! It simply means to take two chemical substances (which, we do not know) and take Adam. The connection for a man of that time was that Adam was made from clay, and therefore, according to the Bible, clay is the *prima materia* of man, the basic secret of man. They no longer meant clay literally: Their knowledge of biology and physiology was sufficient to know that the man made of clay was simply a simile. Therefore, clay stood for the *prima materia.*

239 The man formed out of clay was therefore Adam who, at that time, was a symbol of the Self, or, one could say, the man who has just come from the hands of God, the unspoiled man who has not yet passed through the process of corruption. Uncorrupted man straight from the hands of God is the man who has been kneaded. This is why he does not speak of Adam, for Adam is associated with sin and corruption and Eve, etc., so he prefers to refer to the molded man, and by alluding to Adam in this way, he means Adam in his original, unspoiled form, when he had just been created by God.

240 Obviously this refers to the *prima materia* that we call the Self, which is why in Zen Buddhism it is said, "Show me thy original face." In one of the koans, one of the masters gets enlightened when another master says this to him:

> 241 The gold of the Ethiopian earth generates it [i.e., the man] out of drops and there is some species of ant that brings it up to the surface of the earth and enjoys it.

242 This refers to the famous Arimaspi, who are also mentioned in Goethe's *Faust.*[41] There was a legend in late antiquity that at one time in India, there existed enormous ants—as big as human beings—that dug up gold. For the Greeks, India was the land of wisdom and riches; it was paradise where gold was to be found on the trees and in the streets and everywhere else, and where wise men walked about. Descriptions of India at the time mentioned these Arimaspi, huge legendary ants, that brought gold up out of the earth and were supposed to be the secret of India's great wealth. Olympiodorus is referring to these ants here.

243 If one goes into the symbolism of the ant at the time, one finds that in certain myths, ants resurrected the sun by pushing it over the horizon every morning. They are, then, a complete parallel to the Egyptian scarab that pushes the disc of the sun over the horizon every morning and makes it rise. The scarab is therefore a symbol of the rising sun and of resurrection. In certain traditions in late antiquity huge ants replaced the scarab in this legend but retained the exact same function. Therefore, the reference here is again to the resurrection of the sun, or to the moment of the very first creation of the sun god, which, according to our interpretation, would be the symbol of consciousness.

244 In psychological language one would say, "Go back to the original human being within you; go back to that place where your sympathetic nervous reactions (or your unconscious) link up with the origin of your consciousness." Put more accurately, it means, "Go

[41] Johann Wolfgang von Goethe, *Faust II*, §§ 7106-11.

back to the original point of your consciousness; try to return to the place from which your consciousness comes, to the threshold of the unconscious." The text continues:

245 Then put him [one assumes he means 'Adam'] together with his wife, the vapour, till the bitter divine water issues forth.

246 When this Adam, the original thing, is united with its opposite, which seems to be a vaporlike substance, the two together give birth to a bitter, watery substance. This is the motif of the *coniunctio*, the bringing together of the opposites, and the result is the mystical divine water, the bitter water. Psychologically that would mean to put yourself in an attitude of reflection in which you ask yourself where your conscious processes come from, and link this with the fantasy material—the vapor—that comes up from the unconscious. This creates a living insight, albeit a bitter one.

247 Because the insight we get by looking at ourselves in this way is generally bitter, few people do it; it is *pikros*—bitter—for it corrodes and is very disagreeable to the illusions of consciousness. That is why we speak of the "bitter truth" and of "bitter experience," for self-knowledge is a bitter experience in the beginning. Thus, if we read the text from a psychological standpoint, it is not rubbish but is completely logical. One must view it like a dream. One of Jung's great merits is that he gave us the key to these texts. To historians of chemistry they are officially absolute nonsense, for they see no meaning in them at all, but if we apply the key of Jungian interpretation, it is clear what Olympiodor is driving at, namely an inner experience, an introverted religious experience which those people have in their meditations and experiments with material phenomena, which is the basis of alchemy.

248 ***Question**: Does this reference to Adam refer to him before or after the Fall?*

249 I think before the Fall, for otherwise, in my view, the text would say Adam, and not use this peculiar expression of the molded or kneaded man. The kneaded man refers more to one aspect of Adam,

namely to his creation. The fact that he is made out of clay is what is emphasized, and therefore I would say the man made out of clay is what should be in one's mind when thinking of him, and not the fact that he was with Eve and the snake, etc. I think that can be corroborated by the fact that Olympiodorus knew the writings of Zosimos, who had developed a Gnostic theory about Adam being the unspoiled original man, before the Fall. We can therefore be quite sure the reference is to Adam before the Fall. The text continues:

250 So the sphere of fire keeps the lead and suffocates it, and that is the male thing, and the lead is so demonically possessed, so shameless, that those who wish to investigate it fall into madness through their own unconsciousness, and through their lack of knowledge of Gnosis.

251 This probably alludes to the fact that lead is usually poisonous. This chemical reality coincides with the fact that at the beginning, when one looks at the unconscious, such strong instinctual drives and emotions generally come up that one goes through states that could lead to madness. Alchemists frequently assert that many of them have gone off their heads, which may be taken literally.

252 Many years ago I had an interesting experience showing that there are still mad alchemists here in Switzerland! While working on these texts in the Central Library, one of the officials asked me if I was studying alchemy, and when I said I was, he told me that he had a colleague to whom he would introduce me. He thought it would be great joke. He led me to a little old shriveled-up man poring over an alchemical text and introduced me as a specialist in alchemy. I looked at this man, and when I saw his eyes, I saw at once that he was schizophrenic. I sat down beside him, and after a while he said, "Have you got the secret?" "No, not yet," I replied. And then he said, "I am very close; I think I shall have it in another two or three months." I said that that was marvelous, and then he asked me if I knew Greek, because his trouble was that he knew no Greek, and

that if I could help him with the Greek, we would get it. I said only, "Yes, yes, but not now!" That was a real alchemist who had fallen into the *mania* of the lead.

Lecture 4

253 We were discussing a very obscure passage in the Olympiodorus text where he says one should take the Chrysolithos, the golden stone that was called the male, together with the kneaded man, which apparently refers to Adam, who was kneaded or molded out of clay. There is, then, an indirect reference to Adam in Paradise that would be confirmed by the fact that Olympiodorus knew the writings of Zosimos.

254 In *Psychology and Alchemy*[42] Jung quotes a text of Zosimos in which it is said that Adam, having been created in Paradise from the four elements, fell out of Paradise into the world. The task of alchemy, according to Zosimos, is to reassemble the light sparks of Adam and bring him back to Paradise. Olympiodorus, who lived 200 years later, is obviously referring to this Zosimos text here, to the reassembling of Adam, and to restoring the fallen Adam, who lives as a spark of light in every human being, to the heavenly realm. Therefore, our text is a variation on the idea that, at bottom, Adam, the first man, is in matter in an extended or dissolved form, or in the cosmic figure of a human being (he has various names), and that he has to be liberated or redeemed from matter.

255 I would like to refer to *Psychology and Alchemy* in which, based on various texts, Jung illustrates that the idea of the fallen Adam, or of the fallen anima, mirrors the process of projection.[43] He explains that the myth of an angel, or Adam, or of a cosmic anima figure, falling into matter represents the moment when this figure is projected into matter. This means that such theories, like those in alchemy that spring from the unconscious, bring home the idea that suddenly the symbol of the Self is consciously sought for in matter.

---

[42] Jung, *Psychology and Alchemy*, vol. 12, *CW*, § 456.
[43] Cf. ibid., §§ 405-13.

256 This is clearly the case in our first text that referred to the funeral ritual of Osiris and to Egyptian funereal rituals in general. The search for immortality was actually the search for an incorruptible essence in man that would survive death, for an essential something in the human being that could be preserved. Thus, the search for immortality, for the eternal in man, is to be found at the very beginning of alchemy. This emotional drive and interest in the phenomenon of matter is not comparable to our modern scientific curiosity about the nature of matter; what gave the impulse and libido for the search to understand the mystery of matter was rather a very real emotional yearning and desire to find the immortal part of man.

257 This search continued into the 17th century, with all the later theories of the elixir of life, the *pharmakon zoe*, and so on. Something immortal that survives death, translated into modern psychological terms, could be expressed as an aspect of the Self—the search for the greater, incorruptible, and essential part of man.

258 As mentioned earlier, the next part of the text deals with the ants bringing up gold from the Ethiopian earth and the myth of the Arimaspi of India, for at that time both countries—India and Ethiopia—carried the projection of being the countries where miracles took place and where great piety reigned.

259 In the late Greek novels of Alexander the Great, there are many pseudoletters of Alexander the Great to his mother, Olympia, in which he speaks of India where, he says, Brahmins walk about naked and are the wisest and most pious men on earth. The same idea was also projected onto Ethiopia. In the late geographical novels and reports in Greek, it is always said that the black Ethiopian people were the closest to God and the most pious people in the world. It can also be said that because of their intellectual evolution, the Greeks lost a certain aspect of primitive religion—that immediate primitive religious attitude that, as far as we can see, is common to all primitive civilizations.

260 A study of primitive civilizations shows that having a religious attitude toward life was completely self-evident to them. Religion

was not separated from profane, everyday life, but was rather the self-evident basis of everything they did, believed, and said. In his primitive condition, man is naturally religious, and his religion pervades his whole nature and all his activities. Greek civilization had evolved from that state through the pre-Socratic and the Sophistic philosophy and the various evolutions of Greek philosophy. Perhaps for the first time in history, the learned gentry in Greece had cut away from a primitive religious attitude, and it was then projected onto the Indians and Ethiopians and later, according to late Greek literature, onto the Egyptians and such people, who were then considered to be the highest and closest to God. In their realm, our text says, the alchemical mystery was to be found.

261 A return to this primitive self-evident attitude toward life is a requisite for an experience of the Self that cannot be found through the conscious mind and with the developed part of the personality, but rather by first returning to that primitive human attitude.

262 **Question**: *Would the primitive religious attitude have to do with "participation mystique"?*

263 Yes, it has all the symptoms of primitive religion, namely *participation mystique*, the observation of synchronistic events, the observation of signs, not acting without first observing inner and outer symptoms and signs, or, as it has been defined[44], the constant, careful attention toward unknown dynamic factors. According to this definition, religion never means acting only in accordance with conscious reasoning, but rather paying constant attention to, and consideration of, the unknown participating factors. For instance, if someone says, "Let's have a coffee together after the lecture," if I think only that I have time since I won't be having lunch until 12.30, that would be conscious reasoning, which of course is also correct. But if I am a religious person, I will pause for a minute and try to get a feeling as to whether it is right to do that, and if I have an instinctive feeling against it, or if at that moment a window bangs shut, or I stumble, then I might not go.

[44] Jung, "Psychology and Religion," in *Psychology and Religion*, vol. 11, *CW*, §§ 1–168.

264 One can laugh at this as superstition, and naturally on that level it is not different from superstition, but it is not just a mechanical thing as, for example, the idea that if a black cat crosses your path, you should turn back. It is more that, in such moments, one should concentrate upon trying to get some sign from the Self, or from within oneself. It is tantamount to paying constant attention to the Tao in Chinese philosophy, paying attention to whether what I am doing right now is really in Tao. Naturally, there are also personal arguments—the pros and cons of a thing—but to live in a religious way would mean being constantly on the alert for those unknown powers that also guide one's life. If I get no contrary indication, I can decide to have coffee whenever I have time or because I like it. A bell does not always ring warning us, but if it does and one ignores it, then something goes wrong. A religious and primitive attitude involves constant consideration of these powers.

265 When Jung was in Africa, his safari guide was a Muslim, I believe a Shiite. At breakfast every morning all the black carriers discussed their dreams, after which the leader of the group would go to Jung and say whether or not they would proceed that day. Jung found that when they said they were not going, the general aspect of the dreams had not been favorable, so they felt they should probably wait a day before proceeding. Jung accepted these decisions and even managed to be drawn into the discussion on dreams and to take part. They were very much impressed to find that he knew something about, and was interested in, dreams and that he was even better at interpreting them than they were, and, in this way, he was able to observe what was happening. But an Englishman who went to the same place some weeks later naturally did as most white men do: He accused the men of being lazy and insisted that they had to arrive at their destination in five days' time and used force, and he was killed.

266 This illustrates an attitude of careful consideration of all the irrational aspects. The natives acted as they did because there might have been a thunderstorm that day, or perhaps a rhinoceros might have attacked them, and so on. In nature, one is constantly

confronted with such things and our unconscious knows about these things. When one is living in wild nature, attention to such factors is essential to survival. Animals always receive a warning, be it of an earthquake or some other danger; they get them instinctively, and if we pay attention, we, too, receive them through our dreams. This is why those natives paid attention to their dreams every morning in an adaptable and reasonable way.

267 I had an illustration of something like this the other day when I was at my holiday home when there was obviously a thunderstorm approaching from the upper part of the lake. Naturally, I did not know that it would hail, but my dog suddenly put her ears back and rushed into the house and on up to the top floor and hid her head in my bed. I rushed after her to see why she had behaved in that way and, at that moment, down came the hail! Animals have such warnings by a kind of telepathy, which is only a word meaning to be aware of something far away and explains nothing. We only know that in the unconscious, instinctive functioning of higher animals, including man, there is a supernatural or, better said, a superrational awareness of things about which we could not know rationally, and that it is therefore helpful, healthy and very important to pay attention to such impulses. They seem not only to work for the survival of animals and human beings but also to work for the higher development, the maturity, and the psychological welfare of the individual. This is what we call the preserving and healing aspect of the unconscious.

268 According to our definition, religion, in its most basic form, would simply be constant, alert attention directed toward these facts, instead of allowing conscious rational decisions and our reasoning of the pros and cons to rule and decide our lives. This is why religion pervades everyday life in primitive societies. Before primitives go hunting, there is a hunting ritual, and if there is an accident during it, they do not go. There is nothing mystical, transcendental or special about it; the basic religious attitude is linked to the idea of survival. Being religious, therefore, has an immediate advantage for it can save one's life.

269 When we are confronted with a neurosis, when people get stuck in their difficulties, we try to discover what the unconscious has to say and we guide our analysands to attend more to their instincts, behind which is the whole phenomenon of religious insight and experience. Jung, of course, began as all doctors did, and also on the basis of his contact with Freud, with the idea of helping people become more instinctive to increase their health, but then he discovered that religion is behind instinct, that religion was something instinctive and completely natural, for natural man is a religious man. One therefore has to return to the natural, immediate man within and to a religious attitude, for we cannot have one without the other.

270 There has been an etymological dispute as to whether the word *religio* derives from *religare* or *religere*. Naturally, both have the same root—*legere*, to pick up. Originally, it referred to picking up or collecting, for example, wood. But *legere,* meaning "to read," has another connection, namely one "picks up" or "gathers together" the individual letters, which is how people read at first and how children still learn to read.

271 *Religare* has been accepted as the official interpretation since the time of St. Augustine, with the theological reflection that it means to bind, to bind one back to God. St. Augustine explained that man had been severed from God through original sin and that the task of religion was to bind him back again. This is obviously not a scientific interpretation, but it is very interesting and a good reflection of the Christian idea of religion. Modern etymologists think that the word "religion" probably comes from the word *religere*, which means "careful consideration." I have already given amplifications, for example, alertness to irrational factors. But they are not contained within the word itself, which simply means "careful consideration." The "re" indicates "backward," so it means that one looks backward to find out whether what is behind is coming too, or if it is doubtful. One has always to watch for and ascertain what the other forces have to say about our lives.

272 ***Question****: Could one simply call this superstition?*

273 No! Superstition would be the mechanization of this attitude. Generally one thinks of superstition when one knocks on wood, or when one says that to see a black cat means bad luck, or that a spider in the morning means trouble and is a bad sign. This may all be true, but if applied mechanically, if careful consideration of the signs becomes codified, then superstition comes in. A spider indicates spinning, the spinning of fantasies. The superstition is that a spider means bad luck in the morning and good luck in the evening. Obviously this really means that if in the morning one is slack and sleepy, gets up late and sits around half dressed and just thinks of one's neurotic problems, this would be the spider in the morning, which would certainly bring bad luck. But if, after working all day, one lights a cigarette in the evening and sits in front of the house, as peasants do, and lets one's fantasy run, or if one philosophizes about life, that is quite all right; it is a very good way to prepare oneself for sleep. Therefore, the spider in the evening is propitious. This was probably the original meaning of this widespread superstition. The spider is a negative mother symbol; it is the Maya and everything that goes with that. It is in order if it comes in the evening, or in the evening of one's life, but it is very bad to start the day with it. It would be interesting if someone were to write a thesis on common superstitions and what they mean symbolically, for they are very meaningful. The mechanical application of superstition in the negative sense of the word is just a stupid habit and has nothing to do with a religious attitude.

274 Returning to our text, it says,

> Then put the gold that the ants have brought up together with his wife, or the vapour wife, till the divine bitter water comes out.

275 As mentioned earlier, here we have the motif of the *coniunctio.* One takes the gold that is dug up from the Ethiopian earth, the masculine substance, and puts it together with a feminine substance, that is

also called the wife or vapor, until the child, the bitter water, comes out. The wife is characterized as vapor. Other texts clearly show that vapor or steam is generally regarded as the psyche of matter.

276 In the Swiss military service, right up to 1910, a short course used to be given in general medicine, just to teach people about bones and the circulation of the blood, and so on. Once a teacher said that the brain was like a cup full of macaroni and the steam above it was the soul! He had fallen into the old alchemical pattern! You could say that that fantasy was 2,000 years old, for in the old texts on alchemy the idea of steam or *vapor* always bore the idea of the psyche, of sublimated matter, of subtle body, something half material. If a ghost appears in parapsychological experiences, there is often firstly something like steam, or mist. So we can say that the idea that the psyche has to do with the quality of steam or vapor is an archetypal idea that is somehow linked with, but not identical to, solid matter. As our text was written by a man, there is probably a certain anima factor in it.

277 From the union of the male substance with the vapor comes the divine bitter water. The word "divine" in Greek is *theios*, which also means sulfur, so it can be translated as the divine water, which is the generally accepted official translation, or as sulfur water, since sulfur was regarded as being a divine substance. It is the water, or the liquid, of the divine substance.

278 Water in general, including urine, carries the projection of knowledge and wisdom. In medieval church symbolism they spoke of the aqua *doctrinae*, and in our Swiss dialect, if somebody comes out with a lot of nonsense, just a lot of words, we say he is "urinating." Psychogenic kidney troubles very often have to do with people being filled up with such "bad water," for they do not have the right attitude, or the right connection with knowledge; they just blather a lot of undigested knowledge, and that is like urinating. So one can say that as a rule water has to do with knowledge extracted from the unconscious that can be used positively or negatively.

279 In alchemy water was either the great healing factor, or poisonous and destructive. Usually we interpret it as the water of the

unconscious and differentiate its specific meaning according to the context. If water were rising in a patient's dream, or if there were a big inundation, we would say, "Be careful, the unconscious is overwhelming you!" In this case, the water would be negative. But if you are in the desert and thirsty, it is the water of life. Christ is the well of life, and there are various other well-known similes. In all religions, water is the substance of life, which boils down to the fact that the *extractio* of the anima—that watery knowledge—is what takes place when we interpret a psychological situation or a dream.

280 If someone comes with a problem, instead of arguing with the person, we look at the dream which comments on the situation. Perhaps it can be interpreted in such a way as to vivify the person and give them a feeling of hope and a sense of the problem having a hidden meaning so that there might be a way to solve it, even if is not yet clear how. In a situation like this, knowledge obtained from the unconscious has the quality of the water of life for that person has, as it were, drunk of the water of life, and they will go away with the feeling that now something is flowing and the period of stagnation is over. The analysand is then curious about the next analytical hour and wonders how the inner adventure will continue, and in this way, life gets a new start and flows once more.

281 On the other hand, we have all seen people drowned in the unconscious, namely schizoid or borderline cases, or people in a psychotic episode, who talk knowledge of the unconscious. They sit in bed, or in their cells in the asylum, and talk of the creation of the world, and of what God is, and what should be done to save the world, saying that the doctors in the asylum are all fools and they know better, and so on. This is unconscious knowledge; it is water, and it is even full of wisdom, but the speaker's head is under the water, and this knowledge has gotten the person, not the person the knowledge. These poor people literally drown in the wisdom of the unconscious and they do not want to get out for they feel that they are drowning in something very good and marvelous. This is why most refuse to be cured. Seen from a reasonable standpoint, this is a very bad condition for people to be in, for such people become so

maladapted they have to be confined. They have too much of the water of life, for it *is*, in fact, the water of life, and what they say is not nonsense. If you have sufficient symbolic knowledge, you can understand what a psychotic person says from A to Z, just as though it were everyday talk.

282 In our text we have the normal situation, namely that the divine water has to be produced as a result of the *coniunctio*, which, in psychological terms, would be what we do every day. We unite our conscious attitude with the unconscious, for instance in the interpretation of dreams, and by doing so, we get this vivifying knowledge, a sense of understanding, and this is the water. Now why is the water referred to here as bitter?

283 ***Remark***: *Because it is the truth.*

284 Yes, naturally! Very often we do not have a very happy reaction, for the truth from the unconscious is frequently very bitter. It is often a bitter pill we have to swallow because it contains very obvious criticisms of our attitudes, and that is a bitter experience. This explains the resistance people feel toward psychology, for many do not want to swallow the bitter pill. They have a vague feeling of being badly off track and that they could return to health only by swallowing certain criticism. If it comes from the outside, they are determined to fight it; when it comes from within, it is also extremely unpleasant. The analyst can then wash his hands of it and say he is sorry, but it is the analysand's own dream that is saying it, and not the analyst. And then he has to swallow the bitter pill.

285 Our text continues by saying that the philosopher Petasios also speaks of the work in the same way, saying, "that the sphere of the fire is kept down by the lead." Interpreting himself, the same philosopher says, "This is from the male water." Olympiodorus remarks that the male water seems to be the same thing as the sphere of fire that, as we saw in the earlier part of the text, was the tomb of Osiris, who was suffocated in lead. Therefore, we have Osiris, the sphere of fire and male water, and all three are suffocated in lead, the enemy.

286 In late antiquity, lead was thought of as the metal of the planet Saturn and had the same qualities: on the negative side, depression, and on the positive side, creative depression. Saturn is the God *par excellence* of mutilated people, criminals, and cripples, but also of artistic and creative people. In our modern language it would mean the strange quality in certain depressions when one feels literally like lead. Without thinking of alchemical similes, people often say, "I feel like lead today." In a heavy depression one feels unable to get up from one's chair, or even to open one's mouth to explain that one is depressed; one just sits like a block of heavy matter. Accounts given by people in such a state have innumerable lead similes.

287 As the word implies, a person in a depression is pressed down, compressed, usually because a part of one's psychological libido is below and has to be fetched up; one's real energy for life has fallen into a deeper layer of the personality and can only be reached through a depression. Unless there is a latent psychosis, one should encourage people to go into their depression and really *be* depressed—not to try and escape with the radio or the newspaper. And if the depression says that life means nothing and that nothing is worthwhile, one should shrug and say, "And now?" Listen and go deeper and deeper, until you again reach the level of the psychological energy where some creative idea can come out, and suddenly, in the deepest depths, an impulse of life and creativity that has been overlooked may appear.

288 People who are professionally creative, like artists or great actors and so on, know that before every performance or new piece of work they are likely to have such a depression. One can have it on a smaller scale, for instance, I always have it before a lecture, for the libido firstly goes down. Those are similar rhythms of something that happens on a large scale in a depression. It means that one has overlooked certain creative factors that have constellated below and have attracted the libido, causing listlessness and a lack of energy.

289 It can also be a prepsychotic symptom, as psychiatrists well know. What then comes up is also a creative content, but it wells up to such an extent that it can destroy the personality. In such cases

one must think twice before encouraging a person to go into the depression because, though the mechanism is the same, there is the risk that what comes up may be too strong and burst the personality. Lead is therefore that heaviness, that listlessness, that feeling of nothingness that covers up or suffocates the contents of the unconscious; these are surrounded by, or wrapped up in, such unfortunate things.

290 As the text says, there is even an element of madness in lead. This refers to another aspect, for if you dig up depressive states in a person, there is usually, at bottom, either a creative content or a violent, unsatisfied desire. Frequently depressed people dream of voracious lions or other devouring animals such as dragons, but particularly lions, which means they are depressed because they are frustrated in the fulfilment of their wild desires. They want everything: to be top dog, have the most beautiful partner, money, and everything else. They have childish, wild desires that would like to eat everything up, but at the same time they are intelligent enough to know that life is not like that, that they cannot have what they want, so the desire curls up into a sulky depression. Such a depression has the quality of a sulky, frustrated desire, and this explains why, after an unhappy love affair, people fall into an awful depression. Their lion has been frustrated and has returned, sulking, to its lair. In this sense, the element of a wild and primitive desire is a part of a depression, which explains the devouring, roaring lion.

291 Some people have a frustrated infant within themselves. They are usually very correct and polite and make very few demands on the analyst, but being too polite and correct and considerate is always suspect. One knows that they would like to gobble up the analyst lock, stock and barrel, like a lion. They suddenly make childish demands and scenes because the analyst has stopped five minutes before the time, or answered the telephone, or put off the hour, or even had the flu! Such demanding infantile people compensate by being very correct, knowing that if they admit their demands, the devouring lion will come up, and the analyst will naturally hit back. They have experienced this often in life when,

after hiding their feelings, they one day took the risk and as a result got banged on the head. So the hurt child retires once more, bitterly frustrated, and then comes the depression, the devouring lion. This is a part of primitive nature, of primitive archaic reactions of which the conflict of wanting to eat and not being able to do so is a part, as a result of which the depressive mania takes over.

292 That is the symbolism of the madness in lead, but it also contains Osiris, the immortal man, and if you can only accept that reality within yourself, you will come to the creative content where the Self is hidden. The frustrated child could be said to be an aspect covering up an image of the Self, as is the devouring lion. The image of the devouring lion makes this very clear. If I think I ought to be top dog everywhere, have the most beautiful partner, have money, be happy and so on, then I am having a paradise fantasy. And what is that? It is nothing other than a projection of the Self! The childish thing is actually the desire to experience everything in the here and now. The fantasy in itself is entirely legitimate: It includes the idea of the *coniunctio* and a perfect state—a state of harmony. It is a religious idea, but naturally if it is projected onto outside life and wanted there, in the here and now, it is impossible. The way in which the person wants to realize the fantasy is childish, but in and of itself, it is valuable, and there is nothing wrong or unhealthy about it.

293 So just in that uncontrolled mad spot in a person, in the wild or problematic spot, is the symbol of the Self that provides the drive. This is why people never know what to do for they cannot repress it; or if they are reasonable and just give "it" up because they realize how childish it is and that one should be resigned and adapt to life, they feel they are cured, but that they have been robbed of their best possibilities and are therefore disappointed.

294 I once had an analysand who came to Europe for a Jungian analysis while his best friend went into Freudian analysis. After a year they decided to meet again. The Freudian analysand said that he was cured and was going back to his own country; having realized all his neurotic illusions and nonsense, he was going to begin to earn his living and find a wife and marry. The other said he was not cured

at all but still very mad and in a condition of great chaos, and though he saw his way a little bit more clearly, there was still a great deal which had not yet been solved. The Freudian patient then said that it was strange, but that though all his devils had been driven out, unfortunately so had his angels! A lid had been put on the mad spot, but the religious fantasy in it of perfection, the romantic fantasy, had also had the lid put on it. The fantasy of the Self had also had the lid put on it so that this man could become a resigned, socially adapted animal who functions, while all his romantic dreams of truth and life and real love—admittedly childish fantasies in both those young men—are buried too.

295 To return to alchemical language, the great difficulty, therefore, is to extract Osiris from the lead, to save the fantasy that is life-giving and to cut away the childishness of the wish to realize it. That is so damn subtle! The whole task is to save the nucleus, the fantasy of the Self, and to cut away all the childishness, the primitive desire, and so on, that surrounds it. This is what getting Osiris out of the lead coffin would mean. This is what the alchemist was doing in a projected form when he said that the divine man had to be extracted from the lead coffin, or from the corruptible matter.

Part 2

Arabic Alchemy

Book of the Silvery Water and Starry Earth

296 The Arabic text that we shall now turn our attention to was written by Muhammed Ibn Umail at-Tamimi; it is sufficient to speak of Muhammed ibn Umail because at-Tamimi refers only to the specific Islamic tribe to which he belonged. He lived from about 900 to 960 A.D., that is, at the beginning of the 10th century, according to our dates. One of his writings was published in Arabic in *The Memoirs of the Asiatic Society of Bengal*[1]; it was printed in Calcutta in 1933, as one of three manuscripts that Henry E. Stapleton had found. Stapleton states that there were many other manuscripts by the same author in Hyderabad with most interesting and promising titles, such as *The Pearl of Wisdom*, *The Hidden Lamp of Alchemy*, and so on, but if you write and inquire about them, you get no answer![2]

297 This man has been famous in European alchemy since the 12th or the beginning of the 13th century. The writing I am going to present here was translated into Latin around this time and has become one of the most famous medieval writings in the Latin alchemical world.[3] In these Latin texts his name is given as Senior, and until 1933 nobody knew who Senior was. Even the famous Julius Ruska asserted that Senior was not an Arab: It was a Latin mis-representation. But one cannot always trust Ruska for he is always a doubter; he was completely wrong in his contention that it was mistakenly taken to be an Arabic text. We now have the original and know that the name Senior is simply the Latin

---

[1] H. E. Stapleton, M. Turab 'Ali, and M. Hidayat Husain, 'Three Arabic Treatises on Alchemy by Muhammad Ibn Umail (10th Century A.D.)', in *Memoirs of the Asiatic Society of Bengal*, ed. Turab 'Ali, vol. 12 (Calcutta: Asiatic Society of Bengal, 1933).

[2] For further reading in connection with the life and work of Muhammad Ibn Umail see Abt, et al., *Kitab Hall ar-Rumuz;* and von Franz, *Hall ar-Rumuz.*

[3] Muhammad Ibn Umail, *De Chemia Senioris Antiquissimi Philosophi Libellus* (Strasbourg: Samuel Emmel, 1566); and cf. Jung, *Mysterium Coniunctionis,* vol. 14, *CW,* § 3.

translation for "the sheikh," which actually means "the old man" and explains how Mohammed ibn Umail came to be called Senior.[4] This Latin text was published under the title *De chemia*, to indicate that it is about chemistry, but the real Arabic title is *Kitab al Ma' al-waraqi wa-l-ard an-nagmiya.*[5] The Arabic text is given on one side and the Latin on the other, making it possible to compare one with the other. The Latin translation is quite correct and deviates only in minor details.[6]

298 After Muhammed ibn Umail had left his homeland, his best friend, a Shiite, was burnt as a heretic. In the Islamic world, the Sunnites were the official sect and, expressed roughly, the split between the Sunnites and the Shiites was due to the fact that the latter had a more symbolic and mystical interpretation of the Koran. They did not take the Koran literally but allowed for symbolic interpretation, while the Sunnites insisted on literal obedience to the rules and on its literal truth. The Shiites developed an extensive mystical system of symbolic interpretation and in that way can be compared to the mystics of the Middle Ages, who, in contrast to other religious orientations, also tried to interpret the Bible in a symbolic way.

299 One could also make a comparison with the parallel split between the Talmudic and Cabbalistic trends in the Jewish tradition. The Shiites would correspond to the Cabbalistic tradition, the true introverts who were more directed toward a psychological symbolic interpretation and personal experience of the religious truth, in contrast to the literal-minded people who rather insisted on dogma and the holy text.

300 I shall present the Arabic text just as it is in all its complexities, as I did with both the Greek texts, to allow one to get the full impact of the strangeness of this kind of literature.[7]

---

[4] Marie-Louise von Franz often used the name "Senior" in her lecture, but here his Arabic name is used.

[5] *Book of the Silvery Water and Starry Earth.*

[6] The only published Latin translation of *De chemia* is flawed, according to Theodor Abt, *Book of the Explanation of the Symbols*, vol. 1, CALA, 13.

[7] Marie-Louise von Franz is translating from the Latin text here, for in 1959, at the time this lecture was given, the Arabic text did not exist. This fact does not appear to have essentially affected Marie-Louise von Franz's psychological understanding of the text. In her later interpretations, she was able to consult the English translation by Salwa Fuat and Theodor Abt, cf. von Franz, *Hall ar-Rumuz.*

301 I and my dear Obouail [the ending is feminine] entered the Barba. [Barba means beard, and of course everybody said that one could not enter a beard; no one knew what to say about the word. It simply stands for *Birba* – pyramid.[8] By not understanding this word, the translator caused a lot of confusion.] I entered the Birba and a certain subterranean house, and afterwards I and El Hassan, that is Hassan, saw all the fiery prisons of Joseph, and I saw on the roof the nine painted eagles with their wings expanded as if flying and with their feet open, and in their talons was a big bow, such as is also used by those who shoot with a bow.

302 On the walls of this house, at the left and right of the man entering, I saw the images of human beings standing about. They could not have been more perfect or beautiful, or had more beautiful clothes in all colours. They had their hands extended towards the centre of the room and were looking at a certain statue in the middle of the room near the wall of the inner chamber. And it was facing them. The statue was seated on a throne, similar to a doctor's throne, with its hands spread out over its knees, and in its lap, over its arms, was a marble plate, which was extracted from it [from what is not known] in the length of one arm and as broad as one hand; and the fingers of the statue were clasped over the edge of the tablet which it held. The tablet had the appearance of an open book facing any person who entered, as if the statue wanted to show it to him.

303 This sounds complicated, but it simply means there was a seated statue at the back of the room holding a tablet over which its fingers were clasped outward, and it looked like an open book, which apparently it wanted to show to the person who came in.

---

[8] "Birba" (Arabic) = temple. In the Introduction to *Kitab al-Ma' al-waraqi wa-l-ard an-nagmiya*, M. Ibn Umail describes his visit to the temple of Busir or Abusir, that he also refers to as Joseph's prison. Cf. Theodor Abt, *The Great Vision of Muhammad Ibn Umail.* (Los Angeles: C. G. Jung Institute of Los Angeles, 2003), 11-12. The word 'Abusir' comes from the Egyptian word 'Per-usire, temple of Osiris; cf. ibid., FN 33, reference to H. Bonnet, *Reallexikon der Ägyptischen Religionsgeschichte*, Berlin 1952, under "Abusir."

304 In that part of the room in which the statue sat were images of infinite things, and letters written in a barbaric language [which simply means a language other than Arabic]. The tablet one saw on the lap of the statue was divided by a line down the middle that separated the two sides. On the lower part was the image of two birds bent over each other, one of which was wingless and the other winged. Each held the tail of the other in its beak. Looked at schematically, the birds are lying over each other, each with its head to the tail of the other, one winged and the other wingless. It is as if they want to fly together, or as if the wingless one is keeping the other back, that is, the upper bird wants to carry away the lower, but the lower bird is holding it back and preventing it from flying away. The two birds are bound together, are homogeneous and are of the same substance; they are painted within one sphere, as if it is an image of two things in one.

305 Near the head of the flying bird, and above it, the sun and moon were represented. This was near the fingers of the statue, and on the other side of the tablet – that is, to the right – was another sphere or round object facing the birds. Taken together, there were five time rhythms [that is also something which is unexplained], namely below the birds and the sphere and above is the image of the moon and another sphere.

306 On the other side, near the fingers of the statue, is the image of the sun that emits its rays like the image of two in one. Opposite is an image of the sun with one ray falling downwards and together that would make three, namely the two planets – the sun and the moon – and the ray of the two in one; and from the ray one part goes down and reaches into the lower part of the tablet that surrounds the black sphere and divides it, which altogether makes two, three, and the third.

307 What is clear from the above is that the sun and moon are beside each other, with the moon facing you on the right and the sun on the left, and below is a black sphere that the rays

penetrate. The third has the form of a waxing moon, the inner part of which is white without blackness, but it is surrounded by a black sphere, and the form is like the form of the 'two in one' of a simple sun. And that is the image of one in one and those are again five, and together they make ten, according to the number of the eagles and the black earth.

308 I have now told you all this and have written a poem, and without the grace of God, whose name be blessed, we should not have this secret. So that you may understand and think

> well about it and meditate on it, I have painted for you the image of the tablet, and what the images are will be explained in my poem, and afterwards you can look at the chapters and see what each figure meant. Now I have already explained those ten figures and I have shown the figures in my poem and certainly one could not do without my poem, but I want to manifest to you something which all the wise men have hitherto hidden who produced this statue in this house, in which the whole science is described in a symbolic figure teaching his wisdom on this stone and displaying it to those who can understand. I know that this statue was the figure of a wise man. [This statue represents Hermes, so it means Hermes invented the science and drew the figures.[9]]

309 We now have to find out what this all means. The statue is the figure of a wise man, and on his lap is the secret science that he describes by means of symbolic figures so as to direct the one who knows and understands. The wise one who understands it must look at the inner with subtlety and must know the terms of wisdom and must understand obscure and symbolic language. When he then compares such obscure language with our images, he will open the one from the other and will become the ruler of the secret stone.

310 At this point another part of a text has been inserted that has a new title, *Letter from the Sun to the Waxing Moon.*[10] It begins,

311 In great weakness I will give you light from my beauty till I have reached perfection.

312 At the end of the letter, Muhammad Ibn Umail promises to give an explanation, but, in fact, he simply carries on with the text. The explanation he gives is simply what we would call an amplification—a very meaningful one, it is true, but still not an explanation.

---

[9] On this statue cf. Jung, *Mysterium Coniunctionis*, vol. 14, *CW*, §§ 559-69.

[10] This is the text that Marie-Louise von Franz later (p. 147) interprets at length.

313 Actually we know that Muhammed Ibn Umail was one of those damned robbers who broke open pyramids and emptied the inner coffin chambers.[11] In those times the Arabs destroyed a great number of pyramids, stealing all the gold in them, so that nowadays most pyramids are empty. But Muhammed Ibn Umail did not do it because he, like most of the others, wanted to find gold, but rather because he projected the alchemical secret into the death chamber of the pyramids. As we will discover in the succeeding parts of the book, Ibn Umail thought that the Egyptians knew alchemy and that what was to be found in the innermost chamber of the pyramid was the secret of alchemy. But of course he could not read what was written in the old Egyptian language—as we know, this was before Champollion.[12] He believed that in those mysterious hieroglyphic signs the secret of alchemy was written.

314 As he describes in another text, he found a mummified queen in a coffin made of gold who had a pair of scissors and little bowls of gold with her, and he was absolutely sure that that was the queen of alchemy, as it were, the wise prophetess of alchemy. The instruments hidden in the coffin of the Egyptian queen he took to be symbolic allusions to the alchemical work.[13]

315 That is the strange thing about projecting into the past: Ibn Umail projected the whole symbolism of the alchemical opus into mummification. But what is even more interesting is that alchemy, as I mentioned above, did actually originate from the Egyptian death cult, that the chemistry of mummification played an enormous role, and that the Egyptians mummified their dead in order to obtain immortality and to make the dead person divine; alchemy tried to do the same thing, namely to produce the immortal man, to produce immortality. Thus, there is a very good hook for Ibn Umail's projection—he just projected the whole thing backward into

---

[11] According to oral information given by Theodor Abt, this statement about the pyramids is based upon an incorrect translation of the word *birba* by the Indian Turab 'Ali. This word means temple and has its roots in the Coptic word *perpe*. Still today the word *birba* is used for 'temple' in Egyptian Arabic.
[12] Knowledge of hieroglyphs had long disappeared, and Jean-François Champollion was able to decipher the hieroglyphs only at the beginning of the 19th century.
[13] According to oral information given by Theodor Abt, the text referred to in this paragraph cannot be attributed to Muhammad Ibn Umail.

mummification. Everything he saw in the death chambers of the pyramids he saw from the perspective of the work of alchemy.

316 The picture of this statue holding a tablet is not specific to Ibn Umail but is rather a classic topic found in many other alchemical texts. C. G. Jung's lectures on Zarathustra[14] have made the *Tabula Smaragdina*[15] well known. It is a classical text, the single sentences of which Jung has given an interpretation to, so I need not go into it. The oldest form of such a text was found in the writings of Gabir (Jabir Ibn Hayyan), an author of the eighth century. From this oldest version of the search for the *Tabula* it is clear that the motif goes back to Greek sources. There must have been a Greek story of a Hermes statue found in a tomb, holding the whole secret on its knees.

317 That story is reported in various texts of alchemical literature, for instance in the *Kitab al Habib* (*The Friend's Book*) or also the *Book of Krates*. It always starts off the same way—"I entered the tomb and found a statue with a tablet, on which was ...."—and then follows a kind of explanation. So in Ibn Umail's time this had become a theme in literature, but in this parallel to the *Tabula Smaragdina* there is a new variation. Ibn Umail has added something that we have not found in any of the other tales of the tablet, namely the nine (or 10) eagles that, in the picture, shoot at the statue with bow and arrow. He has also changed the content of the tablet, for on it are no sentences of wisdom, as in the others, but two symbolic drawings—the one of the two birds trying to fly away from each other, and the other of the sun and moon and the black sphere. As far as I can tell, this is Ibn Umail's own contribution.

318 I am now taking some of the information given in the rest of the text, all of which I cannot cite here. The eagles represent the sublimated or volatile substance and therefore bring to mind the wife of the steam in the text of Olympiodor. Flying substances like steam and vapor were often symbolized by birds, and it was said that these substances had acquired spiritual qualities. The bow and arrow are quite mysterious and are never explained throughout the whole book,

[15] Cf. Julius Ruska, ed., *Tabula Smaragdina: Ein Beitrag zur Geschichte der hermetischen Literatur* (Heidelberg: Winter, 1926).

so we must either leave them unexplained or give them a psychological explanation.[16] Hermes sits surrounded by the nine eagles that are shooting at him with bow and arrow, but Ibn Umail ignores this motif in his explanation of the text! The rest of the text, however, makes it clear that the eagles represent the spiritualized substances.

319 What could the bow and arrow represent here? Imagine it was a patient's drawing: What could be the meaning of the eagles shooting at Hermes? We have to firstly amplify the bow and arrow. What does that suggest?

320 ***Remark:*** *Eros.*

321 Yes, of course, that is the first thing that spontaneously comes to mind—the little god of love, Cupid, with his awkward arrows, and the whole literature of antiquity concerning the bow and arrow and how Cupid even sometimes shoots an arrow at Zeus at a very bad moment and gets him into his power.

322 A bow and arrow would indicate direction—something is pointed at an object. The libido has been directed, just as happens if you fall in love: You are minding your own business and are perhaps a little dissociated, swimming along in the stream of life when suddenly you are shot at, and then you think of that woman or man from morning till night. Suddenly all the libido is directed and concentrated there. You do not want to think about it, but then you begin to wonder whether you will meet that person tomorrow at the same place and so on, for that is where the energy is.

323 Therefore, you can say that the bow and arrow have to do with the sudden directedness of the unconscious libido, with a projection, for an arrow is a projectile, and through projection the libido gets pointed. It is just the same if you hate someone. There is even a saying—I believe it is an Indian one—that questions who is closer to God: he who loves him or he who hates him? And the answer is

[16] Cf. the exposition by Theodor Abt, *Muhammad Ibn Umail,* 17, in which he states there was barely an eagle to be found in Egypt. According to Bruno Hugo Stricker, *La prison de Joseph,* (Leiden: Brill, 1943), 101-37; Ibn Umail may have found inspiration from the wings of the vultures that were depicted on the ceilings of Egyptian temples. In the Arabic text that describes these nine eagles, Ibn Umail says that in their claws they were carrying *mustaufi al-'rid,* that can be translated as "sword." Indeed, these vultures are always depicted in the Pharoahs' temples as having long feathers, the symbol of the goddess Ma'at.

the man who hates him, because he will think of God even more often and more intensely than the one who loves him, for his bow and arrow are constantly directed at him. Libido is given a direction through projection.

324 One could say that all the dissociated forces of thought and of the soul are now concentrated upon what is on this tablet, i.e., one's whole psychological attention is now concentrated upon it. The two wings of the tablet are like two parts of a book: On the one side is the problem of the two birds, and on the other that of the union of sun and moon. The problem of the two birds is obviously a variation of the Ouroboros of alchemy, for in the old Greek texts we find a drawing of the snake that eats its own tail. Usually the head has stars on it, and the rest is black, which would be the secret opposition; and it is explained that the head is different from the tail. This is a marvelous image of one thing in which there is an inner opposition between the head and the tail. Therefore, there are such sayings as, "Take the head, but beware of the tail" or "Unless the head has integrated the tail, the whole substance is nothing." There is a great deal said about the head and the tail, and how they should relate to each other; they are good descriptions of the secret that the opposites are, at bottom, one. One could call it a kind of European *tai-gi-tu*—the opposites in one.

325 ***Remark:*** *The eagles give me the impression of having a relation to Apollo for it is said that they can look at the sun, and because of course Apollo has a bow, as has the winged Cupid.*

326 Apollo is the representative of the principle of consciousness, but that does not contradict the interpretation. Apollo's bow and arrow would refer to the attention given by love, the concentration of mental libido through love. According to the scholastic theory of knowledge, you can only get knowledge through love, that you only acquire knowledge by loving your subject, by being fascinated by it. Thus the anima is always behind the search for truth. If you have to learn about a subject you do not love, where you have no projection—which

means that you have no relationship to it—it does not mean anything to you and is not connected with your flow of libido, so you have to toil and sweat at something and learn it for the exam, but 10 minutes later you have forgotten it again. If you are fascinated, however, which means that a projection has taken place, you get emotional and acquire a tremendous amount of knowledge very easily and quickly. That is the whole secret of teaching and learning. You might say that teaching and learning are simply two aspects of what as a general description one might call attention; they are created either by a concentration of consciousness, or by love, and behind both is projection—a fascination based upon a projection.

327 ***Remark:*** *You talk of projection, but these are all archetypal figures.*

That raises the question as to whether archetypes project. I think they do, and it is certainly in our idea of projection. Consider what actually happens. We know quite well that we never make the projection, but that it is done to us. We do not project something—even though that is the way one talks, it is not true. The fact is we suddenly find ourselves in the situation of projecting. Only when we have seen that it was a projection can we begin to talk about it, but not before. For instance, someone who has projected the shadow will insist the other person is a rotter and will carry on like that, but perhaps two years later, in the course of analysis, he will realize how much projection was involved and will be able to say that he did, indeed, project his shadow onto the other person. Thus, the question of *who* is doing the projecting is a great mystery.

328 When the Greeks fell in love, they were modest enough not to say, "I have fallen in love," but expressed it more accurately saying, "The god of love has shot an arrow at me." And that is how it really happens. Seen this way, one suddenly feels a painful sting that one has not made oneself but finds one has been shot. In an instance like this, we would speak of the archetype of the god of love. If you go into the history of Eros, you will find that he is a variation of Hermes; the Eros of antiquity is very similar to Hermes Kyllenios. In olden times, when he was a fertility god of Boetia, he was represented

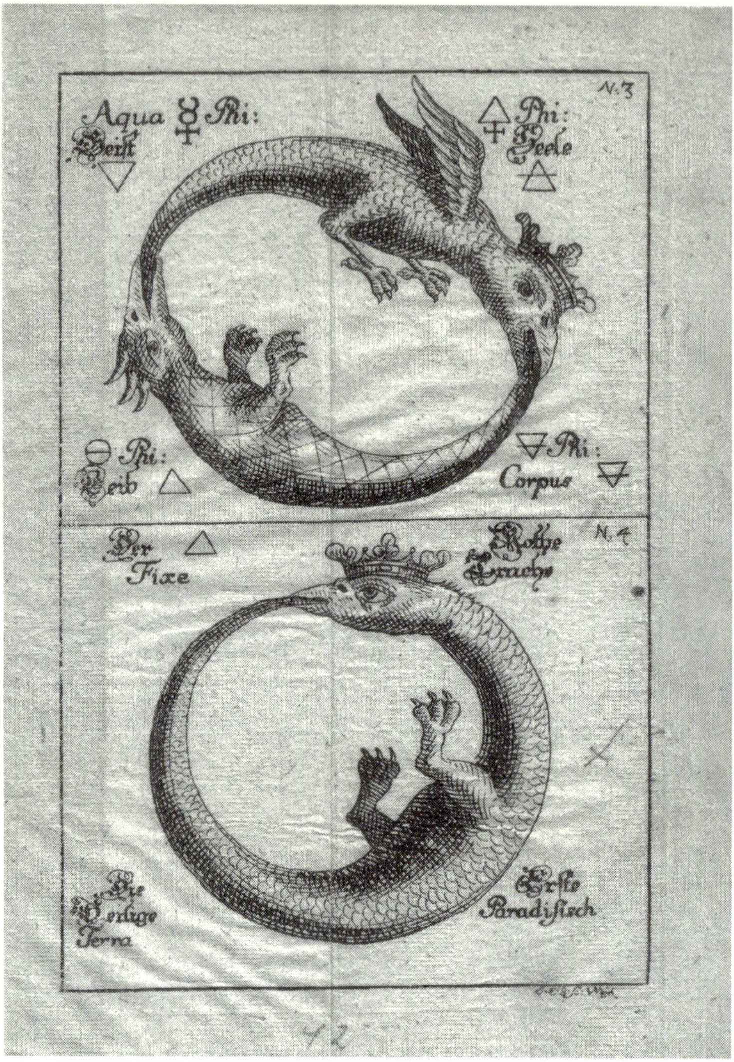

exactly like the priapic Hermes statues. The Greeks apparently meant a variation of the god Hermes. It is a symbol of the Self. The totality makes the projection. I think this is the correct way of putting it. If I find myself projecting something, the Self has arranged it.

329 ***Remark:*** *Here the eagle is connected with Eros, or with Apollo, so in other words, the gods are projecting onto the gods.*

330 Yes, you are quite right. Therefore, in general, we can say that it is always the unconscious, or some aspect of it, that produces the projection. It is a god or the Self that produces the projection. This

means that it is always an archetype and not the ego complex that does it. The next step is to ask onto what does the god of the unconscious project. Usually he projects onto outer objects, either human beings or things. Can it happen that an archetype projects onto another archetype? I think it can, and in my opinion, it is something that occurs frequently; in religion it would correspond to a process of unification. Take polytheism for instance: In most polytheistic systems of religion there is the secret knowledge that all the gods are aspects of one god. The Greeks also knew this; in late Greek Stoic philosophy it is always said that there is really only one god and that all the other gods—Athene, Hermes, and so on—are only different aspects of that one god. So you can say that there is a latent monotheism within Greek polytheism. We see a similar thing with the Elohim in Jewish monotheism. When God created the world He said, "Let *us* create man," and it has always been supposed that the "us" was addressed to the Elohim. So there is also a secret polytheism within monotheism, which is also expressed in the figure of the Malak Jahwe, the angel of God. Sometimes Jahwe interferes Himself and sometimes He sends the Malak Jahwe, who is more or less just one aspect of Himself.

331 In general, it can be said that in any monotheistic system—as in Judaeo-Christianity—there is a secret tendency toward polytheism, which, though not quite realized or admitted, exists, just as in polytheistic systems there is a secret tendency toward monotheism, to ensure that all those many gods are really only different aspects of the one god. In psychological terms, it would mean that the multitudes of archetypal constellations in the Self are all really one. As the Self very often manifests in practical life in single aspects, we prefer to call them different archetypes.

332 The problem is whether there are many archetypes or if the archetype of the Self is really the one archetype? For instance, when someone is dominated by the mother archetype, one speaks of a mother complex, but if we go into that, it will always be found that the whole Self is in it. An archetypal complex always leads to the

symbol of the Self. So here again there is a secret monotheism in polytheism, whether the stress is on the one or the other. If the many point to the one, I would say that in the unconscious there is a tendency toward putting all the energy onto the Self and away from the different single archetypes. The many archetypes tend to concentrate round the one archetype, which mirrors the tendency in the unconscious itself toward greater consciousness.

333 It could be said that the eagles are like an assembly of gods gathering round the one God, which, psychologically interpreted, would mean that many archetypes begin to fall into an order concentrating around the archetype of the Self. The archetype of the Self begins to be dominant, and the dissociation into many archetypes begins to be ordered round a center. If a single archetype is dominant in one's psyche, be it the mother archetype or the animal archetype, or whatever form it takes, then there is a certain amount of one-sidedness in that person. It is only when the archetype of the Self really begins to carry the process that things become unified and everything falls into place. I would say that this symbolizes the moment when the many archetypes begin to give their energy to one.

334 ***Remark:*** *I was thinking of something slightly different, getting a little away from archetypes and more in the direction of the meaning of projection in the primitive religious attitude. For example, if we think of the idea of god or the spirit being in a tree, then, according to what was said earlier, one could ask if perhaps there really is a spirit in the tree, and the archetypes are being projected onto the tree, so God is really in the tree and the gods are projecting onto God. This is a speculation.*

335 Yes it is, indeed, speculation, and I cannot answer it. You can believe it or not, for such a thing cannot be proved. It raises the question of whether, when an archetypal image is projected, there is a transcendental reality that actually makes that projection. We have no means of checking such a thing, so it is a question of belief; you can believe it or not. I do believe it, but I do not intend to try to convince anybody because I have no proof.

336 ***Remark:*** *If you really try to analyze the primitive religious attitude by saying that it is just a projection, then immediately something has been projected. One can only take it on that level.*

337 That is completely wrong, for according to Jung's definition of projection, we can only speak of projection when doubt has arisen. Therefore, it is wrong if we say that the primitive projects onto the tree. That is our way of talking because *we* doubt whether God is in the tree, but insofar as the primitive does not doubt it, we have no right to speak of a projection. If we read Jung's simple definition of projection in *Psychological Types,*[17] it is only legitimate to speak of a projection when doubt has arisen. Only when I feel unsure can I begin to speak of projection, and not before. The concept implies that I am no longer entirely convinced and that I am already out of the *participation mystique*, or archaic identity, to some extent.

338 Naturally the onlooker doubts, which is why if one takes a modern case, for instance X falls in love with Y, the onlooker will call that a projection of the animus. But for the person involved there is no projection, and it would be an analytical mistake to say there was, for that would be infecting the other person with one's own doubt. For X that man is now the beloved, and not simply an image of the animus. If I see things differently, for I have my doubts and do not have the same projection because I am not in the same *participation*, I have no right to poison the other with that doubt. I have to wait until the analysand begins to feel some disquiet, until she tells me the man she loves does not behave as she had expected he would. Once this state of disquiet has manifested, I can say that perhaps she has projected something within herself onto that man. But as long as there is no uneasiness, I have no right to cut into that *participation* by calling it a projection; that is a horrible, poisonous mistake people constantly make, and it is wrong because projections only happen where a semiconscious doubt exists. This is why we say, *grosso modo,* that primitive societies projected their gods onto trees and animals. We see this as a projection as we no longer believe that trees and animals are gods, but it would be wrong to assert that it is

[17] Jung, *Psychological Types*, vol. 6, *CW* (Princeton, NJ: Princeton University Press, 1990), § 793.

projection, for what to us is projection is to the primitive the whole experience of reality. It is their truth, which is why ethnologists do not like to hear us use the term projection, and they protest its usage. They have misunderstood the manner in which we use it; consequently, to some extent they are justified in their protest! They should, however, read Jung's definition in *Psychological Types,* and then they would understand our use of the word.

339 If I were to go to Africa and become "black" myself, emotionally, I would no longer speak as I used to of the primitives' projection but would rather say that I now see the primitives are right: God *is* in the tree. But as long as I am in Europe and the primitive says God is in the tree, I look at it and do not see anything divine about it. In this case I could speak of projection. The use of the word depends on the state I am in. When I doubt, I can use it, but if there is no doubt in me, I should never use the word so that I do not poison another person with it, for that can be very dangerous. If a primitive begins to doubt whether God is really in a certain tree and says that he recently went to the tree and it seemed to him that it was just a tree like any other, then I could say to him that perhaps God has been projected onto the tree, for in this case God would have left the tree long ago and is no longer to be found there! Projections die autonomously, or such events die out and then "it" has disappeared. These things happen completely without conscious cooperation; they are psychological events *per se.* Afterward, I can say there was a projection, but that is only a relative, not an absolute, truth.

Lecture 5

340 I would now like to continue with the interpretation of the images on both tablets.[18] They say almost more than the text that I have already presented. In the final part of the text, which I cannot interpret here, mention is made of these additional images.

341 On one part of the tablet there is a winged bird and a bird without wings. The winged bird is above and the other below, and according to the text, the bird without wings is preventing the winged bird from flying away. Each is eating the other's tail. So here we have a variation of the Ouroboros snake that eats its own tail. Above the birds are the moon and the sun, though this is not mentioned in the description, as well as the sphere to which the text gives different names, for it is called the moon and also the earth and the inferior world, the world below. Therefore, in a way, the moon is double. In the upper picture, it is the bride, or the opposite of the sun, but it is also somehow mixed up with the world below, also called the earth. So there is one moon that is identical to the earth, and one that is the partner of the sun.

342 In the second tablet there are two suns: One emits two rays onto the lower world, while the other emits only one. Both radiate to the lower world. Below is the full moon, described in a later part of the text as being white and surrounded by a black sphere so that if one were to view it from outside, one would see only blackness. But the inside is white, having a white moon substance.

343 In this picture the sun is doubled and in the other the moon is doubled, and each is the partner of the other. In both pictures there is an interconnection between the lower and the upper worlds and,

[18] Cf. Illustrations 9, 11 and 12.

in between, the fight between the birds. The sun radiates onto the lower world. The bottom sphere, which is black outside and white inside, is again called the lower world—the *mundus inferior*—which here means this cosmos below the firmament, or up to the outermost spheres of the planets. In antiquity and medieval times, it was thought that the moon and the corruptible world were below, while the stars and the eternal world were above.

344 ***Question:*** *Why does one sun have one ray and the other two?*

345 That's just how it is! Actually, the rays are not shown on the tablets; an old alchemist who once owned the book (I have the book from Jung)[19] has drawn in two rays in ink on *both* sides, but according to the text this is incorrect, for one sun sends down only one ray. If one reads the whole book, one comes across a very interesting thing on page 17 of this rare and valuable volume published in 1566: Here it is said that the one sun radiates with justice and the other without, and that is the difference between the two, *sol cum justitia* and *non cum justitia*—as the very clumsy Latin translation says. Although the text does not say so, I suppose that the sun with the two rays is the one that radiates *with* justice, for it is balanced: It has the two sides. But both suns radiate upon, and penetrate, the lower world with their rays.

346 We now have to try to understand the text psychologically—I say try, for many parts are far beyond my comprehension. Firstly, we have to refer to Ibn Umail himself and read the amplifications he gives throughout the book. Ibn Umail says of the two birds that they are also sun and moon, but that the one bird is the red sulfur and the winged bird is its exalted soul. Or it is then written that the birds are brother and sister, and the thing beneath them is their basis, as the earth or the lower world is the basis of the moon.

347 Let us consider these few amplifications. Sulfur is one of the most important basic matters in the alchemical process. In *Mysterium Coniunctionis* Jung wrote a whole chapter on it in which he states

[19] For the sake of accuracy, as can be seen in illustration 11, in the book in C. G. Jung's library there are two rays coming from the sun on the left, and one from the sun on the right.

that sulfur is an active and corrosive substance that has a dangerous vapour.[20] As we know, the devil always smells of sulfur in folklore, and when he departs or has been exorcised, he leaves an air of sulfur behind him. Sulfur also produces all colors, is the lover of the

[20] Jung, *Mysterium Coniunctionis*, vol. 14, *CW*, §§ 134-52.

alchemical bride figure, and so on, and it is a thief that interferes with the loving couple.

348 Thus, you could interpret sulfur as drivenness—a state in which one feels driven. It would not be right to speak of the drive itself; it is rather the state or *quality* of being driven or overwhelmed. If you look at it from a certain religious angle, it would naturally be the devil. It is sex, for instance, but in the sense of being driven by sex: sex in its overwhelming form, i.e., something not under one's control.

349 Sulfur is the active part of the psyche, the part that has a definite goal. In a psychological connection, it is a matter of watching to find out where it, and therefore the libido, is driving toward its goal. It may not be sex, but another kind of drivenness; it could be ambition or the power drive, or something else. Sulfur has the double aspect of supplying the original impetus—the male matter, as it is called here, is positive and negative at the same time. Anyone who examines himself, if he is honest, is usually first confronted with that part of the psyche that is in such a condition.

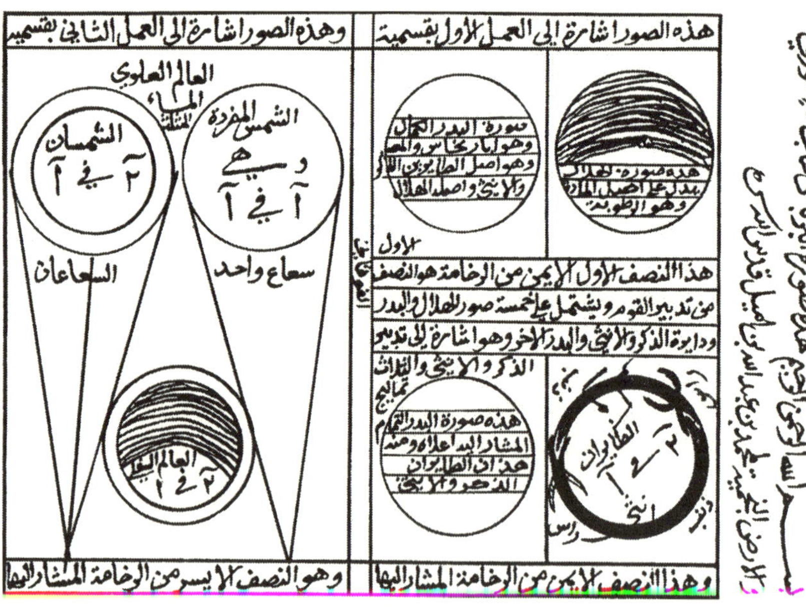

Figure 6
Stone tablet of Hermes-Thoth

350 The red color refers to fire—to the emotional quality. Thus, the wingless bird is the red sulfur; it is the bird below and is also referred to as female. We therefore have a paradox because being driven is regarded as an active male quality, but projected onto the lower bird, it is female. So the characteristics male-female are very vague; the terms are used in different ways in alchemy. It could be said that the wingless bird, the red sulfur, is an underlying factor of the inner psychic life and is always what one has first to unearth, for it is the *prima materia*.

351 To get to the bottom of someone's problem it is necessary to firstly find out the nature of such drives. We all have them in us, and until we bring them up and face them, we have a hidden corner where they live autonomously. They have to do with the unconscious and, as we know, Freud was so impressed by this aspect that when he discovered the "red sulfur," he thought it was the whole thing. He thought that that was it. In a way he was right: He was impressed by the driving nature of the unconscious, by the sex aspect, just as Adler was by the ambitious or power aspect. They both fell upon the *prima materia* of the red sulfur and tried to explain the role of the unconscious from that angle.

352 The winged bird is called "the exalted soul" of the other, meaning that once one has the *prima materia*—that I would interpret here as the basic instinctive drives of the personality—it has to be cooked. As a result, it emanates steam that "flies" above matter, which would be what the alchemists call the soul of matter. We came across this before in the text of Olympiodor in the form of the wife of steam. This steamlike, volatile substance—this flying fugitive substance, as it is called, which explains why the bird is winged—wishes to rise during the cooking process.

353 What does this mean in psychological terms? Let us assume that the wingless bird is the given fundamental human personality and here specifically the strongest basic drives. How do we cook our drives?

354 ***Remark:*** *They are cooked in analysis, surely.*

355 Yes, but how is that done practically?

356 ***Remark:** By making them conscious.*

357 ***Remark:** By allowing a depression to happen.*

358 Well, yes, that would be going to meet the drives. If you do not know them, you have to firstly go into a depression in order to meet them. When you have met them, you are at the bottom, and then you are in the *prima materia,* so to speak, and there is where you touch it. You can meditate upon it and do an active imagination in an effort to find the underlying meaning.

359 Suppose someone is in love but does not get anywhere; being frustrated, one falls into a depression, for it is not possible to get away from the loved one. The whole thing is a continuous torture. One could say to the person that, at bottom, a drive has become active and with it, a dependency, just as it does in a transference.[21] Many analysands resent the transference because of the dependency it entails, but nothing can be done about it for they *are* dependent and driven, calling 20 times a day, etc. The whole business is unpleasant, for both the analyst and analysand. Frequently, as both partners are reasonable people, they agree it is strange and crazy and annoying; nevertheless, the unreasonable drive pays no attention and takes no notice of what consciousness preaches. Anyone who has ever been deeply in love knows this.

360 It is similar with a power drive. You may be madly jealous of a friend who has been successful in his career, and you argue with yourself, saying you should not be jealous, that it is not fair, but your self-admonitions change nothing; your power drive or ambition, which is the cause of your jealousy, is not affected or touched by what you say. The red sulfur remains untouched, so we need stronger medicine to deal with this drive. Instead of arguing with the drives that want to carry us away, we prefer to cook them and fantasize about them and ask them what they want. One has to be quite objective, without opinions and without condemning the thing as unreasonable. One must try to find out amicably what the drive really wants, what it is driving at, for it has an objective.

---

[21] Transference as an attachment between the analysand and analyst is described at length in Jung, "Psychology of the Transference," in *Practice of Psychotherapy,* 2nd ed., vol. 16, *CW* (Princeton, NJ: Princeton University Press: 1985), §§ 353-401.

361 This can be discovered through active imagination, or through a fantasy, or through experimenting in reality, but always with the introverted attitude of observing objectively what the drive really wants or desires to achieve. That would be cooking the red sulfur. Generally, strong drives generate fantasy material that includes a whole bunch of fantasies. To cook something until its soul appears would mean to let the fantasy material emanate from the drive, to allow the fantasy material that is connected to the drive to emerge. That would be the psychological aspect and would correspond to the winged bird.

362 But when you have done that, a terrible conflict begins. Our text says that the wingless bird prevents the winged bird from flying away, while the winged bird wants to raise the wingless bird. Thus, they remain attached, linked together in a kind of insoluble conflict that keeps the whole thing arrested. What would this look like in reality?

363 ***Question:*** *Wouldn't it be a tendency to spiritualize or concretize?*

364 Yes, exactly. If you develop the fantasy material, there is a tendency to quickly conclude that it is all a psychological projection. If you are in love with someone, you can call it an animus or anima, a father or mother projection. By doing so, one is trying to spiritualize or "psychify" it, with the nuance of it being *only* psychological, and the mistake comes in with the world "only." Naturally, on the concrete level I have to be resigned and not start anything; I must behave conventionally and properly, and everything else I have to take within me because it is the projection of a psychological factor, a fantasy. It is the fantasy that binds me to the analyst or to the other person, and if I introject that fantasy, I shall be free. But one also needs to know what happens if one does that: The devil—the red sulfur—insists that there is something real about it all the same, or there should be, for otherwise it is *only psychological*, and a relationship that is "only" psychological is something I do not want. I want the real thing, something concrete—contact, for instance—or, if it is ambition, real recognition, a career, and so on.

365 The introjection of a fantasy concerning ambition would appear as follows: Someone in a humble situation has a megalomaniacal, ambitious drive to be top dog. If one tries to find out what is driving that person, one finds that, like the sex drive, his ambition is acquiescing to the goal of the Self. Such a man might say that he wanted to have a position of authority to realize his ideals and to improve the world; his desire is not based on egoism and vanity, but upon his wish to realize something. If one pursues the issue, it usually transpires that there is a very high ideal behind the ambition. But sometimes there is a hidden feeling of being very special mixed in with ambition. Such people feel their specialness deserves great recognition and do not differentiate this from their ambition.

366 The desire to be something special really comes about through the hunch or intuition of individuation. One has the vague idea of being a unique individual, and without realizing this, it is not possible to individuate. Therefore, *this* aspect of the ambitious fantasy is quite right. But if you say to someone in a humble position that their ambition to be special is quite legitimate and is really an inner thing—the drive to be something and to become something special, to realize oneself as a unique son or daughter of God, deriving from the vague intuition of one's divine inner nature—but that that cannot be exteriorized into wanting to be more than other people, they will feel quite relieved. A part of their ambitious drive will quieten down, but then the red sulfur will insist on the other side. It will ask, for example, if one really has to be a typist in an office for all of one's life? Should it all unfold *only* on the inner level? Can one never have anything in outer life? In this way the phenomenon is cut into the opposites of being "only" psychological or concrete. The devil is the one who wants the concrete thing. He is the great realizer who says that if a thing has no existence in concrete reality, it is just not real, and then the conflict between the spiritualization of the problem and the concrete thing begins.

367 ***Question:*** *What would spiritualization of a problem mean?*

368 Instead of spiritualization, perhaps it would be better to use the word "psychologize" for we are referring to the reduction of a drive

to an exclusively psychic, inner event, although both words are referring to the same thing.

369 Suppose a monk comes into analysis because he masturbates but feels that such behavior is not in keeping with the vows he has taken and with his ideas of morality. In his fantasy, he is always with a beautiful woman. He will be told to look into the fantasy he has of the woman at such times, and he will probably produce—especially as an introvert, and usually only introverts become monks though there are exceptions—a beautiful anima fantasy containing all the material of the Virgin Mary, the Sophia of God, and such figures. Then it can be pointed out that although the fantasy starts on a low level—Christ after all was born in a stable—it is really a fantasy of union with divine wisdom and should be accepted as such. That might solve the whole problem, so that he even no longer feels driven to masturbate for he realizes that the inner psychological factor, which turned up first in a rather disgusting form, is his anima, and he will relate to her. That would be a spiritualization of the factor that would produce the winged bird.

370 But as Goethe says, "Uns bleibt ein Erdenrest, zu tragen peinlich."[22] A little earthiness always remains behind, awkward to bear. Even after the greatest process of spiritualization, there is always something that resists and wants the earth. Ten years after being "cured," a monk like this may still wonder whether, in his fantasy, there had not been the wish for a real woman, too. That thought might nag him from time to time, and if he is still caught in the medieval concept, he will think it is the devil, something he must absolutely refuse.

371 ***Question:*** *Why shouldn't that hold good for 20th-century people too?*

372 If you wish it to, that is for you to decide. You can still say it is the devil if you want to.

373 ***Question****: But do we not all have to live with those dregs within ourselves?*

---

[22] Goethe, *Faust II*, §§ 11954-55.

374 No, certainly not, for that is an individual question that has to do with each person's fate. It is often one's ultimate conflict. There are people who have no peace and think it is simply dishonest to cut the thing off and call it the devil. They feel that to be an absolute dishonesty, while for others it would be a heroic decision, the only right decision that they intend to hold to all their lives. One finds peace of mind in one way and others in the other way, but no analyst can impose his viewpoint upon an analysand; it has always to be an individual decision to be arrived at by each person for himself. There are no recipes. For one it would be pure cowardice to cut that off, and for the other it would be weakness if he gave in to it. But that is the great insoluble conflict.

375 ***Remark:*** *It is also a matter of the words we use in describing our inner feelings.*

376 Yes, and it is a question of the kind of fantasy we have; it is an individual problem that no one can solve for another.

377 Nevertheless, there is a general type of this same problem that can be talked about. This is what the alchemist tries to exemplify in the image of the two birds, of the red sulfur, and the exalted soul. It is an insoluble problem, for the one bird holds the other down while the other tries to rise up. In a way, this picture says that the problem is eternal; it circulates in itself, and its totality of opposites is the whole thing. The one is the lower world, which naturally is connected with the red sulfur, and the other is the higher world. Above there are the sun and the moon, and when we get to interpret The *Love Letter of the Sun to the Moon*, we shall see that they appear in the psychic or spiritual realm and not in concrete reality. The upper part, then, falls into two opposites—the sun and moon—for both characterize the upper part, while the earth and the moon form another pair of opposites in the lower part. So the moon is again divided into the heavenly moon and the terrestrial moon, as expressed in Ibn Umail's words. The text is ambivalent: In one place it speaks of the moon and in another of the earth and of the basis of the two birds. So there is opposition between the lower and upper

worlds, and within the upper world there is opposition between the sun and the moon, and, finally, the two aspects of the moon.

378 It is rather complicated, but unfortunately psychological processes are like that. If you have reached the stage where it is possible to extract the soul from one of your strongest drives and you are torn between the opposites of the spiritual (or the "only" psychological) and the concrete, then you proceed further in the upper part by allowing the conflict to enter into the fantasy material and doing active imagination about your drive. By writing down the fantasy, one is talking to the inner figure.

379 ***Remark:*** *Some of us do not understand active imagination.*

380 Unfortunately, Jungian psychology is so interwoven that every analytical experience is linked with every other experience within one. Expressed in a few words, active imagination consists in making a fantasy about a drive when confronted with it. I cannot go into the question here of how to fantasize, but there are certain important technical points that have to be observed.[23] Suppose you are in love with a beautiful woman and cannot have her and so fantasize or dream about her. You can then continue your dream by meeting and talking to her in your active imagination. If you proceed in this way, some of its meaning will become clear to you. You understand why you fell in love with this unknown woman and that much of it belongs to you; it is part of your pattern and is meaningful to you. Perhaps you then put the fantasy aside because now you understand. But usually the problem I mentioned earlier comes up, and you wonder whether or not you should also ring up the real woman for, after all, she was the origin of the whole fantasy! You can say that it is just curiosity, but people are curious—why was it *that* particular woman? That is the red sulfur talking. But now you have two choices: Either you telephone the woman and fall into the world below, or you ring her up in active imagination and tell her she is your anima, that you have settled that, and that you know she is within you. But something still nags at you, and you would like to

[23] Cf. Marie-Louise von Franz, "Active Imagination in the Psychology of C. G. Jung," in *Psychotherapy* (Boston: Shambhala, 1993), 146-62; and Barbara Hannah, *Encounters with the Soul: Active Imagination as Developed by C. G. Jung* (Boston: Sigo Press, 1981).

meet her in a concrete form. You let the imagined anima deal with the concrete problem and ask what she has to say about that? This would be dealing with the split on the spiritual side, whereby the concrete problem is also raised, for bringing the conflict into your active imagination means a differentiation of it on a spiritual level. Or the red sulfur wins, and you go to the telephone in actual life and ring the woman up. Then you fall into the world below, into the *mundus inferior*, the corruptible earth, which is reality, concrete reality, and then the whole drama begins there.

381 ***Remark:*** *What you are asking your imagination to do is...*

382 You *ask* nothing! There are always two possibilities.

383 ***Question:*** *Should you find out in your imagination what this person will say to you?*

384 Yes, if you go the upper way, you bring your concrete conflict into the upper level by asking the inner woman what you should do about your desire for something more concrete. Then you have to listen to what she has to say about your conflict, and that is a very difficult thing to do and needs quite a lot of practice. Many people cannot do it because they cannot listen to what the inner figure says; they just imagine something themselves, instead of really listening. It really does need a lot of practice. But you can transpose the conflict in such a way and continue to discuss it on the other level, and that would be dealing with it from within. Then the fantasy becomes a wrestle with the inner figure; it is an attempt to win clarity on a psychological level.

385 Please excuse me if I once more bring up the—admittedly somewhat crude—example of the masturbating monk, but the lower world has to be brought in too. Suppose he comes to me and says that it is all very well with regard to Sophia and the inner anima, but from time to time the devil gets at him and says that all the same he is missing something on the real level, and surely that can't be all of it? To his question, "What should I do?" I would reply that he should ask the inner Sophia!

386 ***Remark:*** *Ask inner knowledge.*

387 No, Sophia is much more than that! Sophia is the knowledge of God. You could just as well say, "Ask God!" I cannot settle the analysand's problem; he must speak to the image of the Godhead within him, saying that something still worries him and ask what he should do about it. And then he must listen, after which a lot of things can happen. Most probably he will realize that God has two hands and that He Himself originated the conflict. It is an imagined case, but let's say the monk has realized the inner Sophia and knows that she is the wisdom of God in a form he finds within his own soul. Nevertheless, the red sulfur pushes him into saying that that is not it, or is not the whole of it, and that he should still also have the real experience. I can only say to him that he should ask his inner figure—ask the Sophia within him. I do not say that it is always so, but the inner figure often answers in paradoxes. It might say that in a way reality should actually come in, for otherwise something would be missing, and at the same time it says it is purely psychological. With an answer like this, the poor man will say that he has reached the end of his tether, for this is not a clear answer; it is paradoxical. But if he were able to understand, he would realize that this is the double play of the One and that the conflict is necessary. It is wanted and should not be solved rationally, for the only way the Self can manifest is through conflict. To meet one's insoluble and eternal conflict is to meet God. It is simultaneously the end of the ego with all its blather.

388 It is the moment of surrender, the moment where Job says he will put his hand on his mouth and not argue about God. It is always consciousness that creates the split by saying either-or.

389 I have often seen in such cases that Sophia—or the old wise man, or some other divine figure—answers in an evasive form, if you look at it negatively, and in a paradox, if you look at it positively. This paradox of the psychological factor, or of psychic reality, provokes that quality of consciousness that always generates an either-or and then wants to talk about it. But when the Self appears, debating is over, and the conflict no longer unfolds in the upper part of the personality.

390 It is the moment where the conflict transcends verbal discussion and becomes an intuitive experience of Oneness behind the two. One is between the right and the left hand. Put differently: Something is secretly one, yet it wants to be torn, to suffer, till something happens which is very difficult to describe, and then a switch takes place onto another level. If you let yourself be torn in the conflict, suddenly you change: You change from the deepest root of your being and the whole problem looks completely different. It is as though you tortured an animal so much that it jumped onto a higher level of realization. This can come about in different forms. It is an aspect of the symbol of the cross: one has to be crucified utterly and say, as Christ did on the cross, "My God, my God, why hast thou forsaken me?" And then something happens that outstrips the conflict.

391 ***Remark:*** *If the monk is going to keep his vows, he has to stop masturbating.*

392 According to my hypothesis, he has stopped long ago, since he had his fantasy. But the devil is much more clever and suggests that now he is cured and everything is all right and so on, should he not leave the monastery and have a "real" experience? Indeed, has he not now developed enough to be able to do even that? For instance, in the Middle Ages it was said, "Ubi spiritus, ibi libertas"—"Where the spirit of the Lord is, there is freedom," which was said by St. Paul (2 Cor. 3:17). The devil might introduce doubt by saying that since he has now solved his conflict, is he not free to live?

393 ***Remark:*** *Well, I think he is.*

394 That is *your* opinion, but we are not concerned with opinions here. He has to wait until God tells him what to do. It is not up to you to tell him what to do. You, with your extravert's spontaneity, would say, "Yes, all right, I think you should go ahead," but I would not; I would say he should ask God.

395 ***Question:*** *Suppose the monk has very weak intuition. Would not his answer then have to come from some other place?*

396 It depends on how you mean that. If you mean that is how it generally happens, then you are right, but if you mean it *ought* to be that way, then you are wrong.

397 ***Remark:*** *You said before that the answer would come intuitively, but not everybody can get it intuitively.*

398 Now you are bringing in the problem of the various psychological types and that is something else.[24] Speaking generally, the introvert needs a concrete experience, an outer experience, in order to feel he is complete and that things are total. The extravert, however, does not need this. Which means that if the monk is an introvert, he must have some outer experience—generally speaking.

399 ***Question***: *Sexual experience? Do you mean by that what Freud meant by sex?*

400 I mean, quite simply and concretely, contact with an earthly, human, female being.

401 ***Question***: *You mean a real, sexual relationship?*

402 Yes, quite concretely, but I say that that is in general what happens and not that it ought to. It does not happen in each case; it is a statistical average tendency. But what is important for the individual is his connection with God, not the woman. If God sends him that experience, he has to take it, and if God does not send it to him, he does not.

403 ***Remark:*** *My point is— I speak as a theologian—that God's natural laws are related to him and his relationship with a woman in terms of sex as well. I can say dogmatically that a theologian or priest of the Church who goes out and has a relationship with a woman outside of his vows is doing something wrong.*

404 Yes, because you *know* what God wants in each case, but we do not. We always try to ask Him first from within what He wants.

405 ***Remark:*** *Well, I know He has natural laws involving human beings.*

406 To us, the experience of God is greater and more unknown, and therefore we consult Him again each time. We do not have the idea

[24] On introverted and extraverted types, and on the four functions of feeling, thinking, sensation and intuition that give consciousness its inner and outer orientation, cf. Jung, *Psychological Types*, vol. 6, *CW*, §§ 556-671.

that He has uttered His last word. That is the great contrast between psychology and theology. We think of God as a reality who can speak in our psyche. One never knows what God may ask of an individual. That is why every analysis is an adventure, because one never knows what God is going to ask of this particular person.

407 ***Question***: *Are there limits to that?*

408 No, there are no limits; one cannot set limits upon God. We have a much humbler attitude than theologians. We simply say we should wait and see what God has to say about the situation in each case. We make no assumptions as to what He is going to do; each human life thus becomes a unique spiritual and religious adventure, and a unique meeting with God. God can always set His own limitations.

409 ***Remark***: *But He has not yet done it.*

410 He hasn't in your life, perhaps, but wait until God gives you an order. You are quite right to speak as you do until God makes you think differently. You have the right to say that He has not interfered with your theories. So that is all right for you, but not for others. There are other people with whose conscious theories God has interfered, and very strongly, and they have had to readapt to a new reality.

411 ***Remark***: *The course I am suggesting is on the level of experience, a valid experience.*

412 If we are speaking of a valid, an authentic, experience, then there is nothing further to discuss. Then he is in accordance and at peace with a certain mode of behavior that to him is codified by God so that he is at peace with God, which is the highest aim in human life. Then there is no trouble.

413 ***Remark***: *Think of the prophet Hosea. God told him to marry a prostitute.*

414 Two thousand years later, and after he has been canonized as a prophet, and as it is in the Holy Scriptures, we cannot doubt that it was God who asked this of him, and that is why we can accept it. We understand it as an example of God's paradoxical behavior. But if that happened nowadays to *you*, and you went to a colleague and said God had ordered you to marry a prostitute, what would he say?

He would probably ask if you were really sure it was God's wish. He would almost certainly believe that God could not give such a command, and therefore it could not be God. How would you prove it was God?

415 ***Remark***: *I would want to be sure his motive was genuine, and I would talk to him and ask him who this woman was, and so on.*

416 And then, with your reasonable ego judgment, you would decide if it were God or not?

417 ***Answer***: *It would not be my judgment, but His. All I could do would be to help him to reflect upon his decision.*

418 Thereby bringing the whole thing onto the level of conscious reasoning.

419 ***Remark***: *Not only conscious, logical thought, but feeling and intuition and everything that is involved.*

420 That is the human, rational, conscious way, but it takes the real mystery of God right out of it.

421 ***Remark***: *I don't mean to make God's decision for Him; God has to decide for Himself.*

422 But you are forcing God into a certain concept you have of Him, instead of relating to Him.

423 ***Remark***: *I think God relates through me to some extent or through someone else.*

424 That is an inflation. Why should a person not relate to God directly?

425 ***Remark***: *Because he can't do it. As a human being, I can't do it either. I can't carry on a conversation with God within myself; that is humanly impossible.*

426 Is it?

427 ***Remark:*** *Yes, I have to have some human contact through which I can relate to God.*

428 There are people who cannot risk the loneliness of such an experience. They always have to be in a flock and have human contact, as they call it.

429 ***Remark:*** *I would not deny the efficacy of prayer when God and I work together, but that involves not just myself and God but also*

people with whom I live—my family and what have you. All that I am is in a relationship to God, to the Holy Spirit.

430 There you mention the main thing, but the Holy Spirit bloweth where it listeth, where it will. A theologian identifies with a conscious position and takes that as absolute. From that standpoint one can talk about everything, but one does not notice one's own unconscious identification. If one ponders upon one's own conscious viewpoints long enough, I am sure the Holy Ghost will one day whisper something in one's ear. For us, there is always only the individual and his or her experience of God, and all the rest is secondary. In therapy it is not we who connect the individual with God; even that would be a megalomaniacal presumption. By presuming that they do just this, many analysts have become hidden theologians again. The only way that we can perhaps help is by always saying, "I don't know, but let us ask God!" In this way we can prevent our analysands from drawing rash conscious conclusions, or we prevent therapists from making them. In this way, every religious experience becomes a unique event. God is always experienced in a specific and unique form, and that even includes the red sulfur. This means that if you put the question of the red sulfur before God, God will give you His unique answer in each case.

431 ***Remark:*** *I think God has already given His unique answer in each case.*

432 That is where we differ. You think God has published general rules that He keeps Himself, and we think He is a living spirit appearing in man's psyche that can always create something new.

433 ***Remark:*** *Within the framework of what He has already published.*

To a theologian God is bound to His own books and is incapable of further publications. That is where we lock horns.

434 But let us return to our text. If you raise the conflict to the realm of psychological inner detachment, the problem of the opposites becomes clear: The Oneness becomes visible in the psychological realm and one realizes that we are dealing with a conflict between two aspects of the psyche. But one unsatisfactory factor remains, for one has cut the moon into two. The feminine element remains

divided, and a split remains between what we would call the unconscious and the anima, and the concrete world. This is still an open question. In analysis, this would mean that one realizes the conflict but one cannot yet quite link it up with outer concrete life. As soon as it comes to a problem in the outer, concrete world, there is still uncertainty.

435 Ibn Umail gives no advice as to how to proceed from there, but he switches to the other option, and we may never forget the division into two, the two aspects of the same problem. He presents it in two ways because it can only be described by attacking it from both sides. Here he tries to attack it from the other side.

436 In one picture the sun with its two rays attacks the lower world, as does the sun without justice. The lower world is a secret duality: It is a black sphere on the outside with a white shining moon on the inside.[25]

437 Generally speaking, the sun represents a male principle of collective consciousness; one could say the unknown psychological factor that creates collective consciousness. Wherever human beings flock together, we can see that collective consciousness is created. For instance, the words of a language have an average similar meaning to each individual, and through this medium of language much knowledge is imparted and exchanged. This is how a store of collective consciousness is formed.

438 It is very difficult to say what is individual and what is collective in a person's own consciousness. In earliest childhood one sees sparks of individual conscious reactions, for instance in the marvelous sayings of children and when they ask those wonderful questions. There the child makes an effort toward individual consciousness. Quite naively and employing its own individual consciousness, it asks charming, tactless questions like, "Grandmother, when are you going to die?" But when it goes to school, it is confronted with conventional consciousness. Schools have to be like that. If you tell the children about lions, or bears, and let them write a little essay on those animals, there will be a maximum of three in

[25] Cf. illustration 12.

a class who will say something individual. As a teacher, I often fought with the children, begging them to write what they thought and not what I had told them, until I noticed that children have tremendous difficulty because the tendency of their development in those years is to grow into collective consciousness, and it is the function of the school to support this development. The assimilation of collective consciousness is in fact the function of the school, and therefore the originality of individual consciousness generally fades, and at 20, people are a sack of collective knowledge. If you ask their opinion about anything, they just repeat what their parents or their friends say, or what they have read in the paper, and you have the greatest difficulty bringing them back to one unique, conscious, personal reaction.

439 We can say, then, that the sun is the light within which we all swim; it is the light of all our days. We think we are conscious, but that is not true. We are conscious in the realm of collective consciousness, and we do not even know how little our individual consciousness is. We have to search quite hard to find even fragments of consciousness that are personal. When you analyze an individual, the sun is always shining; that is collective consciousness in which individual consciousness is enclosed, and the conflict is either with the unconscious or with outer reality. When they have a conflict, people are either fighting with outer reality—outside things are wrong and they want them corrected—or they are in trouble with their unconscious. Something from within, or something from without, is in opposition. It is quite rightly said that the enemy with which consciousness is confronted is secretly double, for people come saying they have an outer conflict, but you discover it is an inner one, or vice versa.

440 If there are two suns, there are two principles of collective consciousness. In society this would mean two different forms of relationship to God—Catholicism and Protestantism, for instance. The one lives in the light of the one sun and the other in the light of the other sun. For one group, certain truths are completely self-evident; they are never discussed, for to this group they seem as clear

as the sun; the same applies to the truths of the other group. Thus, there is already a differentiation within the realm of collective consciousness—a split, or something in opposition. This is true of any collective conscious conflict, of two "isms" or two collective attitudes that clash, given it is a collective conflict that is common to many in this form.

441 In Ibn Umail's text, the conflicting attitudes are characterized in the form of two suns, one of which directs two rays toward the opposite, toward the dark thing, while the other sun—the so-called sun without justice—directs one ray. What principle of collective consciousness is without justice toward the world below while the other sun has justice? What would this mean?

442 Clearly there are two possibilities of consciousness, namely a rigid one and one which has a *paradoxical* attitude and therefore does justice to the paradoxical factor of the unconscious. The latter would be what you could call a consciously "open system," an open worldview that is always ready to accept its opposite or to meet its opposite and accept its contradictions. If you have a conscious attitude that is ready to accept the opposite, to accept the conflict and the contradiction, then you can connect with the unconscious. That is what we try to achieve: to bring about a conscious attitude with which the person can keep the door to the unconscious open, which means that one must never be too sure of oneself, or of one's decision, to never be too sure that what one says is the only possibility. One should always have an eye and an ear open toward the opposite, the other thing. This does not mean to be spineless, to just sit there, but rather it means to act according to one's conscious conviction, while always having the humility to keep the door open to being proved wrong. This would be an attitude of consciousness in living connection with the other, dark side. The unjust sun represents an attitude of consciousness that knows exactly what is what, an attitude that blocks contact with the unconscious, while the two-rayed sun has a molding and formative effect upon the unconscious. The latter would be with justice and the former without. I find this highly meaningful.

443 We should not forget that the author, Ibn Umail, lived his life within the tensions that existed between the Shiites and the Sunnites. I could imagine—though this is pure guesswork—that the two suns in his material represent this. In any case, consciousness always tends to be one-sided and sure of itself, and this does harm to the mystery of life. But consciousness can have a double attitude that enlightens the mystery of life and does not harm it. The humble attitude that always keeps the door open recognizes the fact that one may be wrong, morally or scientifically, that one may know something to some extent, but never for certain, and that even the greatest certainty can be negative, or only plausible in relation to my own actions.

444 What is required is a conscious attitude that is connected to a religious attitude that always gives humble and careful consideration to the unknown factor. This would mean to be able to say, "I think this is the right thing to do," and then to watch for a sign, warning that one is not allowing for everything. Consciousness is essential to the unconscious for without it the unconscious cannot live. But consciousness is only a good channel of communication through which the unconscious can flow if it has a double, paradoxical attitude. Only then can the unconscious manifest, and a hardening of the conscious attitude against the unconscious, which means a split in the personality and in civilization can be avoided.

445 There is a secret duality in the object in our text. At a rough guess we can say that this dark world underneath is the unconscious because it is the—it is that which I cannot penetrate with my mind and about which I cannot say I know what it is. The "unconscious" is a concept that simply refers to what is not clear to one's consciousness, and that includes a whole conglomeration of things. There are two aspects, two ultimate unknowns, with which an alchemist would specially deal and of which I spoke in my Introduction. We, too, are still faced with two unsolved mysteries that in some strange way—we do not yet know how—are interdependent: They are psyche and matter. At bottom, the science of physics postulates that matter is something unconscious,

something of which we cannot become conscious. *Per definitionem*, the unconscious is the same thing: It is something psychological of which we cannot become conscious. Indeed, we never know how our descriptions of the unconscious are connected to matter. This creates the whole conflict between the inner and the outer.

446 In the final analysis, it is consciousness that creates the conflict between the inner and the outer by projecting the one as materially real and the other as psychologically real, when, in fact, we do not really know the difference between material reality and the psyche. If we look at it honestly, we are confronted with something unknown that appears sometimes as matter and sometimes as psyche. How the two are linked we do not know as yet. The alchemists did not know, and we do not know either. It is a life mystery that seems to manifest both psychologically and materially. If we describe it from the outside with an extraverted statistical approach, it appears as matter, and if we approach it from within, it appears as what we like to call the unconscious.

447 ***Question:*** *Is there not also a duality between object and subject?*

448 Yes, that is quite correct. Outside, the unconscious presents itself as the *nigredo*, its destructive aspect, which is how we very often experience it, at least when we meet it for the first time. At the beginning, one's dreams are critical, and the unconscious is full of drives and dissociating, destructive factors. But if we penetrate deeper, we see something very light and meaningful. In this way, enlightenment can come from that dark place: If we direct the ray of consciousness upon it, if we warm it up by our conscious attention, something white comes out, and that would be the moon—the enlightenment that comes from the unconscious.

449 Sometimes one has an awkward dream which disgusts one on waking for it is either indecent or obscene, or dreadfully silly or stupid, and it is irritating. One wanted a wonderful archetypal dream, and then this comes! When this happens, I say, "Now wait a minute; let us investigate that, and find out what it means," and generally these are dreams that are the most enlightening if one can get to their meaning. Perhaps their meaning is not immediately clear,

but they have a dynamic content by which you are much enriched. It is just those dreams that are so valuable; they have an unapproachable, disgusting shell of depressing blackness, but within them is the light of the unconscious. It is often in the depressing motifs of the dream that the light is to be found, and naturally it is also to be found in the shadowy impulses that are full of meaning if one can lovingly investigate them with an attitude that accepts the paradox.

450 In Ibn Umail's own consciousness, there seems to be a conflict between two attitudes toward the unconscious at this stage. It might be concerning a life conflict that, from a conscious standpoint, is not seen as a problem at all. Life itself might be bringing up the conflict, represented on the one hand in the sphere of the moon, and on the other in the sphere of the sun. The one is a conscious conflict, while the other is an unconscious conflict. Usually they are interwoven, having something in common, and are two aspects of the same thing, namely the fundamental paradoxical duality of all psychological phenomena.

451 What is not said in the picture but is contained in the text, if you read the book, is that the whole thing describes the philosopher's stone, or the alchemical work. It is said that the one is the first stage of the alchemical work, and, with the second added to it, the philosopher's stone is made, for the life conflict has now been made conscious. Here we are dealing with the later stage of the opus. When we are related to the unconscious, there arises the increasingly subtle problem of how to keep the relationship right, instead of dropping back into one-sidedness. Even people who have had a long Jungian analysis tend to codify their process of individuation. Even after they have had tremendous experiences and life-giving reactions, they do not continue to grow but remain at a standstill if they codify what they have experienced—for example, by simply preaching about it to others. They remain stuck in what was once a lively experience of the unconscious. This is because every conscious phenomenon at some point wears out. For this reason the conflict is eternal and must be sustained. The one-sidedness of consciousness must be

continually confronted with the paradox. This means that whenever a truth has been experienced as such and has been kept alive for a while in one's own psyche, one has to make a complete about-turn, for that truth is no longer valid. As Jung always said, every psychological truth is only a half-truth and that, too, is only a half-truth![26] The analyst himself has always to keep up with his own unconscious and be consciously ready to overthrow everything hitherto attained. This would correspond to a constant double attitude.

452 Therefore, perhaps the sun with the two rays is better adapted to influence—and more able to assimilate—the unconscious by virtue of an open attitude, just as if there were a second consciousness behind consciousness—as if one had in the foreground of one's mind one's ordinary operating consciousness, while at the back something realizes that that is only a part of life. Thus there is a movable "consciousness behind consciousness" that just observes and knows that, for the time being, the thing is as it is. As Jung describes it, this means one finds oneself right in the storm of the conflict and, at the same time, out of it and watching it with serenity.[27]

Love Letter of the Sun to the Crescent Moon

453 Now we will turn to the above-mentioned love letter.[28] At first, one does not know who is speaking, but after a few sentences comes a passage where it is written, "Firstly the sun says to the moon ..." So we can assume that it was the sun speaking prior to this.[29] The sun begins by saying,

[26] "There is nothing quite true, and even this is not quite true." (Multatuli = pen name of the Dutch writer Eduard Douwes Dekker.) Cf. C. G. Jung, *Letters*, vol. 2, eds. Aniela Jaffé & Gerhard Adler, (London: Routledge and Kegan Paul, 1975), 334

[27] Marie-Louise von Franz returns to this interpretation at the beginning of the sixth lecture. Cf. 160-83 of the present work.

[28] Marie-Louise von Franz mentions it here for the first time since page 114. Muhammad Ibn Umail inserted it into the text mentioned above with the promise to interpret it, but then continued with the *Book of the Silver Water and the Sun Earth*. The latter is pursuant with the alchemical poem *Risalat as-sams ila l-hilal* (Epistle of the Sun to the Crescent Moon). An incomplete Latin translation of this with the title *Epistola Solis ad Lunam Crescentem* is published in: H. E. Stapleton et al., *Three Arabic Treatises*.

[29] In Latin, sun = sol, and moon = luna.

454 In great and ultimate weakness, I will give you from my beauty the light through which one reaches perfection.

455 Seen astronomically, the sun is a light while the moon only borrows its light from the sun. So there is a quite natural basis for the sun giving light to the moon. Clearly, it is Sol speaking. In its radiant form, it intends to impart some of its light to the moon so that it, too, may reach perfection.

456 We have to realize what the sun and moon meant to people at that time. The sun in general is an image of the Godhead. Later in the text it is even said that the sun is the spiritual divinity—that in its beauty it emanates goodness, perhaps even without shadow. The sun is beautiful, and it imparts its light to the imperfect moon. Now the moon is feminine; it is a receptacle for the dead,[30] that is responsible for all waxing and waning phenomena on earth: for the growing of plants and their withering, for the menstruation of women, for the ebb and flow of tides, for the process of becoming and of dying—thereby ruling the corruptible world. In short, this is what those people saw in the moon, namely earthly life in its paradoxical reality and irrationality that nevertheless seemed to have a secret meaning. For a man the moon would represent a feminine personification of his unconscious, while for the woman it would personify her vegetative life basis, the instinctual basis of her life.

457 The sun then explains that through it one can reach any height, one is raised to any height; in other words, the sun is that which lifts up. In antiquity, and in later times, people were puzzled by the fact that the sun raised water by warming it, so that clouds formed, and that when the sun disappeared, rain would come; so the sun was often spoken of as the principle of spiritual elevation and was thought to be that which makes things perfect, exalting them and making them visible.

458 Then the moon says to the sun:

---

[30] A universal *receptaculum omnium*, cf. Jung, 'Luna', in *Mysterium Coniunctionis*, vol. 14, *CW*, §§ 154-73.

You need me just as the cock needs the hen, and I constantly need your effect on me because your ethics are perfect, you, the father of all planets, you are the high light, the great Lord and Master. I am the waxing moon, humid and cold, and you are the sun, warm and dry. When we have united within the equal ranking of our house, within which nothing else happens other than that which is heavy and that which is light being together, and in which we will remain in this state, then I will be as a woman who is open to her husband, and this is truly spoken, and when we are united and remain in the belly of this closed house, I will, by flattering you, receive your soul and you will take my beauty from me, and through your proximity, I will become thin, and we will be raised up in spiritual ecstasy.

459 When we have climbed the ranks of the elders [the sheikhs] the light of your light will flow into my light, and you and I shall be like a mixture of wine and sweet water, and I will still my flow after which I shall be enveloped in your ink-like blackness, but after your dissolution and my coagulation, when we have moved into the house of love, my body will coagulate, and I shall be within my emptiness. [This probably means that the moon will completely disappear, i.e. there will be a new moon.]

460 To which the sun replies:

If you do all of this, and do me no harm, O Luna, my body will return [probably back to its original form], and I shall give you the virtue of penetration, after which, in the battle of fire, of liquefaction and purgation you will be powerful, and you will go on without diminishing or darkness, as copper and lead do, and you will not have any conflict against me for you will no longer be rebellious. [So Sol is saying that if, in this *coniunctio* you do not harm me – for Luna could harm Sol – then I will make you strong in your fight against

> fire, you will no longer be corruptible, as copper is, and you will no longer fight me, the sun, for you will no longer harbour feelings of enmity towards me. Thus the moon, that waxes and wanes, and is characterised as being harmful to the sun, and is dark and corruptible, will lose all of its negative qualities and will, like the sun, become a firm light.]

461 Blessed is he who thinks about what I say and my dignity will not be withdrawn from him and the lion, too, will not fail or become cheap, weakened by the flesh [here the lion is an image of Sol], for if you have followed me, I shall not turn you away and withhold from you the increase of the lead, but rather my light will fade, and my beauty will be extinguished, but they will take from the minerals of my pure body and from the fatness of the purified lead, within the harmony of their weight, but without goat's blood, and a difference can be made between what is true and what is false. I am the hard, dry iron and the strong ferment, everything good comes through me, the light of the secret of secrets is generated by me, and nothing can affect my actions. What has light is created in the darkness of the light [everything that shines has been created in darkness]. But when it reaches its perfection, then it recovers from its illnesses and its weakness, and then will appear this great flux out of the head and the tail and these are the two qualities and the ten orders or weights of which five are without darkness and five shine in beauty.

462 That is the end of the letter.

463 At first the sun indicates, so to speak, its superior quality by saying, in a very dignified way, that it is going to give the moon light from its beauty. But then the moon also points out that the sun needs her just as the cock needs the hen, that it is nothing without her, that although she is the imperfect recipient of its light, the sun needs her, too, for what would be the use of a sun that could not shed its light

on something else? Its light would disappear into space for it needs a material object to become visible through reflection.

464 Therefore, the moon, in all feminine humility and submission, points out her absolutely equal right to existence: The sun needs an empty vessel into which it can pour its light; it needs darkness upon which it can shine its light; it needs matter within which spirit can become visible. The moon uses a very vulgar and ordinary simile—"as the cock needs the hen" —which alludes to the fact that there is a purely instinctive, even sexual, attraction between the two principles. She says she needs the sun's constant effect upon her because the sun is perfect, the father of all light. The Latin words *perfectus moribus* mean a particularly ethical kind of perfection, which is something the moon does not have.

465 In mythology, the moon is wicked for it is unreliable. The alchemists frequently quoted the Psalm[31] that describes how, in the darkness of the new moon, the wicked shoot their arrows at ethically just people, implying that the new moon protects thieves and the wicked when they attack the righteous. Thus, the moon has all the wicked poison and unreliability typical of the anima in her original condition and also for feminine beings in general, not only the feminine in man, for in the feminine there is that catty, unreliable cunning and rather doubtful ethics; one could call it the ambiguity of nature. The moon says that she is the waxing, moist and cold moon and the sun is warm and dry, and when they are coupled in a balanced state, then … and so on.

466 Here we are dealing with the conflict between the principle of consciousness and nature—the unconscious, the unknown. This conflict between the masculine and feminine is amplified into a quaternity because both contain two qualities: The moon has the qualities of being moist and cold, and the sun of being dry and warm. This alludes to the late antique and medieval teaching that there are four elements: water, air, fire and earth; and four basic qualities: warm, dry, wet, and cold. Throughout the entire Middle

[31] "For, lo, the wicked bend the bow, They make ready their arrow upon the string, That they may shoot in darkness at the upright in heart." Ps. 11:2.

Ages, these four elements and four qualities were considered to be the basic principles, and they were the categories within which basic matter could be observed.

467 This gives rise, of course, to a beautiful mandala, for fire is hot and dry, and air is moist and cold; the elements and their qualities can be combined in many different variations. However, this was not the case for material reality; even at that time people realized it was a simplification of material phenomena that did not fit reality. As soon as you think more profoundly, it does not fit. This is the same for all archetypal schemes of order that are projected. Even the very first alchemists emphasized that this was not meant to be taken concretely, that it was just a way of introducing order into their ideas. Zosimos, for instance, said this, which clearly shows that they saw an image of totality in the four qualities projected onto matter. Even when they really did not fit, they simply said it was only meant symbolically, and therefore they did fit. So even in those days it was simply a symbolic network that the human mind projected onto matter to bring order to it. We can compare this to our modern use of concepts such as particle, energy, time space continuum and electromagnetic phenomena. Physicists know that these concepts are vaguely interwoven and that they are not at all as simple and clear as we think. They have been created as a means of expression.

468 The four qualities are now added, and they complete the duality of sun and moon. When two people meet, there are basically four: the man and his anima; and the woman and her animus. In an analytical discussion, there are always four elements: two in the conscious and two in the unconscious. Every conscious assertion immediately constellates its opposite, namely negation. If I say a plant is a plant and a dog is an animal, that seems simple enough, but it is a contraposition of two things and contains something more, because if I say a tree is a tree, I express the fact that it is not a mineral or anything other than a tree. Everything I say already has within it the shadow of what is excluded. Therefore, every time consciousness produces something, even two words, there are

always four, because the unconscious is also a part of it. Something unknown is involved that should also be taken into consideration.

469 If we take the counterpositions of physics and psychology; if a psychologist looks at what a physicist does, he sees at once that the latter is full of unconscious projections. This is at once clear. But when a physicist looks at us, he naturally views what we discover psychologically from a physical aspect and says that in this area we are ignorant. The reason for this is that we are not sufficiently developed in our consciousness to keep a contradiction in mind. This is a very difficult thing to do, though it would be necessary nevertheless.

470 Every polarity contains its opposite, which is most obvious when two people discuss together, as they do in analysis, for there are always four: The unconscious of each is always there, too. The fact that everything always has two qualities makes the problem of relationship much more complicated.

471 Let us assume that our love letter—in a projected form—refers to this problem. The sun and the moon say that when they are coupled in a balanced state, where nothing else is involved, it is like a man and a woman who are completely there for each other. So there is the problem of the *coniunctio* in all its various aspects, in which there are two known factors and two unknown ones. But if they are all related, a state of balance and completeness is reached.

Lecture 6[32]

472 A conflict has arisen in the moon, for it appears in two forms. The sun also appears in two forms: the one sun from which only one ray descends upon the earth and is called the sun without justice; and a second sun that sends out two rays and is called the sun with justice.

473 The sun is an aspect of consciousness; it has characteristics that are partly linked with the ego and partly with the Self. One aspect of the sun is open to the unconscious, for the two rays imply a principle of consciousness capable of embracing the opposites, while the other sun is "a closed system"—it is one-sided and therefore destructive. In *Mysterium Coniunctionis* Jung describes the sun as an image of the spiritual divinity, meaning it is, on the one hand, itself, while on the other hand, it is an aspect of the ego.[33]

474 The ego is identical with the Self to the extent that it is the instrument of self-realization for the Self. Only an egotistical, inflated ego is in opposition to the Self. In its rightful function, the ego is the light in the darkness of the unconscious and in some ways identical with the Self. The two suns seem to illustrate this contrast between the destructive and positive aspects of ego consciousness. The sun with one ray would represent an inflated, egocentric conscious principle that is "unjust" toward the unconscious or reality and is opposed to the Self. The sun with two rays, on the other hand, symbolizes the ego as an instrument of realization for the Self, and in that sense, it functions "with justice."

475 The ego of an individuated person would be a manifestation of the Self. It is characterized by its great openness to the unconscious and therefore functions as the sun with justice. Such an ego

[32] The sixth lecture begins with a recapitulation of the image of the two suns and two moons from the fifth lecture. Because of a technical difficulty, approximately the first half of the sixth lecture was not recorded, so Marie-Louise von Franz made a short reconstruction of the missing part.
[33] Jung, *Mysterium Coniunctionis*, vol. 14, *CW*, §§ 130-31.

manifests the Self by having a double attitude toward the unconscious and by constantly being humbly open to the unconscious. In this way, it offers the Self a basis for its realization. On this, Angelus Silesius[34] said,

476 I know God cannot live one instant without Me:
If I should come to naught, needs must He cease to be.

477 Thus, the double sun in Ibn Umail's text shows a conflict between a wrong ego attitude toward the earth, or the unconscious, and a correct ego attitude that allows the Self to manifest. The goal would be to find this double-rayed conscious attitude, namely a capacity for standing the opposites. This would not mean wavering between the opposites but rather holding the tension between them. A tendency to deviate and to become one-sided is inborn in consciousness and is linked with its need for clarity and preciseness. People often say, for instance, that Jung does not write very clearly, but he does that on purpose, for he writes with a double attitude that does full justice to the paradoxes of the unconscious. He describes psychic phenomena from an empirical standpoint. Buddha once said that all his sayings were to be understood on two levels, and Jung's writings also have this double floor, these two levels. People who reproach Jung for this are, so to speak, stuck in the Vishudda-Chakra[35] for they believe in words and cannot grasp the thing itself. But Jung uses a descriptive method, which has now also been adopted in nuclear physics, where facts are described in two complementary approaches that, although they contradict each other, are needed in order to grasp the whole thing. Words are only instruments and not the thing itself.

478 ***Question:*** *Does the* Sol niger *allude to the negative, "unjust" aspect of consciousness?*

---

[34] Angelus Silesius, *The Cherubinic Wanderer*, introduction and notes Josef Schmidt, trans. Maria Shrady (New York: Paulist Press, 1932).

[35] This corresponds to the area around one's Adam's apple—the ether region, cf. C. G. Jung, *The Psychology of Kundalini Yoga: Notes of the Seminar Given in 1932*, ed. Sonu Shamdasani, (Princeton NJ: Princeton University Press, 1999).

479 Yes, the *Sol niger* would be the dark shadowy aspect of consciousness. The sun god in mythology often has a hidden destructive aspect, Apollo, for instance, who is also the god of mice, rats, and wolves. The negative aspect of the sun is especially realized in hot countries where the burning midday sun destroys all the plants. In hot countries, ghosts come out at noon, and in the Bible, for instance, there is the demon of midday; the "destruction that wasteth at noonday" (Psalm 91,6) is literally called the "demon of midday." The shadow side of the sun is demonic.

480 This dark, demonic aspect of the sun finds expression in drivenness, when one's ego is pushed from behind, so to speak. It is a misuse of consciousness to justify the drive when one's ego is not strong enough to decide on the objective facts but is swept away through the weakness of its passions—fear, power or sex. Perfection, too, is in itself hostile to nature; there is a tale in Indochina that the sun was once so hot, a hero shot it down. Thus, the *Sol niger*, that is also Saturn, is the shadow of the sun, the sun without justice, which is death for the living.

481 Man, with his consciousness, is a disturbing factor in the order of nature; one could really question whether man was a good invention on the part of nature or not. There is the myth of the trickster god who is especially stupid, and from a certain angle man is very stupid and does not have enough sense to live in a balanced way. Viewed as an animal, he is disturbed and overly reproductive. Whether he is a mistake or the crown of creation depends on whether his sun shines with or without justice. If consciousness functions as it should, it is helpful to life, but when it gets off track, it becomes destructive.

482 One aim of analysis is to get consciousness to function again according to nature. Inflation is a symptom of "unjust" functioning. If one is driven by a too highly focused consciousness, one has a dark sun. In analysis, people like this try to convince you that they are right, even when they are doing the wrong thing. We are all born in an imperfect and questionable state—to be wrong and split is human nature. The myth of Adam in the Garden of Eden is the original pattern for this, showing that man was flawed from the beginning.

When the Self is not supported, it sends a neurosis, i.e., the shadow of the Self comes into action, and then God and nature become enemies to man. A wrongly functioning consciousness becomes the dark side of God. If consciousness works in accordance with nature, the blackness is not quite so black, or so destructive, but if it stiffens when, so to speak, the sun stands still, it burns and kills life, and then, according to certain Indians, the heart has to be sacrificed to keep the sun moving. Every time we make a rule, we have to make an exception, for otherwise consciousness and life are not in accord.

483 The two moons and the two suns make four. A *quaternio* is always present when two people are together, namely the man and his anima, and the woman and her animus.

484 The *coniunctio* takes place, as our text goes on to say, in the belly of the "closed house," that is, in the alchemical vessel in which the sun and moon unite.[36] The Egyptian coffin is a closed house in which the king marries his mother: Isis and Horus, or Hathor and Horus. The priest says, "Now you stay, uniting in love with your mother," as he closes the door of the funeral chamber. Similarly, a Japanese Zen Master says, "He has closed the door of his heart so that no one can guess his feelings." Oneness with the Self makes one a mystery to others. If you can guess a person's reactions, he still functions collectively. Our sense of "I know how you feel" comes from similar collective reactions. Our empathy is based upon collective qualities. We meet most people on the collective level and know the qualities we share, such as jealousy and love. Without empathy we cannot relate, but that has nothing to do with the uniqueness of the individual. It is a quality of genius to produce the unexpected, to do the surprising thing that clicks and yet is not banal. You can never guess what a creative person will produce, for it is a new creation and there is no knowing what it will be. From the mind come ideas, and from the feeling side come reactions that in such a person are absolutely unique.

485 One's individual developmental process leads to unique creativeness in each moment, and the closed chamber alludes to this

---

[36] Here Marie-Louise von Franz makes a seamless transition from her addendum about the "sun with justice" and the "sun without justice" to a discussion of the *love letter*.

secret center of the personality, the secret source of life. It is the closed chamber of the heart: unique creativity in each moment of life. Where the process of individuation leads to realize this uniqueness others can no longer guess, for they cannot see into the closed chamber of your heart from where the unexpected, creative reactions spring. I would say that unexpected creative reactions come from being at one with the Self, for it is the Self that is uniquely creative in each moment of life. This is why the Japanese Zen master says that one can no longer guess the movements of his heart, for whatever he says or does will always be unpredictable and creatively surprising. The closed chamber alludes to this secret, for ultimately every individual is a unique and closed system that centers around a source of life. If this becomes real in an individual, one feels the mystery of a unique personality. That has to do with closing the house that involves separation from collective entanglements and contamination, not only outwardly, but also inwardly by separating within oneself from what is ordinary and not oneself.

486 ***Question:*** *How does that reconcile with the Satori experience of Zen Buddhism, where the openness to and oneness with nature and with the collective, too, is one of the goals?*

487 That is one of those paradoxes. In the last of the *Ten Cow-Herding Pictures*[37] of Zen, we see an old man at a market. He has a sweet smile and has even forgotten his own enlightenment. There we have a completely collective man who goes to the market with his pupil and his beggar's bowl and has even forgotten his Satori experience with the gods. Subjectively, he does not feel unique, but, as the story adds, the cherry tree blossoms as he goes by. This is something you would not expect of an old fellow with a fat belly who goes to the market with a rather insipid smile. Uniqueness springs from him as a creative act, but it is not intentionally in his mind. He does not feel unique: He *is* unique. Subjectively, he would say that he is a poor old man and what do you want of him? Such people have an extreme, natural humility, in spite of which their uniqueness manifests.

---

[37] Daisetz Teitaro Suzuki, *Essays in Zen Buddhism*, (London: Rider and Company, 1927).

Figure 7
Last image of the Zen meditation "Ten Images of Ox Herding"

488 It is again the paradox of the ego and the Self. The ego must have the attitude of being a human being among other human beings, and then one's uniqueness, if it has been found within, will emanate involuntarily. It is just the opposite of being inflated with one's uniqueness, of feeling so different from others and making remarks such as, "I am so sensitive, nobody understands me." That is just not it. If people say that to me, I always reply that I know a lot of people like that. I do not say it out of wickedness, for it is quite true; it is a very common quality to be so sensitive that nobody understands you. It is very widespread, especially among introverts, who feel unique, but they are not. The enlightened one does not feel unique, but very human. This is why you can say both things, namely that such people are very open to the world and very human with everybody, or you can say they are infinitely unique and incomprehensible—this is a paradox.

489 ***Remark:*** *To express it in another way, I think that the aim is to eliminate subject and object, while at the same time to honestly discriminate between subject and object.*

490 That is absolutely fitting. The "belly of the closed house" illustrates this, namely that the innermost creative being is secluded nature, and not by any artificial act. In a very concrete and banal way, it also has to do with the problem of analytical discretion. As soon as one touches the uniqueness of the partner in an analysis, discretion is imposed. Before it was just a conventional rule, not really necessary, but if the uniqueness is touched upon, it is natural never to talk about it to a third person. One realizes it is unique and quite naturally should never be talked about with anybody else. Basically, it cannot be, and that has to do with the mystery of meeting up with uniqueness, especially in any love relationship. The house then naturally closes by itself.

491 Behind this closed door, the moon receives its soul from the sun, and the sun takes away the beauty of the moon, and it becomes quite thin and weak. This means the *coniunctio* takes place in the new moon, in the underworld. We know that the moon is new when it is close to the sun. When it is directly opposite the sun, the whole moon is lit up, and then we have a full moon, but when it is close to the sun, it is not hit by the sun's rays. This is an enormously deep allegory that Jung writes about in *Mysterium Coniunctionis*[38]—that the *coniunctio* does not take place in the full but in the new moon, i.e., in the darkest night where not even the moon shines. The sun and moon unite in this ultimately dark night.

492 There is an especially interesting nuance here because in medieval Church symbolism the sun symbolizes Christ, and the moon symbolizes the Church—the *Ecclesia*—and the *coniunctio* of the sun and the moon is interpreted as the meeting of Christ and the redeemed Church. But not one of the writers has pointed out the fact that when they unite, the moon is gone, is darkened or blotted out completely. They have tactfully skipped that detail or never questioned why it is so.

---

[38] Jung, *Mysterium Coniunctionis,* vol. 14, *CW,* §§ 21 – 25.

493 The *coniunctio* happens in the underworld; it happens in the dark where no light is shining. When you are completely out and consciousness has given up, something is born or generated. In the deepest depression, in one's deepest desolation, a new personality is born. When you are at the end of your tether, that is the moment when the *coniunctio* of opposites takes place.

494 The sun gives its light to the moon, but, at that moment, the moon is blotted out; the closer it gets to the sun, the more it fades and becomes thin, so it can be said that the sun harms the moon. It is darkened by the sun as it approaches it. And later the sun says, "If you do me no harm in the *coniunctio*, O Moon, then ..." then this and that will happen. Apparently the *coniunctio* is very dangerous for both, for the sun does harm to the moon and the moon harms the sun. This could perhaps be avoided, but the closer the two lights get to each other, the greater is the danger that they will destroy each other, instead of uniting; as we mentioned earlier in our discussion of Ibn Umail's text, the reason for this is that both sun and moon have a shadow.

495 Both have a dark and destructive side, and when they come close, it is like two people who love each other; the more their love increases, the more doubts and distrust increase too. Very often one is afraid to open one's heart, for then the other can do so much harm. If, for instance, a man shows his love for a woman, then he is exposed to her animus. If he does not love her, he just says it is her damned animus, but if he does, then he minds when she makes horrible animus remarks. The same thing holds good for the woman, for if she acknowledges her love for a man, the poison of his anima may hit her. Therefore, there is always this trembling fear in approaching each other. What we human beings experience in love situations is mirrored here in this symbolical process of the sun and moon becoming one.

496 If we take the *coniunctio* on a purely inner level, it can be said that when the conscious and unconscious personalities approach each other, there are two possibilities: Either the unconscious swallows consciousness, as happens when there is a psychosis, or

consciousness destroys the unconscious with its theories, which means a conscious inflation that generally happens when there is a latent psychosis. People then get out of it by saying the unconscious is "nothing but..." with consciousness, thereby crushing the unconscious and its living mystery. When people believe that they know what the unconscious is—namely "It is nothing but ..."—consciousness harms the unconscious by pushing the unconscious aside. Many people leave the analytical process under such conditions. They get closer and closer to the unconscious, and then a disagreeable realization creeps up; the work becomes difficult, and the person puts an end to it, saying he knows all about it, and it is "nothing but ...," thereby distancing himself from it. In such a case, the sun has destroyed the moon. If the unconscious overwhelms consciousness and there is a psychotic interval, the moon has, for its part, destroyed the sun.

497 Always, when conscious and unconscious meet, there is this fear that instead of love, there might be destruction. The two lights in our love letter try to avoid this. The sun says, "If you do not harm me, I will help you," and the moon says the same thing. In this way they do, indeed, succeed in keeping the relationship right. While it is true that the moon at a certain moment becomes very thin and is blotted out, nevertheless they then become exalted, and they join the Order of the Old Men.

498 Since the Latin word *Seniores* is mentioned in the text, this must be the Sheikhs. This is a strange part, and I cannot say I am sure of my interpretation, but there is a parallel text in which the Order of the Old Men is spoken of as the Order of Twenty-four Old Men, referring to the 24 old men of the Revelation of St. John,[39] who sit around the throne of God day and night. This would refer to the hours of the day and night and would mean that the sun and moon go through all the stages of the 24 hours.

499 In the Shiite sect, the mystical movement within Islam, this Order of the Elders also has to do with the secret tradition of Imâm. In each generation there is one Sheikh who is the spiritual initiator,

[39] Gospel according to John 4:4.

known as the Imâm. As the bearer of the light of the Godhead, he represents the incarnation of the Godhead and is the secret Guru, the spiritual teacher in those mystical Islamic sects, for example the Druses. Different sects have different hierarchies, and there are quarrels about who the spiritual leader should be, but in all of them is the idea of the one spiritual leader, the enlightened one, in whom the light of the Godhead has been most incarnated.

500 As we are dealing with an Arabic text, there might be something of this sort here, too, that would also connect up with the other interpretations, namely a multiple aspect of the Wise Old Man in different stages or phases. Practically, that would mean that the archetype of the wise old man, an aspect of the Self, appears multifariously and in specific connections with time—in the sense of how each Imâm appears at some specific world period. This can be compared to the 24 hours of day and night, which is also a symbolism of time. The same idea reappears in Christian symbolism in the figure of Christ and the 12 apostles, to whom the 12 months and 12 hours of the day were attributed.

501 I think it has to do with the simple fact that the realization of the Self, or the process of individuation, has only reached reality when it appears in each moment of this sidereal time. Many people first realize what the Self is intuitively, by reading a book or by the interpretation of a dream, but that does not solve the question as to what they should do this morning and tomorrow evening; in other words, their insight has not yet entered time. They have an intuitive connection with the Self and with the wisdom of the unconscious, but it has not yet entered into the time and space of their personal lives. It is only real if at each moment of one's life—at least theoretically, for one never actually reaches that stage—one is constantly in connection with it, constantly expressing it and knowing what it is. Therefore, it can be said that the Self has only become real when it is expressed in one's actions in space and time. Before it has reached that stage, it is not quite real, but in this way it becomes a factor that brings about change.

502 For instance, what is right for today may be wrong for tomorrow, which is why someone who has reached this stage of consciousness will be unpredictable and always act differently in the same situations. Today the thing is like this, and the person will react in one way, and tomorrow the same situation will occur, and the person will act differently. There are no more rules, for each moment is different, and therefore time acquires a creative quality; each time-moment is a creative possibility, and there is no longer any repetition. In this way, one could say, the Self enters time, meaning it becomes real and is therefore different in every moment, uniquely different.

503 So when the sun and moon unite, they simultaneously begin to move in a circle that has to do with time. In Eastern alchemy, this is symbolized by the circulation of the light; when the inner light has been found, it begins to rotate by itself. This rotation, that is represented, for example, in *The Secret of the Golden Flower*,[40] is called the *circulatio*—the rotation—in Western alchemy, and in many alchemical texts it is said that the *lapis* has to rotate. This is usually connected with time symbolism, for it is said that the *lapis* has to pass through winter, spring, summer, and autumn; it has to pass through all the hours of the day and night; it has to circulate through all the qualities and all the elements; or it has to go from earth to heaven and back again to the earth. There is always the idea that, after having been produced, it begins to circulate.

504 Psychologically, this would mean that the Self begins to manifest in time and space. It does not become something at a certain moment and afterward there is a return to one's former way of living; rather, it has an immediate effect upon one's whole life. Action and reaction are then constantly in accordance with the Self, and it can become truly real and manifest in its *own* movements. The stone, the new light, has its own movements, that is, it can itself move. Naturally we have to allow it to move; we have to listen to it, but if we do so, it can move and can produce autonomous impulses.

[40] Richard Wilhelm, *The Secret of the Golden Flower: A Chinese Book of Life,* com. C. G. Jung (New York: Mariner Books, 1970).

505 ***Question:*** *But are they necessarily the right impulses?*

506 There is no final judgement as to what is wrong and what is right. Some will say it is wrong, and others will say it is right, and subjectively you will sometimes feel it is wrong—or right. If I could say something very personal, I would say that it is not a question of right or wrong, for if one is one with the Self, one does not care anymore. It is so much more important to be connected with the Self, and if it is wrong, naturally one has to pay for it. But the main thing is the connection, and that one is not separated, for separation is spiritual death, while being connected with the Self is spiritual life. If it tells you to do something that is looked upon as being wrong, everyone will attack you, and if you begin to think that it was perhaps wrong, you can still say it was worth it because it was done in connection with the Self.

507 I think if one does something out of a living connection with the Self, paying the price is worthwhile—the price of being accused of wrongdoing and perhaps passing through the stages of thinking it was wrong oneself. Subjectively, one never really feels it is wrong, but one must allow for people saying it is and be tolerant. But if you are happy and feel alive, that is the one thing nobody can take away from you. If I say I am happy, what can anyone else say about it? If one is in harmony with the Self, there is a feeling of absolute happiness and peace, and others can judge as much as they like with destructive intellectual theories, it does no harm. Feeling close to the Self becomes the indestructible thing. Naturally one loses this feeling time and again because it is too difficult to keep for a long time.

508 Then the love letter continues with the moon saying to the sun,

> ...The light of your light will flow into my light, and you and I shall be like a mixture of wine and sweet water, and I will still my flow after which I shall be enveloped in your ink-like blackness, but after your dissolution and my coagulation, when we have moved into the house of love, my body will coagulate...

509 Here we have the admixture of two lights compared to the mixture of wine and water, a symbolism well known in the Christian tradition: When Mass is read, wine and water are mixed, depicting the human and the divine spiritual aspect of Christ—His humanity and His spiritual aspect.

510 Wine naturally belongs to the sun and water to the moon, for the moon is the ruler of all moist things, according to the ancient way of looking at things. This is expressing the idea of the *coniunctio* in a broad and general sense, as it is understood not only in the Christian tradition but also in the Arabic world: the mystical exalted connection of the spiritual substance with the Godhead. In the poems of Hafis and Rumi that appear to celebrate drunkenness, water is generally the corruptible, the feminine, and an aspect of the flow of life and of the unconscious. If the sun and moon come together, the moon will stop its flow and coagulate which, according to the end of the text, is something positive.

511 This means that up to the time of the *coniunctio* the moon flowed, which would have to do with the constant waxing and waning of the moon, the constant flux, but according to alchemical theory, it also produces the dew and moisture, and naturally also menstruation in women—their monthly flow. But since menstruation stops when the child is generated, there is the idea that the flow is stopped when the two lights have united and the new light is born. Something corruptible and nasty that has to do with the changeable nature of the feminine, apparently stops and becomes solid. This refers directly and immediately to the whole alchemical process, which is, as we know, the production of the *lapis philosophorum*, an object of hard substance, something that does not flow and is the highest symbol in alchemy, even symbolizing the Divinity.

512 It is a strange thing that in alchemy the end product—if we look at it naively—is something which, in the order of nature, we look upon as being very low, namely a stone, whose quality is simply to be there. A stone neither eats nor drinks nor sleeps; it just remains there for all eternity. If you kick it, it stays where you kicked it and does not move. But in alchemy this despised thing is the symbol of

the goal. We have to go deeply into the mystical language of the East, of alchemy, and of certain other Christian mystiques to get an idea of what this means.

513 If one has suffered long enough through fighting and meeting the unconscious, a kind of objective personality is established; a nucleus forms in the person which is at peace, quiet even in the midst of the greatest life storms, intensely alive but without action and without participation in the conflict. This striking peace of mind often comes to people when they have suffered long enough. They suffer and suffer and make a great effort and suffer again, and one can do nothing other than suffer with them until one day something breaks, and their face acquires a quiet expression for something has been born that remains in the center, outside or beyond the conflict which, for its part, no longer continues as it did. Naturally, two minutes later it begins again, for the conflict has not been solved, but the experience of there being something quietly beyond the conflict remains, and from then on the process becomes different. People no longer search; they know that this thing exists, that they have experienced it for a moment even if it has disappeared again. Thereafter the opus has a goal, namely of finding this moment again and slowly being able to keep it, so that it becomes something that is constant.

514 In all of life's struggles there is always this one thing that is beyond the struggle; it is, as Jung describes it so beautifully in his Commentary in *The Secret of the Golden Flower*,[41] as if you were standing on the mountaintop, viewing a thunderstorm in the valley below. One sees the black clouds and the lightning and the falling rain, but something in one is above it all and can just observe it. In a certain way you are in it too, but in another way you are out of it. In a more humble way, or on a more minor scale, you have reached this state if, in a storm of despair or in a destructive dissolving attack of a conflict, you can find your sense of humor for a second. For example, when you are being swept away once more by a negative

[41] Jung, "Commentary on 'The Secret of the Golden Flower'" in *Alchemical Studies*, vol. 13, *CW*, §§ 1-84.

animus, you might suddenly be able to say to yourself that you have heard that kind of talk before. Even if you are not able to get out of your destructive animus as it may still be too strong, nevertheless something in you smiles and says it has heard that silly song before. You would like to laugh at yourself, but your pride will not allow it, and you go on with your negative animus and he gets you again. Yet these are those divine moments when something is clear and moving beyond the opposites and the suffering. Usually they are only brief moments, but if you continue working on yourself long enough, the stone slowly grows and becomes more and more the solid nucleus of the personality that no longer participates in the ape-circus of life.

515 This is probably what is meant here: The moon stops influencing life—in so far as it is an ape-circus—and something ceases to participate, something that is eternal and beyond the conflict. The moon coagulates and the life process is seen as something eternal, outside of life. Life itself becomes more solid and steps out of its own rhythm, which is probably the preparation for death, since death is the natural end of life, the fruit that grows out of life. A life that has been fully lived creates an eternal attitude that transcends death. So the moon says:

516 > ...When we have moved into the house of love, my body will coagulate, and I shall be within my emptiness.' To which the sun replies, 'If you do all of this, and do me no harm, O Luna, my body will return [probably back to its original form], and I shall give you the virtue of penetration, after which, in the battle of fire, of liquefaction and purgation you will be powerful, and you will go on without diminishing or darkness, as copper and lead do, and you will not have any conflict against me for you will no longer be rebellious.

517 So the sun only confirms what the moon says, and I think from what I said earlier that it is clear that now, even in the battle of the fire—which means even in the destructive attacks of emotions from within and without—the moon will remain firm and beyond them

and will no longer be rebellious against consciousness. Unconscious and conscious are at peace with each other.

518 Blessed is he who thinks about what I say and my dignity will not be withdrawn from him and the lion, too, will not fail or become cheap, weakened by the flesh.

519 The lion is a well-known symbol of the solstice of the sun, when the sun is at its peak, astrologically speaking, but it is also a symbol of resurrection. We had the lion in our first Greek text, where lion generates lion and I referred to the Egyptian double lions.[42] The lion is a symbol of passionate devouring, of the power drive, not only in the narrow sense of the word, but also generally the desire to possess. Its outstretched paws and its wide-open jaws typify the lion with its powerful, passionate, hot nature. The lion stands for resurrection but can also be "weakened by the flesh."

520 If you have followed me, I shall not turn you away and withhold from you the increase of the lead.

521 The idea is that lead, as mentioned above, is the basic material, the material of passion, and it is now growing by itself. This refers to a stage in alchemy that is often described as growth. Thus, the alchemists say that the first part of the opus is hard work: One is either washing linen, or washing sand, or cooking things, or killing the lion, or bringing forth the *coniunctio*, but afterward, at a certain moment, it becomes what they even describe as child's play, and one has only to water the garden or to play about. No effort need be made, for from now on, the thing grows by itself and one need only attend to it and watch it. All the painful efforts one made earlier are no longer needed. That is the *augmentum plumbi*, the increasing of the lead, as it is called here.

522 It is like the growth of a child in the mother—while the child grows within her, she can only see to it that she herself is healthy

[42] Cf. illustration 6.

and that she does as little as possible. This is a simile the alchemists often use: After one has transcended the stage of conflict, there comes the stage where one is just like a pregnant woman, waiting for the birth of her child; it is a stage where one need not think about whether one is doing the right thing or not. The Chinese would call it doing nothing,[43] just letting things happen. All that is needed now is giving one's constant, loving attention to the process. The text continues:

523 > My light will fade, and my beauty will be extinguished, but they will take from the minerals of my pure body and from the fatness of the purified lead, within the harmony of their weight, but without goat's blood, and a difference can be made between what is true and what is false.

524 Goat's blood—or he-goat's blood—was supposed to have a corrosive effect upon everything, and in late antiquity it was allegorically interpreted as sensuality. The blood of the he-goat is the essence of sensuality, of lasciviousness, of the sensual drive of the he-goat that is so very obvious and destroys everything. The strong, sexual drive destroys everything except the adamant. An old legend says that adamant is the one precious stone that cannot be dissolved by goat's blood, and therefore it stands for the firmness of one's personality that resists the impulse of sensuality.[44]

525 Here is the same symbolism, namely the *coniunctio* of substances of equal weight. This would refer to a state of psychological balance where there is no goat's blood, that is, where sensuality no longer sweeps away the personality. Then one is capable of distinguishing the true from the false, and there arises or grows within the personality what one could call the instinct of truth.

---

[43] The Taoist idea of doing through nondoing, the so-called *wu-wei*, corresponds to "the art of letting things happen" of Master Eckhart, cf. Jung, *Alchemical Studies*, vol. 13, *CW*, § 20.

[44] Cf. the slightly different presentation by von Franz, *Aurora Consurgens*, 323.

526 In general, life is so complicated that if one has to think about things, one is always too late. I am hopeless in this respect and am always too late. If someone telephones and says they must see me that evening, or they need an hour tomorrow, I am not quick enough in deciding whether to say yes or no, or to find an excuse by saying I am not free. My nature, my inferior function, sweeps me away, and I say yes, and afterward I am caught in it and I am upset as it is all wrong. And then I say, "Confound it all! I was too slow again. I should have said no!" but the instinct of truth did not work strongly enough. It was there—something kept telling me to say no—but when reflection and the inferior function came into it, I was once again too slow. Then along comes a bad dream that gives me a good blow on the head, and I wonder if I will ever get out of that stage and be quick enough to not always get caught in the same trap.

527 There is a speeding-up of this possibility by the development of the instinct of truth. This means that when the Self is so present and so strong, the instinct of truth gets through quickly, like a radio telegram, and one reacts rightly without knowing why: It simply flows through one, and one does the right thing. One says yes or no, sometimes doing the one thing and sometimes the other; one can carry on without hesitation because consciousness with its reflection is no longer a disturbance. The action of the Self becomes immediate. But only the Self can accomplish this. It is the same thing as being completely natural and instinctive, when one can discern between the false and the true, but on a higher level. That is why certain theologians refer to the Holy Ghost as the instinct of truth, which is a very good description. The text continues:

> 528 I am the hard, dry iron and the strong ferment, everything good comes through me, the light of the secret of secrets is generated by me, and nothing can affect my actions. What has light is created in the darkness of the light [we understand this now]. But when it reaches its perfection, then it recovers from its illnesses and its weakness, and then will appear this great flux out of the head and the tail.

529 I think the first part is clear. It refers to the generation of a new light, a third thing generated in the *coniunctio*. When a new light is born in the darkness, all neurotic symptoms and illness and weakness disappear and the new thing appears, now called *illud magnum fluxum capitis et caudae*. Here we must remember the Ouroboros, the tail eater, where the opposites—the head at one end and the tail at the other—are one. They are one but have, nevertheless, an opposite aspect. When these opposites—the head and the tail—meet, a flow is born. This is what the alchemists mean when they speak of the mystical or divine water and which I tried to describe as the meaningful flux of life. With the help of the instinct of truth, life goes on as a meaningful flow, as a manifestation of the Self. In this case, it is the result of the *coniunctio*. In many other cases it is described as the philosopher's stone, but in many texts the water of life and the *lapis* are one.

530 It is a very great paradox that liquid—the unformed water of life—and the stone—the most solid and dead thing—are, according to the alchemists, one and the same thing. This has to do with the fact that the realization of the Self has two aspects: Something firm is born, beyond the ups and downs of life, and at the same time, something very living is born that takes part in the flow of life, without the inhibitions or restrictions of consciousness.

531 ***Question:*** *You spoke of the instinct of truth. What do you mean by that?*

532 It is what gives me the truth without reflection; something within me knows the truth by my immediate reaction without my thinking about it or even expressing it. It is very similar to telepathic knowledge. "Telepathy" in Greek simply means "feeling from afar," which does not explain anything, for telepathy is a mystery, and we do not know what it is. Let me give you an example: Somebody proposes that you take part in some business that seems quite all right and clean and straightforward and, from outer appearances, you cannot see anything wrong with it. Naturally, you would say, "Yes, all right, I will participate in that." Then something within you says, "No, don't do it!" And *après la coup* you discover that there was

something unclean or wrong about it. You could not have known, but "it" smelled a rat. That would have been the instinct of truth.

533 Instinct knew something one does not know oneself. One's unconscious, or instinctive personality, knew the truth. I do not mean the religious truth of a doctrine: I mean the truth of the moment. In the already mentioned case of being offered to participate in some fraudulent business, the instinct of truth would have warned one. Or it tells one the truth about a certain situation or of what is being said to one. Somebody may tell you a long story and you just feel it is not true, though you cannot say what is wrong about it. This may be about a marriage problem, and you have the feeling something is not true about it, though you do not know what. In another case, you have the immediate feeling you are being told the truth. If you judge instinctively in this way, it is something inside you that decides, and if it proves to operate consistently well, you can decide to trust that inner thing, for it repeatedly proves to have been correct, even if one only finds out years later. This would be a discernment of truth on an instinctive level that has nothing to do with one's head.

534 ***Question:*** *How does that differ from intuition?*

535 Intuition can be 50% right and 50% wrong. Jung uses a marvelous simile about intuitive people and says either they hit the nail on the head, hit the bull's-eye without any reflection, or shoot away into the woods—20 kilometers on the other side. That is why they should develop another function, because they can sometimes just look at the situation and know all about it, but sometimes they are completely wrong. It is better not to trust intuition all the time, for it may be blurred by projection. An intuitive person is generally right if there is no shadow involved. If the intuitive is not involved with the shadow, or the animus or anima, he has a fantastic way of hitting the mark. But if they are involved, if projection gets in, the same intuitive can still swear he knows the thing is so-and-so, for he thinks he can trust his intuition that is always right, when, in fact, objectively it is all wrong—he is shooting into the woods. So

intuition is a 50-50 business.[45] It is a function, and, like all functions, it is only sometimes right. But the instinctive truth is a manifestation of the Self and has nothing to do with a function. It is something that operates in every human being, like a discreet, quick word that the Self whispers in your ear and which generally you are too slow to catch, or you, yourself, talk too much and then "it" cannot be heard.

536 I have now used up a lot of time for our discussion of this Arabic text; next we shall move on to European alchemy. I am sorry to have given you only one Arabic text, but I think this Shiite alchemist, Muhammad Ibn Umail, is still not sufficiently well known, nor has he been given sufficient recognition; in my view, he was one of the very great men of alchemy.

[45] Cf. Jung, *Nietzche's Zarathustra*, 878.

Part 3

Medieval European Alchemy

Introduction
Lecture 7

537 We shall dedicate the last three lectures to European alchemy. I have three propositions to make and ask my listeners to choose:

538 1. The text of the *Aurora consurgens,* which I wrote a commentary upon.[1] It has been said to be so complicated and difficult that it needs an introduction;

2. Extracts from a text by Petrus Bonus, an Italian of the 14th century, who gives a typical picture of medieval alchemy;

3. A combination of the two.

539 It has also been suggested that I finish up with a text by Paracelsus, but I have avoided this writer because of the many strange words he uses that would require a specific explanation. One has to dig one's way into Paracelsus, as one must with Jakob Boehme, and therefore I do not think much would be obtained from a short excerpt.

540 If you would like a text that, in my opinion, was written out of an immediate religious experience of the unconscious, I would advise the *Aurora consurgens*, but if you would prefer an introduction into the ways and thought, and the more average style, of medieval European alchemy, then I would say vote for Petrus Bonus because the *Aurora consurgens* is not a typical text, but unique and outside of any system. The third option is a combination of the two. I would give a short introduction on Petrus Bonus and then go on to the *Aurora consurgens.* This would be chronologically wrong, but I would prefer to do it that way.

541 (A vote was taken and *Aurora consurgens* was chosen.)

542 I am very happy about this decision because I think this is the most exciting text.

[1] von Franz, *Aurora Consurgens.*

Aurora Consurgens

543 *Aurora consurgens* stands for "rising dawn." The discovery of this text was almost like a detective story. In an old collection of books, Jung came across the text of *Aurora consurgens, Part II*, a rather dry kind of chemical work, with a brief note at the beginning stating that it was the second part of the text and that the printer had omitted the first part because it was blasphemous.[2] This aroused Jung's curiosity, and he spent some time trying to track it down. He discovered that in the monastery on the island of Reichenau, on the Lake of Constance, there had been such a manuscript that was now in the Central Library in Zurich. It is incomplete and begins in the middle of the text we have now published. Jung found that as it was, the text was not legible for it was written in 15th-century Latin stenography; he therefore handed it over to me.

544 After digging my way into it, I discovered there was a complete handwritten manuscript in Paris, another in Bologna, and a third in Venice, so we were slowly able to collect several versions. In most manuscripts the text was ascribed to St. Thomas of Aquinas, which I did not consider for one moment; I knew it was usual to put the name of a famous man onto such a treatise. Thus, someone else might easily have written it, which was the usual reaction of other scholars.

545 This quite amazing text is like a mosaic, combining quotations from the Bible and a few early alchemical writings. If regarded as a puzzle that someone has made for his own amusement, it would be extremely uninteresting, and it is possible that some who have read it superficially have accepted it in this way. But, as we will soon see, it is impossible to explain this phenomenon that way because of the tremendous excitement and emotion it contains. This would not be the case if someone had simply put together a series of quotations.

546 The next conclusion was that it was a schizophrenic product—it sounds rather like one—and this is much closer to the truth. I do not think it is quite that, however, although it was probably written

[2] Cf. Jung, *Psychology and Alchemy*, vol. 12, *CW*, § 464.

by someone overwhelmed by the unconscious. The classic situation of someone in this condition is described as a psychotic episode, but in Jung's opinion, and according to his medical diagnosis, we are dealing with either the outbreak of a psychosis, or a phase in a manic depressive psychosis, or with the description of an abnormal situation written by a normal person who, at that particular time, was overwhelmed by the unconscious.

547 I am inclined to agree with the third theory, though from the document, it is not possible to come to a definite conclusion. I have interpreted it symbolically, like a dream, and have concluded that it is the text of a dying person. The whole symbolism and problem circles round, and is concentrated upon, the problem of death, and at the end there is a description of the mystical marriage, or love experience, rendered in a form which seems to have to do with the experiences many dying people are known to have, resulting in the tradition that death is a kind of mystical marriage with the other half of the personality.

548 Having translated, studied and interpreted the text thus far, Jung suddenly decided we should publish this unique document. He asked me if I would write a brief, historical introduction—the rest was finished—going into the problem of dating it and who its author might be, and so on.

549 I started with the assumption that although the text had been ascribed to St. Thomas of Aquinas, naturally there was no question of that.[3] I intended to continue by saying that the text belonged to the 13th century. But then I realized I knew only quite superficial things about St. Thomas of Aquinas. Why, then, should I write that? So, out of sheer conscientiousness, I decided to look into other writings of his and, in order to be rather more on the safe side, to read a biography. This, however, unsettled me even more, for I found out that, at the end of his life, just a few weeks before his death, St. Thomas suffered from a very strange alteration of his personality. He had been overworking for a long time and, because of this, and

[3] Cf. von Franz, "Was St. Thomas Aquinas the Author of *Aurora Consurgens*?," in *Aurora Consurgens*, 405-31.

for certain other psychological reasons that I would like to discuss in detail later, he began to have strange states of absent-mindedness. For instance, once when reading Mass in public in Naples, he suddenly, although a Cardinal was present, stopped in the middle and remained in a kind of ecstatic, absent-minded state for 20 minutes until someone shook him and asked what the matter was, at which point he came to and excused himself.

550 Many have said that that was the beginning of his illness, while some say that as well as a rational side, he must have had a mystical streak in his personality that broke through from time to time in these strange fits of absent-mindedness. Such states were more frequent in his later years—he died at the age of 49 or 51, we do not know for sure because we do not know exactly when he was born—and then something happened that has never been explained. He used to get up very early every morning and read Mass to himself in the chapel of whatever monastery he was visiting. He traveled all the time. One of his main biographical sources was his friend, Reginald of Piperno, a very humble monk who was his follower and personal servant, and who worshipped him. This monk relates that one morning St. Thomas read Mass as usual, and when he returned, he was quite white. As the Latin report of Reginald literally says, "I thought he had become crazy." In his *Summa Theologica*, Thomas had been writing the chapter *De Poenitentia*, on penitence; but now he pushed aside his writing utensils and just sat there the whole day in a kind of catatonic state with his head in his hands. Reginald of Piperno asked him why he was not writing, and he only replied, "I cannot." This continued for several days. Reginald again went to him and asked why he was not writing and got the same answer, "*Non possum*"—"I can't." About five days later they tried again to find out what was happening to him, for he did nothing all day, neither worked nor preached, but just sat around looking crazy, and he said that he could not write, for everything he had written seemed to him to be like straw—*palea sunt*. In later biographies, written by people who were not present, the words "in comparison with the

magnificent visions I have had" have been added, but those words are not in the original sources and were added later.[4]

551 Reginald of Piperno became very upset about the condition of St. Thomas and, because he had always had conversations with a cousin, an Italian countess, he took St. Thomas to her, thinking he might open up there and say what had happened.[5] But the countess said, "My God, what has happened to Father Thomas? He seems to be crazy." She, too, had the same impression. St. Thomas did not utter a word during the whole of teatime. But then, slowly, he returned to his former state of mind, to the extent that he could again take part in church politics and such things, and he agreed to attend a church congress in Milan or in southern France.[6]

552 On his way there, while riding on a donkey, he hit his head against the branch of a tree and fell. He was a fat, stout man at that time, and it was a very hot summer's day, but he just got up and did not say much about the accident. That night they stayed in a little monastery—Santa Maria di Fossa Nuova. There, in the doorway, he suddenly felt ill again and became giddy and, leaning against the doorpost, said, "This is my death coming; I shall not leave this place." Then he went to bed. The monks of Santa Maria di Fossa Nuova were thrilled to have such a marvelous visitor; they pestered the famous Father Thomas to give a seminar in spite of the dreadful state he was in. Being obliged to follow his Christian obligations, with his last strength he tried to do this and, according to the oldest traditions—though this, too, was omitted in later reports—he gave a seminar on the *Song of Solomon*—of all things! In the midst of it, while interpreting the words "Come, my beloved, let us go forth into the field," he died.

553 Notes of this seminar have never been found, and already at the time of his canonization, in 1312, this last episode is more or less skipped over; nobody showed any interest in his last words, though usually the last words of a saint play a great role in his biography.

---

[4] Ibid., 425: "Everything that I have written seems to me worthless in comparison with the things I have seen and which have been revealed to me."

[5] Cf. ibid. Not a cousin, but his beloved sister, Countess Theodora von Marsico.

[6] Cf. ibid. Instead of a church congress in Mailand: a congress in Lyon.

However, in this case, everything was smoothed over with the oil of roses! These details are not to be found in any official biography, but in the *Acta Bollandiana*, the original Latin sources and reports of the oldest witnesses for the process of canonization.

554 After reading the above, I was even less sure about what I could write on the origin of this text. Obviously, one does not want to think that the great dogmatist could have anything to do with this crazy, psychotic text that was assuredly the work of a dying man. I began to have a terrible suspicion that the *Aurora consurgens* might indeed have originated in the notes of St. Thomas's last seminar. The text is a paraphrase of the *Song of Solomon,* and the last chapter ends exactly at the same place where, according to tradition, Father Thomas died.

555 I was quite anxious about my discovery, for I thought I would make myself very unpopular if I said what I had found. But after struggling with my own vanity and the feeling that I should make myself look ridiculous by saying such things, I published the book as it now stands, stating that there was no proof, but that the evidence was more in favor of than against my theory. Up to the present time, I have had *no* reaction from church people—positive or negative. The official reaction to what I said in the book has so far been absolute silence; not a single specialist has published an article saying that it is all rubbish and that the writer does not even know the ABCs of St. Thomas's life.[7]

556 Of course, I took a great deal of care to establish my statements, as far as I could, but no one has either accepted or rejected what I wrote; there has been nothing but an awkward silence. When the subject is discussed in the press, it is always in connection with Jung's first two volumes of *Mysterium Coniunctionis;* then it is said that the third volume, that is mine, is a very interesting document, but the last chapter, in which I speak of its possible authorship, is simply ignored. I am still waiting to see what will happen—it seems to be a

[7] According to the Preface of the English edition of von Franz *Aurora Consurgens*. X-xi. Marie-Louise von Franz mentions an anonymous author in *Bulletin Thomiste*, (Vol. X, 1957), and quotes passages from a letter sent to her by Father Victor White in which he discusses her comments in *Aurora Consurgens*.

delayed time bomb! Also, I loaded the book with so many learned footnotes, they would, for the most part, cover any dispute, and most people seem to be too lazy to read it to the end. I did that on purpose, in a sense with the feeling of quietly and discreetly putting a bomb inside the Vatican!

557 There is one exception: A Dominican father and teacher of theology reacted very positively. He is a specialist on St. Thomas, and he said that it made complete sense to him, that there was nothing that could not be accepted in such a hypothesis if one were broad-minded.

558 ***Question:*** *Do you have any idea whether the former Pope ever saw it?*[8]

559 No, I do not think he ever did. I did consider sending him a copy with a dedication, but I did not do so. I had to write to him for permission to use the Vatican Library, addressing my letter "alla sua Sanctita"—to His Holiness—and I was very much impressed by having to address him like that, even though it was a pure formality.

560 ***Question:*** *Wasn't this Pope acquainted with the writings of Jung, and friendly toward him? In* The Symbolic Life, *Jung writes that he had the Pope's blessing.*[9]

561 That is simply intimated. I can only tell you that there has been a lot of talk and that Jung has not told me anything about this. The late Pope certainly had a positive attitude toward psychology in general, and at the opening of a psychological congress in Rome, he recommended the study of psychology, and among the different psychologies, the Freudian and others, he seems to have had rather a leaning toward Jungian psychology.

The First Five Chapters from the Wisdom of God

562 I would rather like to focus on the text now. Because of the time available, I cannot translate it all but have selected the most important passages from its approximately 50 pages.

---

[8] Pope John 13.

[9] C. G. Jung, *The Symbolic Life*, vol. 18, *CW*, (Princeton NJ: Princeton University Press, 1989), § 618.

563 The first five chapters are all concerned with the apparition of a female figure that the author refers to as the Wisdom of God. In the *Books of Wisdom*, for instance, in the *Proverbs*, that are all late material in the Old Testament and were influenced by Gnosticism from about the second century B.C.E. till the first century A.D., there is a personification of the Wisdom of God who appears as a feminine figure. She was with God and played before him before the world and mankind were created. This Wisdom of God is mixed up with the Gnostic idea of the Sophia; this female personification was an awkward figure for Christian theologians. What does she embody? In the late writings of the Old Testament there appears a kind of bride or wife of God—certainly a female figure—but who is she? The usual medieval attitude was that she was identical with the Holy Ghost, just a feminine aspect, and wherever the Wisdom of God was mentioned, one should simply read the "Holy Ghost." But some saw her as the soul of Christ—the *anima Christi*—who already existed before Christ incarnated and in this way was identical with Christ before his incarnation. Generally, one thinks of Christ as the eternal word, as the Logos, who has been with God for all time, long before his incarnation as Jesus Christ; but here the Wisdom of God has been looked on as being the same thing, and to explain its feminine character, the expression "the soul of Christ"—*anima Christi*—is used.

564 The third explanation, which to my mind is the most interesting, is that this feminine figure represents the sum of all archetypes—*archetypi*. I am not projecting Jung's concept here, but rather the medieval use of the word—of *archetypi* being the eternal ideas in God's mind when He created the world. To explain: When God created the world, He did not just go ahead with it but instead, like a good architect, He first conceived a plan in which—trees, animals, insects, and all of existence—was present as an idea. Before there were thousands of bears in this world, there was an idea of a bear in God's mind, and before there were millions of oak trees, there was the idea of an oak tree.

565 These ideas, like that of an oak tree, in God's mind were the *archetypi*, the *rationes* or *ideae aeternae*, the eternal plans or ideas. God conceived of the world and then cast His idea into matter and created the real world. If we translate this into psychological language, it would mean that the Wisdom of God represents the collective unconscious, the sum of all the original idea patterns of reality. This would be the feminine side of the Godhead.

566 ***Question:*** *How does one reconcile this with the idea that the word, the idea, the Logos, is connected with the masculine, while the feminine is connected with matter, materialization? I understand only that here one needs to differentiate between the archetype and the archetypal image.*

567 I do not think that comes in yet. I would say that with Logos, the accent is on oneness and spiritual order, while in the feminine parallel, the accent is on the multiple and more pictorial. That is the nuance. The archetypal image does not come in yet; it appears at a much later stage. Here I am speaking in medieval scholastic terms in which it would correspond to the *unus mundus*, a purely spiritual existence that has not yet become an image in anyone's mind, save that of God's. It would be better to make this distinction: Some people primarily experience the secret spiritual order in the unconscious and are most impressed by it, for instance, when they understand the meaning of a dream. This is more the case with thinking types.

568 Although I interpret a good many dreams a day with different people, I am always overwhelmed by the marvelous structure of the dream. There is an exposition, and then the pictures are mixed in a cunning way, and the meaning becomes clear. Because I am a thinking type, I admire the thinking element in the unconscious, the wonderful structure of it. If I were more of a feeling type, perhaps artistically inclined, then, as I often see in my analysands, I would be more impressed by the beauty of a dream image, by the impressive feeling that a dream element conveys. When I say, "Isn't that dream structured wonderfully?" an analysand may say, "Yes, yes," but is actually more impressed by the vivid image or the

impressive emotional tone. A more rational Logos type is impressed by the wonderful structure of something which one might expect to be completely irrational. The logic of a dream is something that always amazes me—the fantastic logic in those series of images.

569 I would therefore say that the Logos would represent the structural element of the unconscious—structure and meaning—while in the feminine qualification, there is more the idea of its pictorial, emotional manifestation. I would rather compare them in this way. In our language, they both mean the unconscious, and even for scholastic authors, it is simply a manner of speaking—it can be called the Sophia or Logos, for they are one and the same thing, or two aspects of the same thing. We could completely agree with this kind of teaching.

570 Another theory that already existed in the Middle Ages comes from the Arabs. The famous Arabic philosopher, Ibn Sina, who was known in European literature as Avicenna, developed an Aristotelian idea about the so-called *nous poietikos,* which is as follows: Within the cosmic reality of the world is a creative intelligence that exists in things themselves; it exists in the cosmos and was created by God. God created the world, and in it He created a creative spirit or, as generally interpreted, a creative intelligence that is responsible for the meaningfulness of cosmic events. This meaningfulness—the fact that the Cosmos is not chaos or an engine that just continues in accordance with causal laws but is also a mystery within which meaningful synchronicities take place—was attributed to the *nous poietikos.*

571 Albert the Great and St. Thomas, his pupil, dug up the writings of Ibn Sina and got into great difficulties because they were absolutely fascinated by the idea of the meaningfulness of the cosmos, the notion that the cosmos has intelligence; they did not know how to reconcile it with their Christian ideas. Albert was an intuitive and a great genius but not a very accurate thinker, and he just remarked happily that this was something like the Holy Ghost. Thomas, who was a thinking type, could not completely swallow that and he therefore divided the *nous poietikos,* saying that in part the

nous poietikos was not in the cosmos but in the human mind, of which it was the basis—in modern terms we would call it the basis of the mystery of consciousness—while the other part, he said, was simply the Wisdom of God.

572 Thus, Thomas divided the Islamic concept into two parts. He put one part into man and the other into the Wisdom of God. This is very interesting, for originally the intelligence, the meaningfulness or spiritual order, of the world was projected outside. Medieval people, like primitives, did not realize that we perceive order through our minds. Causality does not exist in itself; it is simply the way in which we explain the sequence of events: It is a philosophical category. The same thing applies to synchronicity; here, too, we do not know the actual connection between the sequences of events in them.

573 People in medieval times still thought that categories, like causality, etc., existed objectively in the outer world and therefore the outer world had intelligence, which was not such a stupid idea. The idea of an intelligent world struck them very much, for through it, they were able to understand why God created the world and its meaningful connections. Then along came Thomas and introjected the projection, meaning he withdrew it to some extent, and realized that, in part, it is a question of our own mental operations, for there is no meaningfulness unless we see it, and if nobody can describe causality, it does not exist. Both depend on a conscious mind that can observe and describe. Thus, Thomas took the modern step of introjecting the theories of natural science by realizing that the terms we use come from our minds, and because he was a great thinker, he went even further and asked why our own minds produced such ideas as meaningful connections, and this he attributed to the *nous poietikos*. This is the state of consciousness of the man who perhaps wrote the text we are now about to consider.

574 So, this is how the text begins:[10]

[10] von Franz, *Aurora Consurgens*, 157, 160-2, 164, 173, 182. A few additional commentaries given in her English lectures are noted between squared paragraphs [ ] and text that did not appear in the earlier English edition, but did in the German edition, is included between doubled square paragraphs [[ ]].

All good things came to me together with her, that Wisdom of the south, who preacheth abroad, who uttereth her voice in the streets, crieth out at the head of the multitudes, and in the entrance of the gates of the city uttereth her words, saying: Come ye to me and be enlightened, and your operations shall not be confounded; all ye that desire me shall be filled with my riches. Come therefore, children, hearken to me; I will teach you the science of God. Who is wise and understandeth this, of which Alphidius saith, that men and children pass her by daily in the streets and public places, and she is trodden into the mire by beasts of burden and by cattle? And Senior saith: Nought is more base in appearance than she, and nought is more precious in nature than she, and God also hath not appointed her to be bought for a price. She it is that Solomon chose to have instead of light, and above all beauty and health; in comparison of her he compared not unto her the virtue of any precious stone. For all gold in her sight shall be esteemed as a little sand, and silver shall be counted as clay; and this not without cause, for to gain her is better than the merchandise of silver and the most pure gold. [[And her fruits are more precious than the riches of the whole world, and everything you may want cannot be compared with her.]] Length of days and health are in her right hand, and in her left hand glory and infinite riches. Her ways are beautiful operations and praise-worthy, not unsightly nor ill-favoured, and her paths are measured and not hasty, but are bound up with stubborn and day-long toil. She is a tree of life to them that lay hold on her, and an unfailing light. Blessed shall they be who retain her, for the science of God shall never perish, as Alphidius beareth witness, for he saith: He who hath found this science, it shall be his rightful food forever. And Hermes . . . saith, that if a man who hath this science should live for a thousand years, and every day must feed seven thousand men, yet should he never lack. This doth Senior confirm, saying: That such a one is as rich as he that hath a stone from which fire is struck, who can give fire to whom he will and as much as he will and when he will without loss to himself. [Whoever has a firestone can always reproduce fire without any loss.] The same is the intent of Aristotle in his second book *Of the Soul*, when he saith: To the size and growth of all things in nature a limit is appointed, but fire by the addition of combustible matter waxes without end. Blessed is the man that shall find this science and into whom this prudence (of Saturn) floweth; in all thy ways think of her and she shall direct thy steps. As Senior saith: But the wise man and the discerning and ingenious in judgement understandeth her, when his spirits have been enlightened by the *Liber aggregationis*. For then every spirit bursteth into flood and followeth its desire [for desire, the word *concupiscentia* is used here, referring to sensual desire which, for a medieval monk, must have been very shocking!]; blessed is he who meditateth upon my words! And Solomon: My son, put her about thy neck and write in the tables of thy heart and thou shalt find. Say to Wisdom: Thou art my sister, and call Prudence thy friend. For to meditate upon her is a most natural and subtle understanding, which bringeth her to perfection. [Suddenly the text shifts and man has to add perfection to Wisdom, the Wisdom of God. She is the most perfect thing and yet man has to add wisdom to her.] And they that constantly watch for her shall quickly be secure. For she is clear to them that have understanding, and shall never fade away nor fail; she is easily seen by them that have knowledge of her, for she goeth about seeking such as are worthy of her and showeth herself cheerfully to them in the ways and meeteth them with all providence; for her beginning is the most true nature, whereof cometh no deceit.

575 Notice the elated, poetical language and the many allusions to different biblical quotations. If you know your Bible well, a bell will

be constantly ringing in your ears. The quotations are chiefly from the *Vulgata*.[11]

576 At first, one is rather puzzled by this paraphrase of the words of the Wisdom of God. She appears in the streets; she calls for men. This motif is taken from the Bible, in *Jesus Sirach* and the *Proverbs*. If you listen carefully, you notice something very strange. Namely, first there is the Wisdom of God as a feminine being who calls people toward her, saying, "Come and listen to me!" And then the thought shifts, and it says, "This is the thing which is trodden upon in the streets, it is despised by everybody." That is an alchemical quotation that refers to the philosopher's stone in the original text. So, whoever knows this quotation knows that, from the very beginning of his text, the writer identifies the Wisdom of God with the philosopher's stone, that to him they are one and the same thing. He must have had an experience about which he felt that what had entered him was what the alchemists call the *Lapis*.

577 He goes on to quote a few more alchemists, Senior, or Ibn Umail, among others, about the Wisdom of God being very precious but despised by ordinary people. Then there is a long comparison to show how much more precious she is than worldly goods. Then comes a nonbiblical allusion to the fact that one has to work a very long time to find her. It says she is a kind of eternal nourishment or something like fire that can light other fires. And suddenly it says that to find her, only one thing is needed, namely a subtle perception of true nature. This is followed by an even more striking quotation from our friend, Ibn Umail, "If you do that, then your mind will begin to flow and follow its *concupiscentia*."

578 *Concupiscentia*, in medieval scholastic language, means the ordinary lower appetites—sexual desires, desire for food, and so on, but mainly sexual desire, the plain, vulgar basis of higher love. Thomas himself had a theory of love, namely that it always began with *concupiscentia* that had to be sublimated into the love of God.

[11] Ibid., 26. Marie-Louise von Franz draws attention to a difficulty in translation: as the Luther and Zurich Bibles, both well-known, often differ to the *Vulgata*, as they are based upon the Hebrew text, and the alchemical wordplays on the word *Vulgata* are lost, Marie-Louise von Franz depended for the most part upon the Luther Bible, though she also sometimes translates directly from the *Vulgata*.

579 Either we cannot understand this text at all and just say that it is beyond us, or we must look at it like a dream. We can take it as though it were a document from the unconscious, in which case its meaning becomes clear: The collective unconscious has broken into this man's mind in the form of a feminine personification which he feels to be the Wisdom of God. It becomes clear later that he thinks the Wisdom of God and God are one. Thus, we could say a feminine aspect of God has overwhelmed him and that this can happen to one by observing nature in a subtle way and by following your own inner desire; this is something like a subtle truth—the nature of truth—that anyone who has the simplicity of mind to follow his own desire can find. If it means anything, it means that someone has had an overwhelming experience of the unconscious in the form of a feminine personification.

580 From the feeling of the text, I do not believe that we are dealing with an invention of the intellect. It feels to me rather as if someone who was firstly overwhelmed by such an experience, and afterward tried to express it through biblical and alchemical quotations, wrote it. Such a thing can be observed, for instance, in the outbreak of a psychosis.

581 One of the most destructive syndromes in a psychotic interval occurs when people are overwhelmed by emotional or hallucinatory experiences and cannot express them. As soon as they are able to tell someone, they are no longer completely psychotic, for then the first stage is over. If they can say something about it and can describe it even in a stammering way or symbolically, if they can get it out in some form at all, they are no longer lost, and the healing process is already underway.

582 The worst is when the thing is so overwhelming that they simply turn white and sink into bed and become catatonic. One knows they are going through the most tremendous inner experiences, but outwardly they lie in bed like a piece of wood and refuse nourishment. When they get excited and begin to stammer and speak of what they have seen, that is already an improvement, for then they have found a mode of expression.

583 It is therefore extremely important, if you have to reckon with such a possibility, that you treat such people as though they had a latent psychosis and provide them with a tremendous amount of symbolic knowledge. If you suspect a possible outbreak or invasion of the collective unconscious, you must focus as much symbolic knowledge as you can into such people, making them read Jakob Boehme and alchemical texts and mythology as much as possible. They will not know why and might even think it rather strange, but if the overwhelming experience then comes, they can, perhaps, express it, or at least describe it. In some circumstances, one can prevent an invasion and a psychotic outbreak. If you can prepare the ground well enough ahead of time through symbolic understanding, even though the person in question does not realize the meaning or purpose of it all, when the experience comes, they have a net in which to catch and reexpress it.

584 Jung once told me about a case of a very rational, narrow-minded, foreign, female doctor who had studied psychiatry and wanted to have a training analysis. He recognized at once that she had a latent psychosis and that the situation was pretty dangerous. Instead of giving her an ordinary training analysis, he rammed as much symbolic knowledge into her as he could: the history of religion, mythology, as much alchemy as he knew then, etc. Due to her strong transference, she swallowed it all but did not quite see what it had to do with her. She did it all for him, and because of her transference, she assimilated and read it all. Then she went back to her own country, and suddenly the thing exploded, and she jumped out of the window of a hospital where she was working. She only broke both legs, but when brought back into the hospital, she was raving mad and had completely disappeared into a psychotic episode. The doctor who treated her wrote to Jung about the development of the case and described how, after three days of being what one could call completely mad and talking completely psychotic stuff, she apparently began to remember some of the symbolic things she had read and what Jung had said about them. She began to bring that into order, and around this formed the

nucleus of a new ego personality. After three weeks she was right out of the episode and quite normal. What she had heard and read earlier now came to her rescue and enabled her to contain the overwhelming emotional experience within the framework of a symbolic psychological understanding. She recovered, and according to the correspondence Jung had with her for many years—he never saw her again personally, for she came from a faraway country—she never had a relapse. That was her only psychotic episode, and there is every reason to believe that the thing is now really integrated and she is cured.

585 So, one can see how knowledge of symbolism is a net, so to speak, in which one can somehow catch the unspeakable mystery of an immediate experience of the unconscious. I think our author had just such an indescribable and overwhelming experience of the unconscious and that he tried, in a rather chaotic way, through a potpourri of biblical and alchemical quotations, to catch and describe what had happened to him.

586 ***Question:*** *How can one reconcile what you are saying here about giving expression to such an experience with what you said in one of your earlier lectures, namely, that psychotic people would be better off if they didn't talk about their experience?*

587 That is very simple. Naturally, I do not mean here that they should just talk to anyone about such things, but to their analyst. If our author were to proclaim on the street that the Wisdom of God had visited him and that he now knew all about it, that would not be the right thing, but he seems to have written a paper or to have given a seminar on it. If the text really is from Thomas's last seminar, then he was talking in some kind of a coma. I do not think he could still write, so this must have been written up from notes taken, which would fit in with the fact that the manuscripts, even the oldest ones, are very different, some richer and some poorer.

588 We have notes of other lectures given by Thomas. It was usual to take seminar notes at the time, and his pupils collected some of his writings in this way; I could imagine that, as the original report says, he talked in a half-ecstatic way and in a very weak state about the

Song of Solomon. In such a case one could not say that he should have held his tongue, but the effect was that this part of his life and what he said at the time were just set aside later on. We read of this in the earliest reports. Wilhelm of Tocco and Reginald of Piperno, the earliest biographers, recorded the events, but the later biographies do not mention them, because how could this great man with his marvelous, clear, rational mind say such things on his deathbed, even in a half-coma?

589 Normal or not, interned persons who have had such an experience would keep it to themselves or tell it to a few people who would understand. If one has already broken down and is in a mental hospital, then it must be told to someone who will listen, which is better than lying in bed and saying nothing; that would be quite wrong, in my opinion, in such an advanced case. By the way, this kind of speech is not addressed to any one person. It is in the style of an announcement, an ecstatic announcement, "Now I will teach you the Wisdom of God ..." One recognizes the style! One has not necessarily crossed a borderline if one uses such language for it is the style of the unconscious.

590 I remember one of my first pieces of active imagination: A figure came that had such a marvelous feeling and made such announcements that I simply could not write them down! It seemed to me so disgusting that I just blocked it. But Jung explained to me that that was the style of the unconscious. It is in very bad taste, if you want to judge it that way. In one young man's active imagination the Holy Ghost appeared personally and spoke as one would imagine the Holy Ghost would speak, and the poor man's stomach nearly turned at having to write down such pompous stuff.

591 There is something skeptical in us and in our down-to-earth nature that cannot stick it. But that is the style of the unconscious and explains why, as soon as people fall into it, they speak with conviction and begin to have this pompous, emotionally impressive style. It is carried by the whole emotion and is a ritualistic or sacramental style with a lot of repetition and three amens, like those beautiful songs of the North American Indians. When deeper

emotional layers are touched upon, one just has to accept this. One can still observe dispassionately, but if such things are to be allowed expression in their original form, one must allow for the very pompous and emotional way of speaking. This, I think, is where the preaching, ecstatic style of our text comes from.

592 I would like to skip the beginning of the next chapter for it is very tasteless. It says that you should love the Light of Wisdom, for then you will rule the world, that it is a sacrament of God that one should not betray to the common people because everybody would become jealous, and so on. Only at the end is it a bit better where it says if one finds this secret then one can say:[12]

593 > Rejoice, O Jerusalem, and gather together all ye that love me; rejoice with gladness, for the Lord hath been merciful unto his poor. Senior likewise saith: For there is a stone, which he that knoweth layeth it upon his eyes, but he that doth not, casteth it upon the dunghill, and it is a medicine which putteth poverty to flight, and after God hath man no better thing.

594 What has happened to the man here? It is not hard to see what it is as he speaks about ruling the world and says the common people should not be told. Who speaks like that?

595 ***Answer***: *Someone in an inflation.*

596 Yes. He has an inflation in this chapter. The experience of the Wisdom of God was so overwhelming that now, as the one who had that experience and knows all about it, he is naturally the great man. He has the typical symptoms of an inflation: One immediately gets the arrogant undertone of one who is elected, while others are all fools who are jealous. These symptoms are unavoidable after such an experience. I do not think any human being can have such an experience without going through such a stage for a moment; it belongs to the experience; the point is only whether one remains in it.

---

[12] Cf. von Franz, *Aurora Consurgens*, 198-99.

597 The next chapter is even worse. It speaks of "those who do not know this science and who deny it," and his inflation reaches its climax here.[13]

598 This glorious science of God and doctrine of the saints and secret of the philosophers and medicine of the physicians fools despise, for what it is they know not. These will not have the blessing and it shall be far from them nor doth such science befit the unskilled, for everyone who is ignorant of it is its enemy, and that not without cause. For Speculator saith: The mockery of science is the cause of ignorance, and lettuces are not to be given to asses, for thistles suffice them, nor is the children's bread to be set before the dogs to eat, nor are pearls to be cast before swine, etc. For the wise have not spoken to the foolish, seeing that he that speaketh with a fool speaketh with one that is asleep. Morienus saith: If I were to unriddle all things as they are, there would be nowhere any further place for prudence, for the fool would be made equal to the wise; nor would any mortal under the sphere of the moon bewail in step-motherly poverty the pangs of hunger, for in this science the number of fools is infinite.

599 Afterward comes a rather dry chapter that shows a change in the psychological situation. Very dryly he says that the title of his book is *The Rising Dawn* for four reasons:[14]

600 Firstly, it is called Dawn (*aurora*) as one should say the 'Golden Hour' (*aurea hora*) – [that is a play on words]; for so hath this science a (favourable) hour with a golden end for them that rightly perform the Work. Secondly, the dawn is midway between night and day, shining with twofold hues, namely, red and yellow; so likewise doth this science beget the colours yellow and red, which are midway between white

[13] Cf. ibid., 200-201.
[14] Cf. ibid., 45.

> and black. [That is classical alchemical knowledge about the *nigredo-albedo-rubedo-citrinitas,* the four stages of colour. The dawn would be the coming up of the yellow-red colour, the fulfilment of the alchemical work.] Thirdly, (the book is called this) because at dawn they that labour under all the infirmities of the night are relieved and have rest; and so at the dawn of this science all evil odours and vapours that infect the mind of the laborant fade away and weaken, as the Psalm saith: In the evening weeping shall have place, and in the morning gladness. [*Psalm* 30,6] Fourthly and lastly, the dawn is called the end of the night and the beginning of the day, or the mother of the sun, and so our dawn at its greatest redness is the end of all darkness and the putting to flight of night, of that long-drawn-out winter wherein he who walketh, if he take not heed, shall stumble. [*John* 11, 9-10] For of this indeed it is written: And night to night showeth knowledge, day to day uttereth speech, and night shall be light as the day in its pleasures.

601 This last quotation from *Psalm* 139, 12 is the psalm which is sung the night before Easter day in the Catholic Church: "The night shineth as the day: the darkness and the light are both alike to thee." So, we may certainly assume that even if it is not St. Thomas, this man is a Catholic priest, for probably no one else could quote the Bible so fluently. He alludes here to the Mass of the Easter Night and compares the dawn of the science, the rising dawn, with the night before Easter, the moment of rebirth and the resurrection of Christ.

602 As far as the state of the author is concerned, we now see that his ecstatic style has completely ceased and become slightly pedantic; the Aurora is named so for four reasons: firstly, secondly, thirdly, fourthly. Therefore, I would say that he is now out of his inflation and has returned to a relatively sober state of consciousness and now tries to bring order into his experience.

603 This order is very typically fourfold. He gives four explanations of the word "dawn." Whenever consciousness tries to establish itself,

it puts a fourfold order onto things; that is the net with which it catches things and brings them into order. This is why the author now tries to give a fourfold explanation of the rising dawn. The dawn *is* the Wisdom of God, as we shall see later, so he tries to put some distance between what has happened to him and to see what it is. He has met the rising dawn and can describe it with four reasons.

604 His explanations seem to me to be very superficial. Firstly, he makes a play of words—*aurora, aurea hora*—and then he compares it to the morning dawn when people fall asleep after a bad night. What should we think of this?

605 ***Remark:*** *It sounds like his thinking is compensating for his emotional excess.*

606 Yes, it is a thinking compensation for his emotional excesses, but one that goes too far. That happens very often in schizophrenic episodes. There is a play on words and all sorts of scurrilities appear, and then there is a sudden very nasty lightheartedness. This is a compensation for having been pulled too deeply into the emotions. It is understandable as an act of compensation or to escape the emotion, but to the onlooker it is just disgusting. A human being has had the deepest inner experience, in which one participates with one's feeling, and then that same person comes along one day and says it is all rubbish!

607 I have noticed this practically every time someone falls too deeply into the unconscious. It is the defense mechanism of a weak consciousness against a too-overwhelming experience. I would like to describe it as schizoid lightheartedness—taking serious things very lightly, laughing them off almost in a cynical way—but it is the compensation for having been pulled in too deeply. Here we have such a flat reaction.

608 In extreme cases there occurs what doctors and psychiatrists even *want* to reach, namely the "regressive restoration of the persona," when people say what they saw was a part of their illness and they never want to think of it again. They bury the whole experience and go out and try to adapt socially; they take an office job and never want to be reminded of what they said and thought

in that state. They usually go to another town so as not to meet the same people, and if they mention that time at all, it is as something that happened when they were ill.

609 Thus, the experience is absolutely rejected because it is too intense. Its effect at first was too strong and afterward, when they have come out of that state, perhaps by shock therapy, then, as a rule, there comes this flat attitude. If you get people out of such a state, through Largactil or some such remedy, or electroshock—in any case, without psychological therapy—this is generally the reaction. Such people are ashamed of their past when they were crazy; they adapt to reality in a superficial, flat way, and if you meet them, they bore you. You have the feeling they have become boringly normal—all the grist and vitality of their personality has gone.

610 In our text, thank God, it is just a temporary phase, something that often happens and one can understand. It is a normal rhythm in human reactions, illustrated, for instance, in classical antique plays where three tragedies are succeeded by a comedy. One could not go home after having seen Sophocles's *Oedipus Rex* and two others like it; there had to be one of Aristophanes's comedies at the end so that everybody could roar with laughter. Or there is the typical mechanism where, at the height of a very dramatic funeral, one suddenly sees something funny and has the nervous reaction of wanting to laugh. It is this climax of excitement that turns into the wish to laugh, for one can only stand so much of such an exaggerated tragic condition before one is, in certain situations, compelled to make fun of it.

611 A historic example of this is the Mock Mass of the Middle Ages. For 364 days of the year the Mass and the Host were taken very seriously, and on one day it was just taken as a joke. Or, in the North American Indian ritual, there is a clown who belongs to the Thunderbird clan, who makes fun of the holiest ceremonies, making obscene remarks and jokes about them.[15] This shows how a climax of excitement in normal people arouses the desire for some kind of

---

[15] Radin, "The Winnebago Tribe," in *Annual Report*.

compensation. Seen in this way, a reaction like this in a schizoid person who is threatened by the unconscious is quite normal.

612 At home we have a maid who sees ghosts and speaks most graphically of her experiences. To her it is the absolute reality in which she lives, and she talks to the ghosts for hours. It is a great secret into which one has first to be admitted and then she will speak of it with great emotion. But she never ends such a conversation to return to her household duties without saying, "Oh well, you know, ghosts do not exist, that is all rubbish!" And then she gives a broad grin and goes back to her work. That remark is simply a *rite de sortie*, for she cannot switch immediately from her experience with the ghosts to boiling the potatoes; the *rite de sortie* must be observed, for it is her release from something that has moved her deeply. Most people do the same kind of thing when they get too dramatic, if they have any sense of humor.

613 The fifth chapter is entitled *Exciting the Ignorant to Search for Wisdom.*[16]

614 Doth not Wisdom cry aloud in the public places and Prudence put forth her voice in the books of the wise, saying: O ye men, to you I call, and my voice is to the sons of understanding? Understand, ye foolish ones, and mark the parable and the interpretation, the words of the wise and their mysterious sayings; for the wise have used diverse manners of speech in making comparison with everything that is upon the earth, and beneath the sphere of the moon they have multiplied parables in this science. If a wise man hears the wise people, he will become more wise and he will understand and when he understands this science, he will know it. This is Wisdom, namely the Queen of the South, who is said to have come from the [the Orient] like unto the morning rising, to hear, to understand, yea and to see the wisdom of Solomon, and there was given into her hand power, honour, strength, and dominion, bearing upon her

[16] von Franz, *Aurora Consurgens*, 209-10.

> head the crown of the kingdom shining with the rays of twelve stars, prepared as a bride adorned for her husband, and having on her garments written in golden letters in Greek, in barbarian script, and in Latin: Reigning I will reign, and my kingdom shall have no end for all them that find me and subtly and ingeniously and constantly seek me out.

615 Now the author tries to deal with his experience in another way—he suddenly understands that all the symbolic texts he has read before, in the Bible and in alchemy, point to the same experience. He is probably now capable of reading alchemical texts and feeling that he knows what they mean, for he can link them up with his own experience. He thinks that the entire Bible and the whole alchemical tradition are symbolic, a kind of simile or symbolic description of what he has just experienced.

616 What I described earlier is now happening: He is trying to comprehend, to consolidate, and to understand his inner experiences by amplifying them with other texts. He recognizes possible amplifications in the Bible and in alchemical literature. And this figure, that is really the key figure of the whole experience—Wisdom, the Queen of the South, the Rising Dawn—appears again, and he praises her. She is the queen who will rule her kingdom forever. She is called the Queen of the Midday, or the South Wind—in Latin, *auster* stands for both "south wind" and "midday"—and this refers to the biblical text in Matthew 12:42: "The queen of the south shall rise up in the judgment with this generation, and shall condemn it: for she came from the ends of the earth to hear the wisdom of Solomon; and behold, a greater than Solomon is here."

617 This text, which is more or less the same as Luke 11: 31, refers to the famous Queen of Sheba, who came to visit King Solomon and had a love affair with him, from which the present Abyssinian kings still stem. The Queen of Sheba was an Ethiopian heathen queen who was converted by Solomon to the true religion. With her black servants, she slept with him and then returned to her kingdom pregnant, where she gave birth to the first king of Abyssinia. This

love affair of the aging Solomon became *the* great theme of European love literature.

618 In the Orient, as we know, especially in Persian mysticism and in some Islamic mysticism (mostly of the Shiite tradition, to which Ibn Umail belonged), are books which could be said to constitute the literature of the *coniunctio*, literature on the union of an outstanding man and woman, a king with a queen, for example. One could take this to be an image of the union of the soul with God, the soul of man that was thought of as feminine: in the moment of highest religious ecstasy, the anima unites with God, and therefore, in that moment, the mystic is a bride who marries the Godhead. In the very earthy and understandable love poems of El Hafis, it is said that they must be read with their mystical meaning in mind and that El Hafis is *not* describing an ordinary love affair with a woman but uses this language to describe the *unio mystica* of the soul with God. The same applies to Rumi.

619 The *Love Letter of the Sun to the Crescent Moon* is a typical variation of this kind of love literature. It symbolically expresses that the problem of the phenomenon of transference is connected to the process of individuation in the most beautiful way. The experience of the anima for the man and the animus for a woman goes beyond any real experience with a human partner. The extent to which the human partner plays a role—as only a faraway image or as a genuine connection—varies from case to case, but this experience is *the* paramount one leading towards an experience of the Self.

620 We can therefore say that in every deep love experience, an experience of the Self is involved, for the passion and the overwhelming factor in it come from the Self. This experience was much better understood and more cultivated in non-Christian cultures, where there was a more balanced attitude toward the female principle. With few exceptions, this kind of love literature and the problem of the love union with God were more rejected in the Jewish and official Christian traditions. In the Jewish tradition it is chiefly the Kabbalah that has taken up this theme again, and in the Christian tradition there are a few mystics like St. John of the

Cross who used this kind of language in his famous poem[17] that is a paraphrase of the Song of Solomon. As he lived in Spain, St. John of the Cross probably knew a great deal about Islamic literature.

621 By contrast, in our civilization there has been a split. The Church has not encouraged this kind of mystical religious literature, which, as a result, deeply affected the half-religious literature of the medieval novels, in particular the poetry of the Grail cycle and the Grail legends. Here the whole love mysticism, as you might call it, penetrated. The legend of the Queen of Sheba played a great role in this.[18] At this time, her story had already given rise to a very romantic novel of which there were various Ethiopian, Abyssinian, and Islamic versions. The novel portrays the path from mystical love to the conversion to God. This was picked up by medieval novels of knightly chivalry and influenced all those beautiful love stories that the Church did not directly reject but cast a rather mistrustful eye upon.

622 The Queen of Sheba has therefore a long tradition. She represents an anima figure in the Christian tradition that is not quite as sublime as the Virgin Mary. The Virgin Mary is an adequate symbol for the sublime aspect of the anima—but upon whom is one to project the less sublime aspect of the anima? The Queen of Sheba with her dark shadow, her dark-skinned servant, became a fitting object upon which this aspect of the anima could be projected. Many novels therefore elaborated upon the love story of King Solomon.

623 How very legitimate this was is supported by the following legend: While on her way to King Solomon, the Queen of Sheba came to a river over which there was a little bridge; it is said that the wood from this bridge was later used for the cross of Christ. With her mediumistic farsightedness, the Queen of Sheba refused to step onto it. She preferred to wade through the river and wet her feet than to step onto that wood. As she foresaw that this wood would become the cross, she was looked upon in medieval legend as a prophetess, as a seeress who foresaw the life of Christ and His death upon the

[17] St. John of the Cross, *The Spiritual Canticle* (Cantinas espirituae).

[18] Cf. Rivkah Schärf-Kluger, "The Queen of Sheba in Bible and Legends," in *Psyche in Scripture: The Idea of the Chosen People and Other Essays* (Toronto: Inner City Books, 1995), 57-100.

cross. Thus, she legitimately entered Christian literature through this back door. By this act she was legitimized, despite her dark shadow and her earthly love affair with King Solomon. It was all tolerated because she had foreseen the death of Christ.

624 So, the Queen of Sheba is a highly interesting anima figure of the Middle Ages; it was to her that Matthew 12:42 alludes, and our author alludes to her by equating her with the Wisdom of God and the rising dawn.

The Seven Parables on the Development of the Nigredo to the Albedo

625 The beginning of the next chapter, called *The First Parable of the Black Earth Wherein the Seven Planets Took Root*, is astonishing.[19]

> 626 Beholding from afar off I saw a great cloud looming black over the whole earth, which had absorbed the earth and covered my soul, because the waters had come in even unto her wherefore they were putrefied and corrupted before the face of the lower hell and the shadow of death, for a tempest hath overwhelmed me; then before me shall the Ethiopians fall down and my enemies shall lick my earth. Therefore there is no health in my flesh and all my bones are troubled before the face of my iniquity. For this cause have I laboured night by night with crying, my jaws are become hoarse; who is the man that liveth, knowing and understanding, delivering my soul from the hand of hell? They that explain me shall have eternal life, and to him I will give to eat of the tree of life which is in paradise, and to sit with me on the throne of my kingdom. He that shall dig for me as money and obtain me as a treasure and shall not disturb the tears of my eyes and shall not deride my garment, shall not poison my meat and my drink and shall not defile with fornication the couch of my rest and shall not violate my whole body which is exceeding delicate and above all my soul [or dove] which

[19] Cf. von Franz, *Aurora consurgens*, 57 – 65.

without gall is wholly beauteous and comely, in which there is no spot, who shall do no hurt to my seats and thrones, he for whose love I languish, in whose ardour I melt, in whose odour I live, by whose sweetness I regain my health, from whose milk I take nourishment, in whose embrace I am made young, from whose kiss I receive the breath of life, in whose loving embrace my whole body is lost, to him indeed I will be a father and he shall be to me a son; wise is he who rejoiceth his father, him whom I place first and highest among the kings of the earth, and I will keep my covenant faithful to him for ever. But if he shall forsake my law and walk not in my ways and keep not my commandments aforesaid, the enemy shall have advantage over him and the son of iniquity shall have power to hurt him; but if he shall walk in my ways, then shall he not fear in the cold of snow. And for all his household there shall be covering, fine linen and purple, and he shall laugh in that day when I shall be satisfied and my glory shall appear, for he hath looked well to my paths and hath not eaten his bread idle. Therefore were the heavens opened above him and there thundered the voice of him who holdeth the seven stars in his hand, which are the seven spirits sent forth into all the earth to preach and to bear witness. He that believeth and is well baptized shall be saved, but he that believeth not shall be condemned. And the signs of those who believe and are well baptized are these: When the king that is in heaven judgeth over them, they shall be whited with snow in Selmon and shall be as the wings of a dove covered with silver, and the hinder parts of her back with the paleness of gold. Such shall be to me a beloved son, behold ye him, beautiful above the sons of men, at whose beauty the sun and moon wonder. For he is the privilege of love and the heir, in whom men trust and without whom they can do nothing. But he that hath ears to hear, let him hear what the spirit of the doctrine saith to the sons of the discipline concerning the seven stars, by which the divine

> work is wrought. And of these Senior treateth in his book in the chapter of the Sun and Moon, saying: After thou hast made those seven which thou has distributed through the seven stars (and hast appointed to the seven stars) and hast purged them nine times until they appear as pearls – this is the Whitening.

627 Because this chapter makes a peculiar impression upon one, I would like to comment upon it. It begins with somebody in a state of despair. Sometimes it seems as if it were the author, but then it rather looks as if it were that feminine being, the Wisdom of God; and the chapter ends with the statement that after a process something has been whitened, that the stage of whitening has been reached.

628 So, from praising a personification of the unconscious that has broken into the conscious realm of the author, the text now changes into an effort at describing a process, a sequence of events. As we will see, this happens repeatedly in the following chapters. Every chapter begins with a black, chaotic state and ends on a positive note. The author is now beginning to digest the experience in the form of a process. Before, he described the full impact of what had happened to him, and now he is trying to express the process itself, but all he can do is to explain it again and again in the same way.

629 He is now trying to circumambulate the experience by describing it as a process. This is what happens when somebody is overwhelmed by the unconscious, becomes inflated, laughs it off, and then recovers his balance again and says he must face it; he finally begins to think about it and tries to describe how it began, what happened, and what the results are. This stage is only arrived at after a certain time, for when people begin to regain consciousness, at first they can name only one detail. Only afterward, when they are a bit more conscious, can they begin to repeat step by step what had happened.

630 People who have suffered a psychotic episode say that, at first, they just felt tired and then listless, and then they heard a voice, and then "it" suddenly happened—whatever the "it" was. They can thus go back and digest what happened. Here the experience was so

exciting and overwhelming that Thomas needs seven chapters to describe it. He chews over the same process again and again, always describing it from a different angle. This is typical behavior for someone whose psyche has been overwhelmed by the invasion of a content of the unconscious.

631 One can see the same mechanism on a minor scale when someone has experienced something exciting, for example, a car accident. They will recount it at least three times that day; they have to tell and retell it. Repetition helps to assimilate the shock. Thus, if you have had a psychological shock, you tend to digest it by repetition until you have integrated all its aspects; this is how you get your balance back. Something similar must have happened here.

632 The same thing happened to Niklaus von der Flue[20] who, after he had had his frightening vision of the Godhead, tried to digest it by making a painting and explaining it to a number of people, over and over again. In this way he assimilated the shock. Actually, from that time on until his death, he was really only concerned with assimilating the shock of his vision of God, his original experience of the divine.

633 I have an analysand who has had tremendous experiences of the Godhead. Recently, she asked me how many years it would take until she had digested them. I answered that I supposed it would take at least 10 years. "So long?" she replied. She became thoughtful and then said she thought I was probably right. One cannot digest such an experience immediately. This means that every time I see her, we have to talk about it from yet another angle. This is not abnormal: in such unusual circumstances it is quite normal.

[20] Cf. von Franz, *Niklaus von Flüe,* 115-17.

Lecture 8

634 The so-called first parable begins quite differently to the first five chapters in which the author talked about the overwhelming appearance of a feminine personification of the wisdom of God. From the many ways he described her, we deduced that St. Thomas was at first quite overcome and that he then identified with the image and became slightly inflated, saying that he would now tell people about her, etc. Later the inflation turned into a kind of scorn for the uninitiated who could not understand—which is still a symptom of inflation—and then he fell out of the inflation and into a state of emotional flatness. He again described the experience but in a rather prosaic way, which is typical of those who surface again after having been pulled into the unconscious. There is a kind of dry disappointment about the whole thing that compensates for the inflation. This is even more extreme in people who have been treated with psychotropic drugs or given electric shocks after suffering a psychotic episode.

635 In this parable, the author himself enters the picture. Earlier, the writing had been in the style of a pompous announcement of the truth. This is typical of identification with contents of the unconscious, which explains why the style of this document is also to be found in primitive religious literature and certain poetry.

636 When the author begins by saying, "From afar off I saw a great cloud looming black over the whole earth," one feels it must be the author who sees the black cloud that has covered the earth from above. Later, however, this person, who asks who it is that can save her, is the Wisdom of God. One of the most interesting things in this text is that the "I" as seen from the context is the author on one line, and two lines later is the Wisdom of God. So, there is genuine

confusion, and we see how the author has identified with the Wisdom of God and fallen into the unconscious.

637 Firstly, he sees the black cloud hovering over the earth that covers everything. The black cloud is a well-known alchemical symbol for the state called the *nigredo*, the blackness which very often occurs at the beginning of the opus, for if you distill the material, it evaporates, and for a while you see nothing but a kind of confusion or cloud. The alchemist compares this state to the earth being covered by a black cloud.

638 In the language of antiquity, the cloud also had a double meaning, sometimes being compared to confusion or unconsciousness. There are many late Hermetic texts where it is said that the light of God cannot be found before one has come out from the dark cloud of unconsciousness that covers people. In religious language, clouds have a negative connotation. In Christianity, the cloud is a product of the devil of the north and out of whose nostrils blows a constant cloud of confusion and unconsciousness over the world. But one finds the cloud in early medieval texts also in a positive connection, namely as the unknown, bewildering aspect of the Godhead. *The Cloud of Unknowing*, a medieval mystical text, describes the fact that the closer the mystic gets to the Godhead, the darker and more confused he becomes. Such texts say in effect that God lives in a cloud of unknowing and that one has to be stripped of every idea, every intellectual conception, before one can approach the light which is surrounded by the darkness of utter confusion. Here the cloud has the same double meaning: It describes the state of utter confusion, of utter unhappiness, that is simultaneously the beginning of the alchemical work.

639 Seeing deepest hell and, as is said sentences later, seeing his own sins, has frightened the speaker. Then there is mention of the Ethiopians. This refers to *Psalm* 72:9 that speaks of victories over enemies and of the Ethiopians bowing before the Israelites. But the Ethiopian here naturally represents the *nigredo*; this is its classical meaning, that also appears very early in Greek alchemy.

640 We came across Ethiopian earth earlier in the text of Olympiodor. Ethiopia was the country whose people carry the collective projection of extreme piety and religious fervor on the one hand and of being unconscious heathens on the other. In alchemy, the Ethiopian is often the symbol of the *nigredo*, and it is obvious what that would mean in psychological language, for it is not very different from the form in which black people still turn up nowadays in the unconscious material of white people, namely as the primitive, natural man in his ambiguous wholeness. The natural man in us is a genuine man but also the man who does not fit into conventional patterns and who, in part, is very much driven by his instincts.

641 The Ethiopians appear in this *nigredo* of the author, and then this figure suddenly asks, "Who is the human being who knows and understands, who will save me from the hand of the underworld?" And the very person who was drowned by the unconscious, who one first assumed to be the author but who later turns out to be the Wisdom of God, says, "They that explain me shall have eternal life, and to him I will give to eat of the tree of life which is in paradise, and to sit with me on the throne of my kingdom." Then comes the passage I have already commented upon: "He that shall dig for me as money and obtain me as a treasure and shall not disturb the tears of my eyes ..." after which comes the declaration of love.

642 It is Christ Himself who, as God, promises to share His kingdom, so we must conclude that the person speaking—and the adjectives used in relation to the "I" are always feminine—is the Wisdom of God. It is the one who is in absolute identity with God and Christ, who speaks out of the darkness of the *nigredo* and calls for help, asking for a human being to save her soul from the underworld. This shows the tremendous turnabout that has taken place, for suddenly it is the Wisdom of God who is crying out for help from the depths of the earth and who needs a human being to pull her out of the darkness. She firstly appeared as an overwhelming divine factor from above, and now she calls from below as a helpless feminine being who needs the understanding of a human soul.

643 This is one of the most striking sections and illustrates what Jung, too, in *Psychology and Alchemy* describes as one of the great mythological themes of alchemical thinking,[21] namely the idea that the divine soul, or the Wisdom of God, or the *anima mundi*—a kind of feminine figure—falls off the original man, the original Adam, into matter, and then has to be rescued. Jung explains in this chapter that this illustrates what happens when a projection takes place, namely that there exists an archetypal idea of the divine man, or the feminine Godhead, and this archetype is projected into matter, which actually means the image falls into matter. Such myths amplify what the alchemist did not know consciously, or only in part, namely that in fact they were looking for the unconscious, or the image of the feminine Godhead, or the experience of the divine man in matter. This is what they were actually seeking, as I tried to explain with the text of Olympiodor.

644 An equivalent in our modern life would be to think of a modern man getting to know a woman he is very much attracted to and then dreaming that an image of the Goddess has entered her. The image of the Godhead was already carried within him, and now it has entered this woman. This is how the unconscious proceeds with a projection; it is not something we do or even realize, it just happens to us, and that is why dreams often show us that a projection has taken place, quite like the example above. Here in our text the alchemical imagery is saying that this has happened and that the alchemist is unconsciously searching for such a figure.

645 This process has already begun in the Jewish religion. From the beginning, they had no feminine Goddess, yet the Hebrew word for primordial chaos *Tohu wa bohu*, is essentially an allusion to the Babylonian goddess Tiamat. One could say that in the Jewish tradition the great mother Goddess does not appear personified in the Bible but only exists in a hidden way in these few allusions. The feminine reappeared in the late Gnostic fantasy of the Wisdom of God, but only a sublime aspect of this feminine goddess appears in the Bible. The feminine aspect of the Godhead is not properly

[21] Cf. Jung, "The Spirit in Matter," in *Psychology and Alchemy*, vol. 12, *CW*, §§ 405-24, § 557.

represented in the Judeo-Christian tradition. There are a few obscure allusions to a dark chaotic mother-mass below that is identical with matter, and a sublime feminine figure that is the Wisdom of God, but even she was eliminated in Christianity, for God was declared to be identical with the Holy Ghost and the soul of Christ, while matter was said to be of the devil.

646 This pronounced lack of a feminine personification of the unconscious has therefore been compensated by radical materialism that has increasingly taken hold of the Christian tradition. One could say that practically no other religion began with such a highly one-sided spiritual accent and has landed—if you think of communism as the end form of Christian theology—in such an absolutely one-sided materialistic aspect. The swing from one to the other is one of the most striking phenomena we know of in the history of religion. It is due to the fact that, from the very beginning, there was a lack of awareness, an unbalanced attitude toward the problem of the feminine goddess and therefore of matter. The feminine godhead in all religions is always projected into and linked up with the concept of matter.

647 I would like to make a short digression here that seems interesting to me. Only yesterday I had a book by Hans Marti entitled *Urbild und Verfassung*[22] in my hand. Marti shows that since man originally conceived of the constitution of the democratic state—he is mainly concerned with the Swiss Constitution—a secret switch has taken place from the patriarchal concept of the state (the juridical state, the state being a legal concept, a kind of father spirit) to what he calls the welfare state. In its beginnings, let us say until the last 50 years, a club of men chiefly administered Swiss democracy—women in Switzerland still cannot vote.[23] The basis of the Constitution was a certain number of laws, the main object of which was to guarantee freedom of the individual, freedom of religion, freedom of ownership, and so on. As Marti very beautifully

[22] Hans Marti, *Urbild und Verfassung: Eine Studie zum hintergründigen Gehalt einer Verfassung* (Bern: Hans Huber, 1958).

[23] Women have the right to vote on a federal level since 1971. Some cantons gave them the right to vote on a cantonal and community level prior to this date, others even after this date.

points out, another idea slowly crept into this, namely that of the welfare state—a mother archetype where the state has to care for the health of its people, their material welfare, their old age pensions, etc. Marti points out very clearly that this is a switch, that the state is no longer the father but has become the mother who is interested in the physical welfare of her children. He shows how, according to Swiss law, the state now has the right to impose certain regulations on the possession of land, to protect agricultural areas, for instance.

648 In order to protect people, the state assumed control over water rights—water is a feminine symbol—some years ago, since the water was becoming so dirty and unwholesome, and slowly it has acquired the right to issue laws to fight epidemics. If, for instance, there is some kind of plague, or rabies, the state can issue regulations that did not exist previously. Formerly, mankind was not so interested in the physical and material welfare of people. If they died of the plague or were bitten by mad dogs, it was just a part of life and not particularly important; the emphasis was upon spiritual freedom while physical welfare was rather neglected. Over the last 50 or 60 years, physical welfare has gradually become an important concern of the state, and with that it has by degrees become more and more the carrier of the projection of the mother and less of the father image. Slowly and without noticing it, we are gliding into a matriarchal situation. Marti shows very clearly how certain emotional factors are unconsciously at play, how the people conceive of the state in some very archetypal form and how, from that standpoint, they vote for certain laws. But what seems to be self-evident—that the state should look after its children—is really a projection of the mother image, and that is *not* self-evident. He ends his book very intelligently by saying that we should become conscious of what we are projecting onto the state and begin examining our motives. We should not change our laws by projecting a mother image.

649 This book describes a small aspect of a slow change, which, on a large scale, has happened throughout our entire Christian civilization, that one could call a secret, unobtrusive return to

matriarchy and materialism. This enantiodromia has to do with the fact that the Judeo-Christian religion did not face the archetype of the mother consciously enough. To a certain extent it excluded the question. It is well known that when Pope Pius XII declared the *Assumptio Mariae* his conscious aim was to strike a blow against communistic materialism. In a manner of speaking, by elevating the symbol of matter in the Catholic Church, he took the wind out of the communist party's sails. There is a much deeper implication, but that was his conscious idea. The only way to fight the development of materialism would be to raise the symbol of the feminine godhead and with it matter. Since it is the Virgin Mary's body that is raised to heaven, the emphasis is upon the physical, material aspect.

650 In our text we have the image of a Godhead that has completely fallen into matter from where she cries for help. If we were to take this as the personal drama of the author, what would that mean?

651 ***Answer***: *That his anima has become lost in the material world because he had no relation to her.*

652 Yes, he was outside of any relationship to her. We must conclude that he had no prior relationship to the feminine principle. It is quite obvious from the text that he is a clerical man, and I would imagine he had a negative mother complex and either for this or some other reason, he had no relationship with the feminine principle, neither to his own feminine side, nor to women in general. In such a case, an overwhelming influx of the feminine Godhead would take place.

653 There is a striking parallel—that of the famous mystic, Jakob Boehme. As you know, he was a very poor shoemaker and somewhat of a borderline case who had the most tremendous religious experiences and was capable of expressing them in his difficult writings. This man was an introverted intuitive of the prophetic type. His marriage was very unfortunate; they felt nothing but mutual contempt and hatred, understandable on both sides, for his wife was a down-to-earth woman who thought he would be better employed mending shoes and earning money rather than writing books about the Holy Ghost while she and the six children he had had with her had nothing to eat. So, she made constant scenes, saying he should

provide his children with food instead of writing books about the Good Lord.

654 He, on the other hand, felt quite naturally that she was a worldly woman who weighed him down, someone who hampered his spiritual creativity. It was one of those classical tragedies. Boehme rejected the feminine completely—that is, until the later phases of his life he had only a negative attitude toward the feminine. Shortly before his death, he was suddenly completely overwhelmed by an image of the Wisdom of God, of the Sophia—so the same image—and he left a text in which he praised this figure in the most ecstatic loving terms, so much so that it is even rather distasteful; in his love song to the Wisdom of God a very strong sexual note shines through, and all the dirt that had been rejected becomes visible and wells up in this great experience.

655 I suspect that our author was in a similar state, that he had no relationship to the feminine principle and is now overwhelmed by it in its most impressive form. This would be a typical compensation for the scorn and contempt he must hitherto have had for the feminine. In such cases the unconscious breaks through with such tremendous force it can no longer be avoided.

656 What is for consciousness a realization of an archetypal image is for the archetypal image itself a great downfall. Imagine the ego with its field of associations as a spider in its web. When an archetypal image approaches the field of consciousness, it is for the ego a condition of great enlightenment, a state of elation, etc., as was seen in the first five chapters of our text; for the poor archetype, however, it is just the opposite for it falls into something very small and quite inadequate. Therefore, seen from one side, it is a great realization, while from the other, it is a very bad downfall.

657 Many creation myths describe the creation of the world as the Godhead falling from heaven. This is how it is depicted in a dream of the French poet in Gérard de Nerval's book *Aurélie*.[24] This book describes the onset of his psychosis. One of the most frightening

[24] Gérard de Nerval, "Aurélie," in *Oeuvres*, vol. 1, ed. Albert Béguin and Jean Richer (Paris: Gallimard, 1952-1956), 357-414.

dreams he had during this time was that he went into the backyard of a typical Paris hotel where there were old dustbins with cats eating out of them. Such dark courtyards are to be found everywhere in Paris. Here, to his horror, he saw an angel of God, a tremendous, overwhelming archetypal figure with colored wings who had fallen into this backyard and was jammed into this constricted space. He had the sudden frightening realization that if the angel were to free itself, if it were to make the slightest movement, the whole building would collapse. This would have meant the outbreak of his schizophrenia, which did occur soon after. Compared to his genius, his conception of life was much too narrow. He had a great unconscious genius, as evidenced by the angel, and his conscious concept of life was exactly that of the typical French rationalist of Paris with its backyards. His conscious mentality was therefore not adequate to his real makeup and his own inner destiny.

658 Very often the reason for schizophrenia is not so much the invasion of the unconscious but rather that it happens to someone who is either mentally or emotionally too narrow for the experience. People who are not broad-minded and have not enough generosity and heart to open up to what comes, are exploded by the invasion.

659 Gérard de Nerval's life illustrates this very clearly: He fell in love with a girl and was overcome with the most romantic, emotional feelings for her, but instead of accepting them, he revolted against them, saying, "*C'est une femme ordinaire de notre siècle*"—she is an ordinary woman of the present day—and he ran away from her. Afterward he felt extremely guilty, but she did not pardon him. His guilty conscience came from the fact that he was running away from his own feeling. During this time, he dreamt of the angel, showing that his narrow-minded, rational, backyard idea of life and of love was not up to his experience; this explains why he later hung himself in the gutter.

660 I only mention this dream as an illustration of the fact that what is seen from a conscious standpoint as a realization of an archetype is for the archetype itself a falling down into matter. We find the same thing in the theological teaching about the *kenosis* of Christ

that refers to the place in the Bible where Christ sheds His plenitude to come down as a servant and incarnate in man.[25] Based upon this, theologians developed the theory that Christ was identical with God the Father and the Holy Ghost, that He lived in plenitude and expansion in heaven, and that it was a tremendous self-sacrifice when He emptied and reduced Himself to enter human life and incarnate. Thus, from His side it meant humiliation and a reduction in His condition. As an archetype, He would be the Godhead, the Logos that entered miserable human life, but for mankind it was a revelation of the light of God.

661 This is not a unique case. Whenever an archetype approaches human realization, it means a great narrowing for the archetype; this accounts for the catastrophic visions and dreams of the fall of a divine being onto the earth. As can very clearly be seen from the case of Gérard de Nerval, understanding is the essential factor at such times. If he had understood what was approaching him when he had those tremendous feelings and fantasies about the girl he loved, he would not have gone off his head; but it all seemed crazy and stupid to him and had to be repressed, which resulted in the catastrophe.

662 In our text the fallen Wisdom of God calls for a human being of understanding to rescue her from where she had fallen. She asks where the human being is who lives and will understand her, and she promises eternal life to that person—he whom she loves and in whose embrace her whole body melts away, etc. This is a passionate declaration of love to the unknown person who should understand her and get her out of matter. Then comes a most surprising statement, for she says, "He for whose love I languish, in whose ardour I melt, …*to him I will be a father and he shall be to me a son.*" This is taken from *Hebrew 1:5*, where God says this to Christ. When reading the text, it is easy to overlook these strange allusions, but the Wisdom of God clearly says here that she herself is God the Father and that whoever saves her is the Son of God himself. This sentence is the key to all that follows in the text. The Wisdom of God

[25] Philippians 2:7 in DV 2:6.

is simply an *experience of God Himself, but in His feminine form*, and the beloved bridegroom of this feminine appearance of God is the author who replaces Christ and becomes Christlike.

663 Christ Himself predicted that through the spreading of the Holy Ghost many would do greater works than He, leading to the idea of the Christlikeness of each individual. Christ is not the only case of the incarnation of God, but through the Holy Ghost this continues and spreads among the many, so that every individual can, to a certain extent, become Christ and therefore be deified. This was predicted in the Bible by Christ Himself[26] but has been ignored in theological interpretation because it is an awkward statement that means nothing less than every human individual being potentially capable of living the same fate as Christ and being identical with the Godhead.

664 This aspect was ignored in medieval theology and not brought out into the light; it was carefully not preached about because it is nothing other than the process of individuation. It means that to follow Christ is not to follow outer rules, not to imitate Him outwardly, but to take upon oneself the total experience of Christ Himself and to realize it in a different, completely individual way, that means to go through the whole process oneself. Because this was too difficult, or people were not up to such a task, it was ignored. This is why it reappears here as an unconscious pressure in the form of God who, as a woman, elects a human being as her bridegroom, a human who understands her. She wants to unite with him. And, as the text says, this is the relationship of God the Father and God the Son.

665 She then says that if she can find such a bridegroom, she will appear in her glory and will manifest in all her beauty. In this context the appearance of God at the end of all days is announced, as in the Apocalypse. She compares herself to a dove—a silver shining dove, appearing once again very clearly as a feminine spiritual symbol.

[26] "He that believeth on me, the works that I do shall he do also; and greater *works* than these shall he do." John 14:12.

666 The chapter ends rather flatly or dryly with the words, "After thou ... hast purged them nine times until they appear as pearls (in likeness)—this is the Whitening." Here there is a sudden return to purely chemical language that says that the whole experience comes practically down to washing the stars until they are as white as pearls.

667 I want to comment briefly on the last part that says:[27]

> But he that hath ears to hear, let him hear what the spirit of the doctrine saith to the sons of the discipline concerning the seven stars, by which the divine work is wrought. And of these Senior treateth in his book in the chapter of the Sun and Moon, saying: After thou hast made those seven which thou has distributed through the seven stars (and hast appointed to the seven stars) and hast purged them nine times until they appear as pearls—his is the Whitening.

668 The seven stars were mentioned earlier in our text; they are the seven stars the Godhead holds in His hand when He appears at the Apocalypse. At that time they naturally referred to the seven planets. Seven metals are attributed to the seven planets, and it is quite customary in alchemy for the seven metals—tin, copper, lead, iron, gold, silver and mercury—to be attributed to the seven planets, but they are more than that for they are, so to speak, the same thing as the seven planets. Iron equates to Mars, and copper to Venus; one can therefore call iron the earthly Mars, and copper the earthly Venus, etc. That was a common way of speaking about the metals in those times, so the seven stars are really the seven metals in the earth, and these earthly stars have to be distilled and cleansed nine times, at which point they become white; this is the process of the *albedo*.

669 In alchemical literature it is generally said that the great effort and trouble lasts from the *nigredo* to the *albedo*; this is said to be the hard part, after which everything becomes easier. The nigredo—the

[27] Cf. von Franz, *Aurora Consurgens,* 63-65.

blackness, the terrible state of depression and dissolution—has to be compensated by the hard work of the alchemist and this hard work involves, among other things, constant washing. This is why the work of washerwomen is often mentioned in the text, or constant distilling, which is also done with the object of purification, for the metal evaporates and precipitates into another vessel, thus removing the heavier substances.

670 This is clearly a psychological analogy to the first hard part of an analysis in which Venus, the love problem, must be washed, and then Mars, the problem of aggression, and so on. In life, all the different instinctive drives and their archetypal background generally first appear in a disturbed form, that is, in the form of a projection—people love or hate somebody or they have a boss who suppresses them and they do not know how to defend themselves.

671 If a projection is on the outside it means that Mars has fallen into matter, that is, the principle of aggression and all it covers up is seen in Mr. So-and-So; or if Venus has fallen, then an analysand talks about the ups and downs of a love affair and sexual difficulties, for in his case the whole thing has fallen into matter. She must first be taken out of matter, so, as the analyst, one suggests leaving Miss So-and-So out of it for the moment, to look at what is going on within the analysand instead.

672 This is the *prima materia* that has to be constantly washed and distilled. The first activity of the opus is to distill, wash and clean, over and over again. Here it says nine times, others say fifteen times, and some say ten years. It is really a very long process and sometimes means going over the same problem in its different aspects endlessly. This is why alchemical texts always point out that this part can go on for a long time and is characterized by endless repetition—just as we unfortunately fall into complexes that have not been sufficiently worked out, and have to be looked at time and time again. But through this hard work the matter becomes white.

673 Whiteness suggests that purification has taken place and one is no longer contaminated with matter, which we technically, and so lightly, refer to as taking back our projections. This is by no means

an easy thing to do; it is very complicated and difficult, and it is not enough for one to understand that one has projected something and to therefore resolve not to do it anymore. It needs a long process of inner development and realization for a projection to be taken back. But when it has been withdrawn, the disturbing emotional factor vanishes.

674 As soon as the projection is *really* withdrawn, a sort of peace establishes itself; one becomes quiet and can look at the thing from an objective angle. One can look at the specific problem or particular factor in an objective and quiet way and perhaps do an active imagination about it without constantly becoming emotional, or falling back into the emotional tangle. This corresponds to the *albedo*. It is, in a way, the first stage of becoming quieter and more detached and objective, more philosophically detached. One has a standpoint *au dessus de la mêlée*; one can stand on top of the mountain and observe the thunderstorm below, which naturally is still going on, but which one can look at without fear, or feeling threatened by it.

675 So the whitening of the alchemists refers to the material they are working on reaching such a degree of purity and oneness that they can begin to combine substances. After the metals have been melted out of the minerals they must be cleansed—which would be the analytical work—and then the chemical synthesis can begin. This is an exact parallel to what happens in analysis with firstly its analytical and then synthetic approach. The *albedo* is characterized as being something wonderful, for, the alchemists say, from now on one has simply to feed the fire, keep it going, but the hard part of the work is done. But, as we will see, the process of getting from the *nigredo* to the *albedo* is repeated many times. Here it is described seven times.

676 ***Question****: When did the alchemists begin to have doubts about their projections?*

677 I would say that our author has not yet had any doubts. Some skepticism appeared at the end of the 15th or the beginning of the 16th century, though of course this is not very precise, for there were

medieval alchemists even after the 16th century, and some had doubts earlier. One could say that doubt set in around the time of the Renaissance. Afterward, alchemical symbolism became an allegory and was no longer a genuine symbolic experience; the old texts were thrashed out allegorically.

678 Basilus Valentinus, for instance, and Michael Maier, and then later developments through the Rosicrucians and the Freemasons are examples. The Freemasons still use symbolism, as do the Rosicrucians, but to them it is only an allegory. They explain the meaning of each detail completely rationally; others continued along chemical lines but without speaking of such things as the bride and bridegroom, which they took to be just flowery language; and others used symbolic language but no chemistry. One could begin to speak of a projection, for now the element of doubt had entered. They no longer really believed that the thing was to be found in matter, or they only half believed it, or pretended to do so to themselves, but it was not a clean attitude. This is why there came the nasty boasting, half-religious gold-maker style into it that brought alchemy into such disrepute. In this text there is an inflation, but nothing of the charlatan, whereas the writings of Basilus Valentinus are written in an arrogant gold-maker's style. But Gerard Dorn, who lived at the end of the 16th century, was still a genuine alchemist. I would say it was approximately then that the first doubt arose. In our text it is still a genuine projection, or what we would rather call an archaic identity; the Wisdom of God was *really* in matter. A real belief was brought about through archaic identity.

679 The second parable is called *Of the Flood of Waters and of Death, Which the Woman Both Brought in and Put to Flight*. It again starts with the *nigredo* and describes the whole process anew, until it again comes to the *albedo*; it is the same thing seen from a different angle, which is exactly what we experience. How many times in analysis has one got a little bit out of the problem, really feeling at peace and to some extent at one with oneself so that the worst seems to be over, but three weeks later it all begins again, as if one had done nothing at all? Many repetitions are required before the experience

is consolidated, until finally the work holds. The way from the *nigredo* to the *albedo* has to be repeated eternally.[28]

680 When the multitude of the sea shall be converted to me and the streams have flowed over my face and the arrows of my quiver are drunk with blood and my presses are fragrant with the best wine and my barns are filled with the corn of wheat and the bridegroom with the ten wise virgins hath entered into my chamber and thereafter my belly hath swelled from the touch of my beloved and the bolt of my door hath been opened to my beloved, and after Herod being angry hath slain many children in Bethlehem of Juda and Rachel hath bewailed all her children and a light hath risen up in darkness and the Sun of Justice hath appeared from heaven, then the fullness of the time shall come when God shall send his Son, as he hath said, whom he hath appointed heir of all things, by whom also he made the world, to whom he said of old time: Though art my Son, today have I begotten thee: to whom the wise men from the East brought three precious gifts; in that day, which the Lord hath made, let us be glad and rejoice therein, for this day hath the Lord beheld my affliction and sent redemption, for he shall reign in Israel. That death which a woman brought into the world, this day hath a woman put to flight, and the barriers of hell are broken down; for death shall no more have dominion, nor shall the gates of hell prevail against her, for the tenth groat, which was lost, is found, and the hundredth sheep is restored in the wilderness, and the number of our brethren from the fall of the angels is fully made up. It is meet therefore, my son, to make merry this day, for there shall be no more crying nor any sorrow, for the former things are passed away. He that hath ears to hear, let him hear what the spirit of the doctrine saith to the sons of the discipline concerning the woman who brought in death and put it to flight, which the philosophers

[28] Cf. von Franz, *Aurora Consurgens*, 67 – 71.

> declare in these words: Take away his soul and give him back his soul, for the corruption of one is the generation of another, that is: Take from him the corrupting humour and add to him the connatural humour, through which shall come to pass his perfecting and life.

681 Again, there is a catastrophe at the beginning that is described as a flood and is compared to the slaughter of the children in Bethlehem. But although it again starts with the *nigredo*, with a disaster, the positive aspects are given at greater length. There is a description of a love union, of a bridegroom entering the bridal chamber, and the pregnancy of the feminine figure, followed by a long and rather conventional allusion to the birth of Christ to whom the three Magi bring their gifts, and finally the triumph that death has been overcome by this birth.

682 So it can be said that although the process is repeated, there is already a lighter aspect, one of which was not hitherto mentioned, namely that in the catastrophic moment, a birth takes place. When the *nigredo* was at its darkest, a secret birth took place in the unconscious. Within the catastrophe, in the midst of depression and confusion, the new symbol of the Self was born. It was born in the unconscious, so the author has not yet realized what has happened; he only vaguely realizes that although he fell into a terrible depression and the anima figure fell to the earth, something was also born.

683 As Jung has shown in his essay *The Psychology of the Child Archetype* about the divine child,[29] when a hero is born—and the birth of Christ is no exception—there is always an outburst of destructive powers. Thus, if a person in therapy has a suicidal tendency, it will always be strongest at that moment that one might call the crisis of the healing. In a deep depression, or in a completely schizophrenic confusion, only rarely and exceptionally is the danger of suicide great, though it does exist under certain circumstances.

[29] Jung, *The Archetypes and the Collective Unconscious*, 2nd ed., vol. 9/I (Princeton, NJ: Princeton University Press, 1980), § 282.

But if such a case is on the threshold of healing, there is often an acute danger of suicide. Then you must watch the person concerned day and night, a well-known fact in asylums.

684 Naturally, this is only an extreme illustration of something that happens in analytical work on a less dramatic level—I call it the last attack of the devil. The devil sees he is losing the game and so makes his last desperate attack. The same is true when fighting the destructive animus, when someone has slowly begun to fight and to take a stand against him, but the battle has not yet been won, for he is still lurking around the corner; the devil has not quite been driven out, and if a little more fire is put into the thing, along comes the final attack, which is generally so bad it looks as though one will have to start all over again, for it is as bad as it was at the very beginning. Everything appears to be lost, and the devil is raging worse than ever before.

685 This is generally a very good sign for it simply means that hell is now losing its power and the devil must use the last of his ammunition. Saying goodbye to a neurotic attitude is a very sad business, and nobody has ever got out of a neurosis without feeling sad, for unfortunately it is a beloved condition that one resents being separated from. So when one reaches the final stage, where once and for all it is necessary to say goodbye to some kind of infantility, or animus opinion, or some other thing, there is always some kind of a crisis. Mythology illustrates this for at the moment the Savior child is born, all the powers of darkness attack with more force than ever before. In our own Christian myth we see this in the slaughter of the innocents in Bethlehem. Naturally, the divine child always escapes, for it is a last outbreak of darkness against something that is already so powerful it can no longer be suppressed, even though it is only newly born.

686 The author is describing this by saying it is the light born in darkness. We recall that in Ibn Umail's *Love Letter from the Sun to the Crescent Moon,* it was also said at the end that the light was born in utter darkness. This is also the moment when God chose to send his son, that one could call the adoption of Christ by God. When St. John the Baptist was baptizing Christ, the heavens opened, and a

dove came down, and the voice of God said, "This is my beloved Son in whom I am well pleased."[30] At that moment it was made manifest that Christ was the Son of God.

687 Here, God is feminine, represented by the Wisdom of God, and the son is the author. So it is a repetition of Christ's life, but it is the author who has been accepted as the son by the Wisdom of God. This means that the archetypal figure that burst in has adopted him as a son. He becomes a child of the Wisdom of God. He then sums up the experience by saying that this is the death that the woman introduced and that the woman has put to flight.

688 In the official church allegory, the woman who brought death into the world was Eve, by the apple of Paradise, and the Virgin Mary drove death away when she gave birth to Christ. So in the patriarchal tradition there are these two different female figures. Our text is unusual for the 13th century in that somebody dared to say that the woman who brought death into the world and the woman who drove it out were one and the same. There is only one woman—Eve and Mary are one.

689 The text is so confused that unless you think about it, you might not notice or realize what the author is saying, but that is typical of him: He says the most shocking and amazing things, but in such beautiful biblical language that one wonders what he is really getting at, and then one realizes that from a medieval point of view, he is saying the most terrible things. I think this springs from the fact that he spoke unconsciously; he was overwhelmed by the image of the unconscious and proclaimed its compensatory truth without quite realizing the enormity of what he was saying. He just felt his own experience: that an image of a woman he thought to be the Wisdom of God had killed him and then restored him to life. This is why he describes her as the woman who brought in death and afterward restored life.

690 He amplifies this in purely chemical or alchemical language by saying:[31]

---

[30] Matthew 3:17.

[31] Cf. von Franz, *Aurora Consurgens*, 71.

691 Take away his soul and give him back his soul, [. . .] take from him the corrupting humour and add to him the connatural humour, through which shall come to pass his perfecting and life.

692 In chemical language, *extractio animae*, the extraction of the soul, means distillation. If you evaporate a chemical substance, the vapor that forms is its soul, and if you precipitate or coagulate it again, the soul returns to the body—an obvious simile. The simile of the humidity comes in then, too, for the corruptible humidity has to be distilled by fire, and then the verifying humidity is poured in.

693 This has been described in other alchemical texts, for instance by saying one must reduce everything to ashes, the driest substance on earth. Whoever has ever poured water on ashes knows how much water can be absorbed. This is why they say everything has to be burned to ashes, to ensure that every bit of destructive humidity has left the substance; then pure water must be poured on it to restore it to solid form.

Figure 8
Marriage of water and fire: the union of the incompatible.

694 Pouring water on the pulverised ashes would be nourishing them with living water. This corresponds to our analytical work, for it is in effect what we do when we drive out the corruptible humidity. In practical language, this means all the different kinds of unconsciousness, all the blind and unconscious spots that hamper living existence. We do not even know in how many ways we are hampered in our fullness of life by unconscious assumptions or feelings. This is something that is often more obvious to an outsider than it is to oneself. If such an unconscious spot is hit, we might say, "but I thought …," for an assumption has been made.

695 There are, for instance, many people who live far below their spiritual level because they assume they are nobodies and are so sure of it that they never even think of questioning the fact. It is so self-evident to them that they would not think of speaking of it to the analyst, for they do not think there is anything to discuss. But then, one day, a dream shows what is within them, and they are quite amazed, for they thought it true that they were nobodies. That would be the corruptible humidity, a spot of unconsciousness that has crept into the system—with women in the form of animus opinions, or shadow drives, or whatever it may be. It is so self-evident that one does not even think of driving it out. It is the task in dream analysis to discover such things, whereby it is quite a shock to realize that one has always thought something about which one might have thought quite differently.

696 This is only one of a thousand possible examples of what corruptible unconsciousness means. Unconscious feeling, or thinking in a certain way, is a corruptible humidity that we do not notice, and it is the aim of the opus to cook all of it out. The dreams focus upon a certain fact, and by interpreting and integrating what they say, we slowly get rid of the corruptible humidity. But if we go on too long, if we overanalyze, we miss a certain very decisive moment in the process that should be continued only for a certain time. If it goes on too long, people become unspontaneous.

697 We all know such overanalyzed people who have lost any kind of spontaneity in life. Before they even greet you, they say they know

they will project the anima onto you, or they come and say that they hate so-and-so and are sure it is a shadow projection. Why should one not dislike somebody? Overanalyzing, continuing the process too long, creates a second neurosis, which is a very general disease that is very difficult to cure. Naturally, it is a kind of unconsciousness, too.

698 Thus, there follows a second phase we could call the return to the water of life, a return to spontaneity, to an immediate, natural and spontaneous way of living, without forgetting what one has learned. To climb out of the water and sit in the sun only to have to jump back into the water again is a very dangerous business. One can just fall back into the former state, but that has no merit. One should return but keep the second form of analytical consciousness—being aware of the shadow and the anima and so on. This second kind of spontaneity is a conscious spontaneity in which the participation of consciousness is not lost. This is a very difficult thing, as it is so much easier to go on overanalyzing, or to slip back into one's former state of unconsciousness.

699 ***Question***: *If people are overanalyzed, is it not the fault of the analyst, namely that he gives too much interpretation and is too active, and thus does not leave the analysand to his own process?*

700 I would not say so. I think that might contribute to such an unfortunate state, but in general, in my experience, that is not the only reason. I know analysts who are completely passive and who excel in not interfering and can still produce an overanalyzed analysand because the latter does it to himself! What was positive in the beginning, namely the need to find out and to reflect and to realize what is going on, is experienced as something very redeeming. They have got out of a problem by reflection, by thinking it over, and naturally, because it had such a redeeming quality in the beginning, they keep on with it and miss the right moment to stop.

701 I even think it is *necessary* that each case reaches a period of being overanalyzed, that it is a necessary phase of the work, a stage that must be reached so that there can be a conscious return to spontaneity. One has to realize that this return to spontaneity is

necessary, again and again, for otherwise one slips back unconsciously.

702 The alchemist Gerard Dorn says that the anima is caught in the body of a man, and it requires a mental effort on his part to fish her out; but this is then the death of the body. That is the way he describes it. He says it would be as if a monk retired from the world and meditated and got his anima out of his body through asceticism and then, he says, if he went on with it, he would just die. If you reject the body, you cannot live, so you have to get your body back.

703 Imagine the mind and the soul and the body as entities. As one's mind for a Christian is a little higher—it represents good intentions and a positive program of life—one's soul can be fished up again through a period of asceticism. Dorn compares it to the monk who meditates instead of living. The mind pulls up the anima while the body lies dead below. The body has nothing more to say because the projection has been completely withdrawn and that would represent a condition of complete mental introversion—the *unio mentalis* between mind and anima. Dorn says he does not want to stop here, for what is to happen to the poor body? He says that now comes the terrible danger because the body should be redeemed too; but if mind and soul go only a bit toward the body, they fall plumb into it, like being drawn by an iron magnet, and then the whole work fails.

704 Therefore, the body has to be approached with wisdom, and Dorn does this by means of a chemical active imagination: Instead of snapping back into the body, *the body itself* has also to be raised onto a higher level. Then the two are united but not in their old state. This is what is meant when it is said that the anima must unite with the body again, without simply falling back into it. The latter would correspond to someone saying one should forget about projection and the shadow and so on, and just live.[32]

705 This is why I think it is necessary to prolong an analysis for a time. One has to go that far so that the *unio corporis* can be accomplished, to avoid falling back into the old pattern. In an

---

[32] Cf. Marie-Louise von Franz, *Alchemical Active Imagination,* (Boston: Shambhala, 1997), 40-51.

indirect way the analyst allows a mistake to occur, but in certain circumstances, you have to allow for that in order to make the return in the right way. I think the mistake an analyst can make is not to know about the necessity for the return, and thus, when the dreams announce the need for the change, it is overlooked.

706 I remember the dream of an analysand who had overanalyzed and who dreamt he was near water where a man was fishing. He saw a beautiful golden fish in the water and he told the fisherman to get it. But the fisherman, a very natural, simple man, said no, the man should jump in and join the fish! That is a beautiful illustration showing that now the moment of return had come—the unconscious could not have spoken more clearly. To jump down and join the fish instead of fishing it out would be completely *contra naturam*, but the process could not have been better illustrated. This was someone who had had eight years of analysis, beginning with a Freudian analysis, and now he should swim with the fish. I think this has to do with taking away the corruptible humidity and bringing back the natural humidity so that one gets back into the flow of life.

707 The third parable *Of the Gate of Brass and Bar of Iron of the Babylonish Captivity* says:[33]

> 708 He who brake in pieces my gates of brass and my bars of iron shall also move my candlestick out of its place, and shall break asunder the chains of the prison of darkness and feed my hungry soul, which hasted in thirst for his face, with the fat of wheat and with honey out of the rock, and shall prepare a large dining room for my pilgrimage, that I may sleep in peace, and the seven gifts of the Holy Spirit who hath had mercy upon me, may rest upon me. For they shall gather me together out of all the countries, that they may pour upon me clean water, and I shall be cleansed from the greatest sin, and from the noonday devil, for from the sole of my foot unto the crown of my head there is no soundness found in me.

[33] Cf. von Franz, *Aurora Consurgens*, 73-79.

Therefore they shall cleanse me from my secret faults and from those of others, and thereafter I shall not remember all my iniquities, for God hath anointed me with the oil of gladness that there may dwell in me the virtue of penetration and of liquefaction in the day of my resurrection, when I shall be glorified by God. For this generation cometh and passeth away, until he come that is to be sent, who also taketh away the yoke of our captivity, wherein we sate seventy years by the rivers of Babylon; there we wept and hung up our instruments, because the daughters of Sion were haughty and walked with stretched-out necks and winkings of their eyes and made a noise and went at a measured pace. Therefore the Lord will make bald the crown of the head of the daughters of Sion, and will discover their hair, for the law shall come forth from Sion and the word of the lord from Jerusalem. In that day when even women took hold of one man, saying: We eat our own bread and wear our own apparel, why doest thou not defend our blood, which is poured out as water round about Jerusalem? And they received the divine reply: Rest ye still for a little time, until the number of our brethren is filled up, which is written in this book: then every one that shall be left in Sion shall be called saved, when the Lord shall have washed away the filth of his daughters of Sion with the spirit of wisdom and understanding; then will ten acres of vineyard yield one little measure and thirty bushels of seed yield three bushels. He that understandeth this shall not be moved forever. He that hath ears to hear, let him hear what the spirit of the doctrine saith to the sons of the discipline concerning the Babylonish captivity, which endured seventy years, of which the philosophers tell in these words: Manifold are the alternations of the seventy precepts.

709 This chapter is not as interesting as the others, so I can finish it briefly. There is again the idea of a prison being broken open, and of the daughters of Jerusalem who have been arrogant and luxurious

and have to be washed and punished by the spirit of wisdom and insight. Then there is the notion of Babylonian captivity in which one has to stay on for 70 years, till one is freed from it, and afterward comes an allusion to the fact that this captured being will experience a resurrection. It says, "The day of my resurrection, when I shall be glorified by God." The analogy to the former chapters is clear, but before it was firstly the dark cloud that was the negative thing, then the water and Herod killing the innocents; now there is the aspect of being in a prison and being punished for arrogance and that from this kind of captivity, which lasts a certain time, one will also be freed. One notices the repeated mention of the number seven. Earlier we had the seven stars, and now there are the 70 years of Babylonian captivity. This has to do with the fact that from the standpoint of number symbolism, seven was viewed as the number of development. One thinks of the seven planets that are the constituents of every human totality represented in a horoscope, and the seven days of a week after which the cycle begins again, and the seven notes of an octave. There is always the idea that seven has to do with a process of slow evolution in time. This is why the time factor is in the foreground here. It expresses the problem of having to stay in prison for a certain length of time, which is characterized by evolution, after which a resurrection will take place.

710 It compensates what we all also know from our own experience of the unconscious, namely a tremendous conscious feeling of impatience. People wonder why they are not making progress and whether or not they can yet do this and that, and so on. One has sometimes to tell people that they have to remain in their depression and difficulty as long as it lasts. They often ask how long it will take to get rid of their symptoms, or problems, and one can only say until the evolution has concluded. For there must be some development for relief to happen, but from the standpoint of sidereal time, no one knows how long this will take. It can go slowly or quickly because, as Jung says, one does not solve conflicts: One outgrows them. Therefore, to come out of a problem means an evolution must happen, either long or short.

711 The problem here in our text is certainly one that cannot be solved; the author can only outgrow it through an inner transformation. That is the meaning of the endless repetition of the same problem; this is why it is bound to a number that stands for development and evolution through time. This man has fallen into a problem that he cannot solve intellectually, and that is destiny. He has been hit by fate and can only grow from it when he has recovered his balance, if there is still time. If St. Thomas was the author, he died in the middle of the process.

712 The motifs of death and resurrection, the idea of eternal life, are beginning to show up, for instance, when we read, "He that understandeth this shall not be moved forever." When one is resurrected, the figure says, one has the power of penetration on the day of resurrection. The power of penetration is a very strange expression in this text. From the times of ancient Greece onward it was said that the philosopher's stone had the capacity to penetrate every other object, and this is linked up with the idea of Egyptian funeral rites and the idea of life after death.

713 The Egyptian concept was as follows: If somebody did not go through the process of resurrection properly, after death that person would be imprisoned in the coffin chamber; whereas someone who had gone through the process of becoming Osiris, and was therefore divine, would be able to appear in any shape every day. According to certain papyri texts, the dead could leave their coffin chamber and their pyramid grave and walk about in the daylight, and they could change shape. They could appear as a crocodile and lie about in the sun by the Nile, or they could fly about as an ibis.

714 The highest goal of the resurrection was thought of as the ability to be completely free to change into any shape and move about through anything in this material world, to be a kind of ghostlike being that could walk through closed doors and manifest in any desired form. Egyptian prayers for the dead, written on some papyri, state that this was the highest goal of life after death. The alchemists connected this idea with their concept of the philosopher's stone, that divine nucleus in man that is immortal and ubiquitous and able

to penetrate any material object. It is an experience of something immortal, lasting beyond physical death. In parapsychological reports this is sometimes mentioned as a typical quality of the soul of a dying person.

715 In this connection, I recall the story of a man who, after a severe operation, woke up from the narcosis and, feeling quite well, got out of bed and walked through the hospital. He noticed, but without much of a shock, that he could walk through closed doors. As he did not take this very seriously, for it did not quite come to his consciousness, he walked on, right out of the hospital onto the street and suddenly a voice said to him, "If you want to return, this is your last chance, quick!" In a panic he rushed back into the hospital, and at that moment he really woke up from the anaesthetic, and the doctor was saying, "My God, we almost didn't bring him back." His heart had failed, and they had brought him back through heart massage at that very moment, but subjectively he had had the experience of just walking out, and the specific experience of walking through doors, which he half-consciously thought was rather odd.

716 This is a parapsychological experience of the subtle body. The ghost of the dead is already capable of walking through shut doors. These reports have to be taken as they are: We cannot discuss them psychologically. We can believe them or not; we cannot make a point out of such things because they are reports of unique situations—but it is probably from such experiences that the generally widespread idea that ghosts, the surviving soul, can walk through matter has arisen. It exists in all countries where there is a belief in ghosts. It was looked on as proof of the immaterial, immortal aspect of the psyche.

717 If we take this "power of penetration" not as a near-death experience, but as the experience of a living being, it could point toward the influence of the unconscious on its surroundings; I am not thinking of an intentional influence but rather that something is felt when one is in connection with the Self. The Self begins to have a certain effect on other people. As soon as one *intends* to exert

such an influence, it generally disappears, but an unintentional influence can certainly happen. If one is connected with the Self inwardly, one can penetrate all life situations. Insofar as one is not caught in them, one walks through them; this means there is an innermost nucleus of the personality that remains detached, so that even if the most horrible things happen to one, the first reaction is not a thought or a physical reaction, but rather an interest in its meaning. Some part remains concentrated upon the meaning, so that one is never pulled into the outer situation. By concentrating on the meaning, one remains more or less objective.

718 It is as if a part of the conscious alertness of the personality remained steadily concentrated on the meaningfulness of any event in life, so that one is never unconsciously lost or caught in it. Psychological captivity refers to an emotional factor; being caught is simply being caught in something emotional or instinctive. If one is caught in a projection, a feeling of hate or love, it is not so easy to get out of it, which is why people often say, "I'm awfully sorry, but I can't help it." That is a sort of prison, for a prison is any kind of psychological factor that traps one, whereas if one has a constant alertness to the Self, one is no longer caught in anything; there is an innermost part of the personality that remains free and can no longer be caught. There is an end to the state of helplessness in which one was caught by one's own inner processes. This amounts to a tremendous steadying of the innermost core of the personality. This is comparable to the philosopher's stone, which is a symbol of what forms through this constant inner experience.

719 ***Question:*** *Would you connect this with what you said earlier about the overanalyzed person who had to jump into the stream with the golden fish? That person was also staying outside real experience.*

720 Yes, but if he returns now and swims with the fish, he will not think he is a fish, and he will not be caught in the fish existence. One returns to experience, naïve experience, but one is no longer caught in it. To return to the water, to use the metaphor of the dream, would mean to go with the fish and to swim, but to remain a human being, and not become a fish again, that means to go completely and

spontaneously into the experience while "it" remains outside. It is as if a second part of the personality were watching the experience, or to use Eastern terms, one goes on living spontaneously but one part of you is concerned with the Tao all the time. One's focus is no longer caught by what is happening but is directed toward the Tao. If one can detach oneself from life as much as that, one is already dead and has reached immortality. This is something that cannot be altered, even by death. Death then becomes a chance event that does not affect the *nucleus* of the personality. This is, at least subjectively, an experience of being immortal.

721 ***Question:*** *Does jumping into the water mean jumping consciously into the unconscious?*

722 No, in this case I would say it means having conscious experiences, for it is not always jumping into the unconscious, but rather it is often a conscious jumping into an experience of life. This is often what it means for introverts. That man had jumped into the unconscious long ago, but here it is about him going into life, about simply living without always thinking, "That's my anima," and so on.

723 ***Remark:*** *It would mean the river of life.*

724 Yes, he simply needed to get into the river of life.

725 ***Question:*** *But isn't spontaneity incompatible with consciousness?*

726 Yes, this is a paradox that has to be reached—conscious spontaneity. It is being spontaneous but with a slight delay. Consciousness becomes something like delayed spontaneity. In practical terms, imagine a situation in which you get angry and spontaneously wish to let your anger out. You are not going to be unspontaneous by holding back for a moment. Yet it is not like just flying into a rage—for then the rage has you—but rather, you have *it* in hand. You stop for a moment, say yes or no to it, and then let it out. That is the paradox of conscious spontaneity.

727 The other may accuse you of putting on an act, saying you were not really angry; but it *was* honest anger, only consciousness had it absolutely in hand, and in that way it was consciously active. It is a paradox for you are actively conscious and yet spontaneous. I would

call it conscious spontaneity—completely spontaneous behavior yet always knowing what you are doing.

728 ***Remark:*** *The water was transparent in the dream, so it could not be referring to the unconscious.*

729 That is right; in this man's case the water was not unconsciousness, but life. He was an introvert and had overanalyzed so much that he did not live anymore. He simply had to go and live, in spite of all he knew.

730 For instance, he had a terrible boss in his profession, a brutal military officer who liked to shout at people if the work was not brought punctually. He treated them like dogs, and that naturally had a castrating effect upon other men. My analysand's spontaneous feeling was to hit back, but that kind of thing he could not do. He always said his boss must be a shadow figure for him and always analyzed his aggression. So jumping into the water meant, among other things, just being aggressive for once, but to time it right because he could have hit this man and knocked him out, but to knock out your boss would not be a good thing as you depend on him for a living! So he had to delay his reaction a bit, but one day he shouted back and said he was not going to be treated like that, and he got up and walked out of the room and slammed the door. The result was that his boss invited him to supper and even offered to raise his salary. He said he was a real man, and he made friends with him. That was the result of for once jumping into the water and living, instead of always analyzing his own aggression and the awfulness of his aggressive shadow—but he had to do it consciously, because his naïve, spontaneous reaction would have been to knock out his boss's teeth, which would have been a bit too much!

Lecture 9

731 We are currently discussing the *Aurora Consurgens* and are in the middle of a circular process. Each chapter seems to begin with the same situation, namely with a *nigredo,* to use an alchemical expression. Then follows a description of a certain treatment of matter, and each chapter ends with some aspect of the *albedo.* At first, we had a black cloud that covered the earth, and the soul or a woman is redeemed from it. Then came a flood that covered matter, followed by the woman who introduced death and drove it away again, after which the white pearls appeared. In the last chapter we commented upon, the *nigredo* took the form of the Babylonian captivity that lasted 70 years and from which the daughters of Jerusalem and of Zion were later able to escape. The transformation was described either as a washing process—matter had to be washed again and again—or in the form of an anointing with the holy water of the Church, with the *chrisma*, so that the power of penetration enters the object treated, and so on.

732 But the big question is just what this object is. Sometimes it is said that the *prima materia* is the matter treated in the alchemical process, but then from the dialogues it is clear that it is the Wisdom of God that has, so to speak, fallen into matter and become identical with it; at other times it is the author himself, for he speaks in the first person using "I": "For this cause have I laboured night by night with crying ..." Thus we must conclude that the spirit in matter and the author are sometimes contaminated—the difference between the two is blurred, and the alchemist has become literally identical with the mystical object he is cooking in the vessel.

733 This borders on, or gets very close to, a psychotic state; typical of the latter is for ego consciousness to be swallowed up, after having become identical with certain complexes of the unconscious,

generally of an archetypal nature. This also happens in what Jung calls a "voluntary psychosis," namely in active imagination. Jung said that, *cum grano salis,* active imagination is a voluntary psychosis. We therefore do not quite know and cannot quite judge by the manuscript itself whether we are faced with an involuntary psychosis or with what one could call a voluntary psychosis, namely with the product of a certain form of meditation.

734 If my hypothesis is correct and Thomas of Aquinas wrote this document in his death struggle, then both these assumptions are not quite true. But there is a third possibility, namely that it is an irruption of an archetypal content of the unconscious that cannot be called a psychotic episode, but rather a premortal invasion of the unconscious. Such a thing may look quite similar, but is not reached by meditation, but rather by a sudden breaking through of the collective unconscious into a very rational mental system of an unusual personality. Then these chapters would show how, in a death struggle, the personality still tries to assimilate this shock, to digest it and find a right attitude toward it, and to integrate the content that has broken in. That is my hypothesis about this text. It is not more than a hypothesis; I can only say it is probable, but I cannot declare it as a certainty.

735 In the next chapter, the fourth parable, "Of the Philosophical Faith, Which Consisteth in the Number Three," follows a confession of faith on the triune God image. This is a very long chapter that is slightly shortened here.[34]

736 Whosoever shall do the will of my Father and shall cast out this world into the world, I will give him to sit with me upon the throne of my kingdom and upon the throne of David and upon the seats of the tribes of Israel. This is the will of my Father, that they may know him to be the true (God) and no other, who giveth abundantly and upbraideth not, unto all peoples in truth, and his only begotten Son, God of God, light of light, and the Holy Spirit who proceedeth from both, who

[34] Cf. von Franz, *Aurora Consurgens,* 81-89.

is equal in Godhead to the Father and the Son, for in the Father inhereth eternity, in the Son equality, in the Holy Spirit (is) the bond of eternity and equality; for as it is said, Like as the Father is, so is the Son, and so also is the Holy Spirit, and these three are One, [which the Philosopher would have to be] body, spirit, and soul, for all perfection consisteth in the number three, that is, in measure, number, and weight. For the Father is of none, the Son is of the Father, the Holy Spirit proceedeth from both; for to the Father is attributed wisdom, by which he ruleth and sweetly disposeth of all things, whose ways are unsearchable and his judgments incomprehensible. To the Son is attributed Truth, for he in his appearing took upon him that which he was not, subsisting perfect God and man of human flesh and reasonable soul, who at the behest of the Father with the co-operation of the Holy Spirit restored to the world lost by the sin [of the first parents]. To the Holy Spirit is attributed Goodness, through whom earthly things become heavenly, and this in threefold wise: by baptizing in water, in blood, and in fire; in water by quickening and cleansing, when he washeth away all defilements and driveth out murkiness from souls, as it is said: Thou dost fecundate the waters to give life to souls. For water is the nourishment of all living things, whence when water cometh down from heaven it plentifully watereth the earth, and the earth by it receiveth strength which can dissolve every metal, wherefore it beseecheth him saying: Send forth thy Spirit, that is water, and they shall be created, and thou shalt renew the face of the earth, for he breatheth upon the earth when he maketh it to tremble, and he toucheth the mountains and they smoke. And when he baptizeth with blood, then he nourisheth, as it is said: He gave me to drink of the saving water of wisdom, and again: His blood is drink indeed, for the seat of the soul is in the blood, as Senior saith: But the soul itself remained in water, (which [today] is like to it in warmth and humidity,) and therein consisteth all life. But when he baptizeth in flame, then he infuseth the soul and giveth perfection of life, for fire giveth form and completeth the whole, as it is said: He breathed into his face the breath of life, and man, who was aforetime dead, became a living soul. Of the first, second and third the philosophers bear witness, saying: For three months water [preserveth] nourisheth the foetus in the womb, air nourisheth it for the second three, fire [also] guardeth it for the third three. The infant will never come to birth until these months are expired, then it is born and quickened by the sun, for that is the quickener of all things that are dead. Wherefore the aforesaid Spirit by reason of the excellence of his sevenfold gift is said to have seven virtues in his operation on earth. Fire, penetrating and subtilizing by its warmth, consumeth all earthly parts which are wholly material and not formal; for as long as fire hath matter, it ceaseth not to act, seeking to imprint its form on the passive substance. And Calet the Less: Make warm the cold of the one by the heat of the other. And Senior: Set the male upon the female, that is, the warm upon the cold. In the second place he extinguisheth the intense imprinted fire by ignition, of which saith the Prophet: A fire was kindled in their congregation, and a flame burned the wicked upon earth; he extinguisheth this fire by its own temperament, whence it is added: Thou art coolness in the heat. And Calet the Less: Extinguish the fire of the one by the coolness of the other.

737 A few additional quotations emphasize the same thing, namely that you have to put out fire with fire.

738 In the third place he maketh soft, that is, he liquefieth the hardness of the earth and dissolveth its condensed and exceedingly compact parts. And elsewhere it is written: Woman dissolveth man and he fixeth her, that is, the Spirit dissolveth the body (and softeneth it) and the body hardeneth the spirit.

739 In the fourth place he enlighteneth, when he taketh away all darknesses from the body, of which the hymn singeth: Purge the horrible darknesses of our mind, enkindle a light in our senses, and the Prophet: He conducted them all the night with a light of fire, and night shall be light as the day. And Senior: And he maketh all that is black white and all that is white red, for water whiteneth and fire enlighteneth. For he shineth through the tincturing soul like a ruby in colour, which it hath acquired by virtue of the fire, wherefore fire is called the Dyer. And in the *Book of the Quintessence*: Thou seest a wondrous light in the darkness.

740 Fifthly, he separateth the pure from the impure when he removeth all accidents from the soul, which are vapours, that is, evil odours, as it is written: That fire separateth those things that are unlike and bringeth together those things that are like. Wherefore the Prophet: Thou hast tried me by fire, and iniquity shall not be found in me. And again: We have passed through fire and water, and thou hast brought us forth into rest and refreshment. And Hermes: Thou shalt separate the dense from the subtle, the earth from the fire. Alphidius: Earth is liquefied and turned into water, water is liquefied and turned into air, air is liquefied and turned into fire, fire is liquefied and turned into glorified earth. And this fifth virtue doth Hermes refer to in his Secret, when he saith: Thou shalt separate the earth from the fire, the subtle from the dense gently (etc.).

741 In the sixth place he exalteth the lowly, when he bringeth to the surface the soul deep and hidden in the bowels of the earth, of which saith the Prophet: Who bringeth out them that were bound in his strength. Again: Thou hast delivered my soul out of the lower hell. And Isaias: The Spirit of the Lord lifted me up. And the philosophers: Whosoever shall make the hidden manifest knoweth the whole work, and he who knoweth our cambar (i.e. fire), he is (our) philosopher.

742 In the seventh and last place he inspireth when by his breathing he maketh the earthly body spiritual, of which it is sung: Thou by thy breathing makest men to be spiritual. Solomon: The Spirit of the Lord hath filled the whole world. And the Prophet: And all the power of them by the spirit of his mouth. And Rasis in the *Light of Lights*: Heavy things cannot be made to ascend save by alliance with light things (nor can light things be brought down to the depths save by combination with the heavy). And [in] the *Turba*: Make bodies incorporeal and the fixed volatile; but all these things are brought about and fulfilled by our spirit, for he alone it is who can make clean that which is conceived of unclean seed. Doth not the Scripture say: Wash yourselves in it and be clean. And to Naaman (the Syrian) was it said: Go and wash seven times in the Jordan and thou shalt be clean. For there is one baptism for the remission of sins, as the Creed and the Prophet bear witness. He that hath ears to hear, let him hear what the (holy) spirit of the doctrine saith to the sons of the discipline concerning the virtues of the sevenfold spirit, whereby all the scripture is fulfilled, which the philosophers set forth in these words: Distil seven times and thou hast set it apart from the corrupting humidity.[35]

743 It is striking that the tone of the text is no longer ecstatic. From time to time there is the odd beautiful poetic quotation, but in general there is a rather monotonous tone throughout this chapter. At the beginning there is a nearly literal repetition of the Creed: God of God, light of light, and the Holy Spirit who proceedeth from both, and so on; it may vary in expression in the various creeds, but there is no great difference. Here, naturally, we have the Catholic version. As we recall, at the start of the process, the author, in his elation, praised an overwhelming, positive invasion of the Wisdom of God; then he seemed to get into an inflation: He scorned those

[35] Cf. ibid., 89-99.

who know nothing of such an experience and was aggressive toward ignorant people. He then lapsed into a boring wordplay on the words *aurora - aurea hora*. After this first phase begins what I would call the circling of a spiral: He always begins with a dark process and describes what has been done and then ends with a positive result, whereupon the whole thing repeats itself. In this chapter we are in the middle of the spiral. But we need to ask how this chapter differs from the other chapters. There is a striking return to the official Christian approach! At the beginning he even literally repeats the Creed, the official version of the Confession of Faith: I believe in God the Father, and so on. Why does he do this? What does it show?

744 ***Answer***: *That he is more or less back to being himself.*

745 Yes, he is in the process of returning to his conscious self; he is trying to return to his former conscious attitude, or as one might say, to flee from the flood that drowned him.

746 Here one can see the value of an official creed, or of having a religious attitude: It is a boat into which one can retire when the sharks attack.

747 One can go out bathing in the unconscious, but if the sharks come, there is a boat to get back into, which is why the Church has been compared to a boat, or to an island, to which one can retire when the influx of the unconscious becomes too strong. To have only my human faculty of reason and to simply tell myself to be reasonable is not enough to keep back the influx of the unconscious. But to have a belief that exists in consciousness is like having a boat, a place to which one can flee.

748 We must therefore conclude that our author was not a heretic and did not doubt his Creed but believed in it, as one would expect of a cleric of the 13th century. He was a truly believing Catholic, a medieval Christian, and he therefore now tries to retire to his belief. But there is *one* change! If we look at the balance, we see he first confesses that he believes in the Father, the Son and the Holy Ghost, and that lasts for about the first 10 lines of the first page. But the remainder of the chapter is then concerned with the effects of the Holy Ghost. That is amazing. The Holy Ghost fills the whole of one

of the longest chapters in the entire book; it is concerned solely with its different alchemical effects. The whole emphasis of his Creed has suddenly shifted toward the Holy Ghost.

749 Here we catch *in flagranti*, so to speak, what happened at about this time—in the 12th and 13th centuries. If one knows the history of the spiritual development of Christianity, one is aware that at that time sects of the Holy Ghost appeared everywhere. Some were heretical, while others endeavored to remain within the Church; the Holy Ghost, however, became *the* occupation and concern of the people. There was much theological discussion, and there were many movements, such as the Brethren of the Holy Ghost (the Humiliated), the Poor of Lyon, the Loyal Heart, the Big Heart of the Tertiarians. They all confessed that they were especially devoted to the adoration and following of the Holy Ghost.

750 In the Bible, Christ Himself predicted that after his death, God would send a Comforter who would bring comfort to the people for His having left the earth and His death, and that those who received the Holy Ghost would be able to do works even greater than He Himself had done. Therefore, from the very beginning, the Holy Ghost has been a very awkward aspect of the Christian image of God, for, according to the Bible, it is said to enter the individual directly. One could no longer directly communicate with Christ, for He had returned to Heaven after His resurrection. God Himself had never come down to earth—that is not exactly true, because all three are one, but I am now speaking here as if they were not. But, according to the Bible, the Holy Ghost is supposed to descend upon individuals again and again, and this is not restricted by time.

751 Tradition tells us of Christ's contemporaries meeting Him again and again, but we cannot communicate with Him now except through visions or through prayer. On the other hand, throughout history the Holy Ghost has been supposed to be able to descend upon people, which conveys the idea of an individual being filled directly with the spirit of God, or, as certain theologians have clearly seen, even continuing the incarnation of God. God did not incarnate only once in the person of Jesus Christ; through the workings of the

Holy Ghost, any individual in the Christian community can again become a vessel of the divine spirit, which would be an incarnation of a little bit of the Godhead.

752 These thoughts became suddenly so emotionally important that certain sects in the Middle Ages drew quite amazing conclusions. For instance, there is a saying of St. Paul: *ubi spiritus, ibi libertas*—where the Spirit, i.e. the Holy Ghost, is at work, there is freedom; therefore, they thought that if they were filled with the Holy Ghost, they no longer needed to obey the Church, or go to Confession, for they had their own direct connection to the Godhead through the Holy Ghost. This interpretation naturally became a danger to the organization of the Church, for people felt they no longer needed the Church now that they were filled with the Holy Ghost.

753 Also, some sectarians said that if one were filled with the Holy Ghost, one could read the Holy Scriptures oneself and understand them directly, and therefore the interpretation of the Church was no longer necessary. One could understand the Bible symbolically and spiritually oneself. These people began to read the Bible and interpret it for themselves. Other sects went so far as to say that if someone were filled with the Holy Ghost, he could commit any sin and it would not be wrong—adultery, for instance—for "where there is the Spirit, there is freedom."

754 It is easy to imagine that the Church did not approve of such interpretations and that some sects of the Holy Ghost were therefore partly condemned while others were badly persecuted; most had to close down. As was seen long ago, they anticipated the Reformation at the beginning of which there was also an attempt to claim that each individual had the right to communicate with the Godhead directly, without the intermediary of any human organization. These movements are usually known as pre-Reformation movements as they share the idea of an individual, direct communication with God, though in other ways, of course, they were different.

755 As our author, who has passed through religious experience, wants to uphold his Christian attitude, he naturally refers to the Holy Ghost. By understanding his suffering as having been conveyed

upon him by the Holy Ghost, he is able to integrate it into his conscious point of view.

756 So here he clings emotionally to this idea as one clings to a life ring. He describes the Holy Ghost through three forms of baptism: by water, by blood, and by fire. He then describes the seven processes through which the Holy Ghost affects matter. Afterward, the text shifts amazingly, for suddenly the Holy Ghost becomes a kind of chemical agent that cooks, cleanses, purifies alchemical matter and makes it subtle. It is here conceived of as a kind of energy—something like fire or electricity—that has an effect upon matter. Here the idea of "spirit" returns to its original, archetypal form, namely as mana.

757 From the comparative history of religion we know that one of the oldest concepts of the divine in many primitive religions is the concept of mana, *mulungu*, the idea of a divine power that many ethnologists have compared to a mystical kind of electricity. It is something like a divine energy that pervades certain objects and strikes certain people. A king has mana, a chief has it too, as does a menstruating woman and one who has just given birth. A tree that has been struck by lightning is also full of mana.

758 Mana must always be treated with respect, either by keeping away from it through taboos or by approaching it according to certain rules. It can be destructive or positive. A menstruating woman, for instance, has negative mana and must stay away from the tribe and tribal rituals during her period, for she is loaded with destructive electricity, so to speak. Mana can also be neutral, for if the chief of a tribe has mana, he can bestow fertility on the tribe, the cattle, and the soil in his dominion, or, if it is approached irreverently, he can bewitch people, making them ill and so on.

759 This is an archetypal idea. Psychologically, one could say it is a representation of the effects of the Self, or of psychic energy that, on this level, is not experienced as a personified image of God, but rather as an impersonal aspect of divine power. In later religious and sometimes geographically different developments, there are other aspects of the Divine, namely as gods, demons, ancestral ghosts, etc.,

that are all more or less personified, more or less anthropomorphic figures. They are spoken of as if they were personalities. The climax of this is to be found in the Greek religion, where the gods have human form—they represent the archetypes—and in the Judeo-Christian religion, where God is also conceived of as a being in human form, with semihuman reactions.

760 In Christian art, for instance, God is generally represented as an old man with a white beard. That is the classic image. The mana aspect, the aspect of the Godhead as something like nonpersonified power, reappears suddenly in Christianity in the form of the Holy Ghost. He is water, wind and fire: A wind filled the house; flames appeared on the heads of the apostles at Whitsuntide; and he also appears in baptism as water. Thus the archetypal idea reappears here in this interpretation of the Holy Ghost as an impersonal power with a semimaterial aspect.

761 It is to this idea that our author clings when he describes the Holy Ghost quite naively as a kind of semimaterial physical agency that works upon the *prima materia*: firstly by washing it and then by filling it with blood—that is by vivifying it—and then by heating it up with fire, which would be giving it life and resurrection. He amplifies this even further by comparing it to the birth of a child who is preserved in water for three months, then nourished by air for three months, and finally is protected from fire for three months, until it is born. So the activity of the Holy Ghost—the impact it has on matter—simultaneously involves generating, bringing forth, and nursing the divine child, a comprehensive midwife. Here we see that our text is a typical description of how the *lapis philosophorum* is produced, for it is often compared to the whole process of childbirth; it is the Self, born within the psyche as a divine child.

762 After the earlier allusions to the motif of the *coniunctio*, now it is said, "Make warm the cold of the one by the heat of the other. ... Set the male upon the female, that is, the warm upon the cold."[36] Here we have the idea of the *coniunctio oppositorum*, the male and female coming together, and also a depersonalization through the

---

[36] Cf. ibid., 89.

ascription of qualities, so that warm and cold are brought together, which would be a bringing together of opposite powers. It was a general medieval idea that men were hot and women were cold, physiologically speaking.

763 Then comes a more subtle idea, namely that this bringing together of opposites means they are secretly one, for the fire has to be put out by fire or has to be cooled by its inner fire. How would you interpret that psychologically?

764 ***Answer**: It sounds like the Ouroboros.*

765 It is, in a way, though on a more primitive level because the Ouroboros symbolizes the natural process of this; here it has already been brought forth and is in the vessel. To a certain extent, you are right, but what would you say that it is psychologically? What is fire?

766 ***Answer**: Emotion.*

767 Yes, and what is positive about emotion? It transforms, cooks, and enlightens, which is how fire brings light: If I am emotionally gripped by something, I can understand it; if I am not emotionally wrestling with my problems, or something else, then nothing comes out of it. Where there is no emotion there is no life. If you have to learn something by heart and it is of no interest to you, there is no fire; it does not register, even if you read it 50 times. But as soon as there is emotional interest, it need only be read once and you know it. Therefore, emotion is the carrier of consciousness; without emotion, there is no progress in consciousness.

768 The destructive aspect appears in quarrels and arguments; there, it eats up both oneself and one's opponent. You know how enjoyable it is if you keep an affect to yourself; if you do not let your negative emotion out, it just eats you up from within. There is a growling dog within you for hours.

769 In our text there is an allusion to evil emotion:

> "A fire was kindled in their congregation, and a flame burned the wicked upon earth."

770 It is the burning of wicked people, of sinners. And then it is said:

"He extinguisheth this fire by its own temperament."[37]

771 Psychologically, this is very revealing. Again and again people in analysis say that they are in love with you or that they hate you. Although they say they know it is quite unreasonable, and they say to one, "I am not crazy; I can behave and be reasonable, but the thing is still there. What can I do about it? Please redeem me! It is not enough for me to know it is all nonsense." The response to this is a sad one: The fire has to burn the fire—one just has to burn in the emotion until the fire dies down and becomes balanced. That is something that unfortunately cannot be evaded. The burning of the fire, the emotion, cannot be tricked out of one's system; there is no recipe for getting rid of it—it has to be endured. The fire has to burn until the last unclean element has been consumed. All alchemical texts say this in different variations, and we have not found any other way either. It cannot be hindered but only suffered until what is mortal or corruptible, or, as our text says so beautifully, until the corruptible humidity, one's unconsciousness, has been burned up. That is the meaning: It is the acceptance of suffering.

772 If one is filled with 10,000 devils, one can only be burned by them until they grow quiet and are still. The infantile demand on the analyst, or anybody else, to redeem one with some kind of comforting trick does not help. If an analyst pretends he can do that, he is just a quack because there is no such thing, and it would be meaningless anyway. If he tries to get analysands out of their suffering, he takes away from them what is most valuable. This is why cheap comfort is wrong, for by taking people away from the heat of their passion, you are taking them away from their process and from the place where the process of individuation takes place.

773 Sitting in hell and roasting there is what brings forth the *lapis,* for, as it says here, the fire is extinguished with its own inner measure. Passion has its own inner measure; there is no such thing as a chaotic libido, for we know that the unconscious itself, as pure nature, has an inner balance. The lack of balance comes from the

[37] Ibid.

childishness of the conscious attitude. If you simply follow your own passion according to its own inclinations, it will never go too far; it will always lead to its own defeat.

774 Inordinate passion seeks defeat. Where love is concerned, people who have an inordinately passionate nature, a kind of devilish nature, search for a human person, or situation, against which they can knock their heads, and they despise any partner or situation in which their passion wins out. Instinctively, they seek defeat. It is as though something within them knows that this devil has to be hit on the head. This is why one does not help the person if one is friendly or weak or understanding toward such a fire. Generally, such people walk out of analysis because that is not what they want. Basically, the fire of the passion looks for that which will extinguish it, and that is why the urge for individuation, as long as it is a natural inordinate urge, seeks impossible situations; it seeks conflict and defeat and suffering because it seeks its own transformation.

775 Let us say someone is possessed by a power devil. If he can dominate people in his surroundings, he is not happy but remains restless; he dominates the whole family and goes on dominating outside and in his professional life, but he is still restless. He is really searching for someone who can overcome him; that is what he longs for, though naturally he does not like it. It is an ambiguous attitude, for he hates the idea, but at the same time he longs for someone or something to overcome him and put an end to his power. It is very important to know this in the treatment of borderline cases, for they usually suffer from tremendous emotions and always try to let the whole impact fall on the analyst in the hope and fear that he will hit back, precisely because fire knows its own inner measure.

776 Then the spirit breaks up or modifies what is hard and hardens what is weak. This seems understandable, but how would you interpret it?

777 ***Answer**: It is the coniunctio between the male and female.*

778 Yes, the hardness would be the male; it is a conjunction of opposites, but how would this look in life—to soften what is hard and to harden what is weak?

779 ***Question:*** *Has it to do with the four functions? The main function is what is strong and the fourth function is weak.*

780 Yes, but the main function is not always hard.

781 ***Question****: Couldn't the hard thing be resistance?*

782 Yes, resistances, or, for instance, a rigid attitude in some corner where one literally hardens, which is a typical complex reaction. When, for instance, an analysand refuses to discuss something, that would be a hardening that covers up a weakness; obstinacy and rigidity are hard, and that usually has to do with destructive and negative childhood experiences. Such people write off love, or this or that, and in the process, they even write off themselves. They set their will on success and money, or something of that kind, and inwardly they are as if frozen.

783 Very often the analytical process is concerned with softening the hard corners of the personality, which is generally in a painful cramp. To harden is a symptom of weakness, so solidifying what is weak would be part of the same process, for it is where one feels weak that one stiffens, whereas one remains flexible where one is strong. The rigidity of people springs from weakness and fear. Fear stiffens them, and out of fear, one becomes inflexible. Therefore, weakness has to be strengthened—ego weakness or feeling weakness, or whatever it may be; there are many weaknesses. So the psychological process is often concerned with softening up those parts of the personality that have stiffened, and at the same time solidifying the nucleus of a personality, the Self; this would be bringing together the opposites of male and female.

784 Then comes the fourth effect (of spirit): illumination. That is the moment in which one experiences a feeling of comprehension, when certain problems become clear. This is also called the coloring and the whitening, for things become clear, and one's feeling for life begins to flow again. Spirit then segregates the pure from the impure so that all accidental things, all unimportant side effects, are removed—bad odors, and so on.

785 To comment on that alchemically, very often the philosopher's stone is surrounded by foreign material that does not belong to it

and therefore has to be either washed or burned away. It is a fact that in the alchemical process not everything has to be integrated; there is something called dammed earth, *terra damnata*, or *res extraneae*, exterior or outer things that have to be cast out and not integrated. They simply have to be thrown away. Often people who have read a little about Jungian psychology think that everything, whatever happens, belongs to the process and must be integrated. This is only true *cum grano salis,* for it is a fact that not everything belongs. Like all psychological truths, in a certain way it all belongs, yet in another, not at all. What are those outer things that have to be thrown away?

786 ***Answer**: Collective attitudes.*

787 Yes, for example, those collective attitudes that hamper the development of the individual or identification with other people. Many people do not get to themselves because of their admiration for some other person, perhaps of the same sex. They always strive to be like that person and thereby lose the possibility of becoming themselves. As a snake stares at a rabbit, they stare at someone else, or at a collective idea, but that is something outside: It is not who they are. It does not belong to them, and such things do not have to be integrated. Their dreams will tell them to get away from that, to leave it alone; it is not theirs and is none of their business. Thus, individuation also means separation, differentiation, and the recognition of what is yours and what is not. The rest has to be left alone. Libido and energy should not be wasted on things that do not belong to us. It can be said, therefore, that there needs to be just as much separation as integration, and this would be regeneration through fire. This lasts until, as the text says, one reaches a condition of tranquillity. When people can let go of wrong ideals or collective attitudes, they suddenly become peaceful; one can relax and say, "Thank God, I always thought I had to be brilliant, and now I find I don't have to." They had just stared at someone else who was. In this way one is redeemed from the constant effort of having to achieve something in the wrong direction.

788 The whole process is then described as earth changing into water, water into air, air into fire, and fire into earth. Here we have the

classical idea of the *circulatio*, of moving through the four elements, of repeating the process but always on a new level. This circling of the Self through the four elements and forms, this *circumambulatio*, is, among other things, the process of individuation through the four functions and different phases of life. In the process of individuation the same problems very often come up again and again; they seem to be settled, but after a while they reappear. If we look at that negatively, we are discouraged, saying here it is again, the same old thing, but when looked at more closely, one generally sees the *circulatio*, for it has simply reappeared on another level. For instance, it may now have become a feeling problem.

789 If we look at the intellectual, intuitive types who run very quickly through an analytical process and seem to understand a lot of Jungian psychology and what is going on inside, they assimilate a great deal, but it has not become an ethical problem to them. Their feeling is left out, and with that the ethical aspect is omitted. This means that in their ethical behavior in the world, they continue in the same old style, perhaps acceding to reason or collective influence. They speak of the process of individuation as if they had arrived there and knew all about it, which in a way is quite true, for they have assimilated it, but only in fire, not yet in earth. So fire has to change into water and water into earth, and the whole thing has to be lived through once more as an ethical problem. Such people sometimes suddenly discover that they are right at the beginning again, that they have not even learnt the ABCs of the shadow problem, or something like that, and they say now at last they understand the problem, for hitherto they had only understood it partially.

790 This is what goes on constantly with psychological understanding; there are many layers, and something can always be understood on a new and deeper level. You understand it with a part of yourself, and then the penny drops deeper, as it were, and you realize the same thing but in a much more living and rich way than before, and that can continue indefinitely until it becomes completely real. Even if you feel you have realized something, you

should always have the humility to say that that is how you feel *for the time being*; a few years later you may say you did not know at all before, but now you can understand what was meant.

791 That is what I find so beautiful about this work—it is an adventure that never comes to an end, for each time you turn a corner, a completely new vista of life opens up before you. You never know and have it all settled, even in the case of things that, for the present, feel sorted out.

792 The last section refers to the spirit that makes life real, and to the spiritualization of the body. The body becomes incorporeal and the spirit concrete. This is another aspect of a *coniunctio*, of bringing the opposites together, but again it has a different nuance. How would you look at that? The body, the material thing, becomes spiritualized, and the spirit in turn becomes concrete. What would that mean in practice?

793 ***Answer**: The end of the split between body and spirit.*

794 Yes, but what does that look like?

795 ***Answer:** It would be a totally different attitude toward the body.*

796 In what way?

797 ***Answer:** It would be putting analytical or spiritual experience into actual life.*

798 That would be solidifying the spirit. That is correct. If you apply a psychological realization, you incarnate what was previously spiritual. If you recognize something as right and put it into action, it becomes real. Now what would the other part involve?

799 ***Answer:** A conscious attitude that retires in part from spontaneous experience, while looking at it symbolically—a kind of spiritualization of experience.*

800 Yes, I would say if I am able to understand a concrete situation symbolically, that is the moment I am able to hold back my spontaneity. If I can keep to what Goethe says, "*Alles Vergaengliches ist nur ein Gleichnis*"—"All that is transient is but a parable"—if I can see the symbolic aspect in a completely concrete material situation, and take myself out of it, then I spiritualize it—it becomes a parable for something psychological. In a way, all outer events in

life are only parables—parables of an inner process, of synchronistic symbolizations. We have to look at them from that angle to understand and integrate them; this would be spiritualizing the physical.

801 **Question:** *Isn't there a danger of, for instance, losing the taste of good roast beef?*

802 Certainly, that is why we have to solidify the spirit again! We have to do both. It is what the Zen master said, "At the beginning of the process water is water and mountains are mountains and streams are streams"—this equates to the taste of a good steak, but for the ego only, and that is not enough. That is why we have to go into a state where mountains are no longer mountains, streams are no longer streams, and water is no longer water, which means we see them as parables—and this would be where the beefsteak loses its taste. But at the end of the process mountains are again mountains and water is water—spirit has again become concrete.

803 That is why you are quite right, for to get stuck in the middle, one way or the other, would be bad. The process needs both movements to not become destructive. This is so beautifully illustrated in alchemy: The body has to be spiritualized and the spirit has to be incarnated—both things must take place. This is an example of Jung's view, namely that alchemy compensates the one-sidedness of Christian spiritualization. It is that underlying movement that is not anti-Christian but rather completes it by bringing the opposites closer together. It brings physical life and all that goes with it more into the field of perception and thereby draws attention to it.

804 ***Remark:*** *I have often observed that in Jungian analysis there is a danger of intellectualizing the spirit.*

805 Yes, and then it becomes awfully thin! The spirit turns into intellectual concepts and loses its original emotional and gripping quality. Then exactly what you say happens, and that is *the* great danger: Spirit becomes thin and is trapped in the bottle.

806 ***Question***: *Couldn't one say that whenever there is a real spiritual experience, it should become manifest?*

807 I think a real spiritual experience—I don't know exactly what you have in mind when you say that—*shouldn't* become manifest. If it is real, it *manifests.* Mythos means communication. If you are overwhelmed by a spiritual experience, "it" wants you to communicate it, i.e., to manifest it. That is the meaning of the word mythos. There is no religious experience where there is not a need to tell of it; that is natural. But one need not add the word "should." If it is true, it *will* become real; its natural flow will be into reality.

808 This is very beautifully illustrated in the book *Black Elk Speaks.*[38] As a boy of 9, and in a kind of coma, Black Elk had a most tremendous spiritual experience. He kept it to himself until he got a thunder phobia. Then he went to a medicine man who said, "Your experience has not been given to you only: You owe it to your tribe." So he told his tribe of his visions, and the phobia disappeared.

809 I would say that a real spiritual experience flows naturally into communication, but there is no "should" about it. If it is real, it will manifest involuntarily. Even if you try to hold it back, it will flow out of you and manifest in reality *because it is real.* If one has to tell people that a dream *does indeed* mean something, and that it must be acted upon, that is already bad. One of the most positive experiences in analysis is when an analysand brings a dream whose meaning you tell, but without commenting upon it, and the next time the analysand says, "Do you know what happened? You gave me the interpretation of that dream, and as a result I did such and such a thing!" We do not need to play the part of a governess and say one should do what the dream says; that is not the right way. Normally, if a person is morally sound, it will come about quite naturally.

810 Let us say, for example, that a grown-up son still tries to get money out of his mother, and she, being softhearted, cannot say no, but, thinking he might be hungry, sends him the money at once. Suppose such a mother had a dream that to send money to her son meant poisoning him. You don't need to say, "Don't send him

[38] John G. Neihardt, ed., *Black Elk Speaks: Being the Life Story of a Holy Man of the Oglala Sioux.* (Albany, NY: Excelsior Editions, State University of New York Press, 2008).

money," but rather "The dream says if you send money, you are poisoning or castrating your son." The next time this woman will tell you she has made up her mind not to send money anymore. This is how it happens if people are morally sound—and therein rests our hope.

811 I have sometimes met cases where I thought there was practically no hope, horrible cases, but if the analysands had that quality, I was sure they would get out of trouble, even quickly. This kind of moral integrity, even naivety, that just says "yes" speeds up everything. It says in the Bible, "Let your yea be yea, and your nay, nay."[39] Such people are morally sound. The opposite would be those who understand, who nod their heads to everything, but need heaven knows how many electric shocks from within and without before they realize they have to do something about it.

812 Mothers often say they know they should not eat their sons, but they never think of changing their behavior. They do not even notice what they are doing. The other day I heard from a woman that her mother had telephoned her three times on a Sunday to say she should come home at once. The same mother swore to me in her analytical hour that she never made any demands on her daughter and always gave her complete freedom. She looked me straight in the eye and swore she made no claims. What the daughter had told me was in confidence so I could not make use of that illustration. I sat there furious but could do nothing. I asked, "Are you sure?" "Yes," she said, "absolutely." In this instance the spirit never materialised. Such people can analyze for years and the result is absolutely zero. They can talk about Jungian psychology as though they know all about it, but there is no change.

813 We are now up to the fifth parable, "Of the Treasure-House which Wisdom Built upon a Rock." We know of the famous simile in *Matthew* 7, 24-28 of the house that was built upon sand, and the one built upon rock. We also know of the simile in *Proverbs* 9, 1-5

[39] 2 *Cor.* 1:17; and *James* 5:12.

of Wisdom who built her house on seven pillars and invited the Israelites to eat there.[40] The text says,

814 Wisdom hath built herself a house, which if any man enter in he shall be saved and find pastures, as the prophet beareth witness: They shall be inebriated with the plenty of thy house, for better is one day in thy courts above thousands. O how blessed are they that dwell in this house; for therein everyone that asketh receiveth and he that seeketh findeth and to him that knocketh it shall be opened. For Wisdom standeth at the door and saith: Behold, I stand at the gate and knock: if any man shall hear my voice and open the door, I will come in to him and he to me, and I will be satisfied with him and he with me. O how great is the multitude of thy sweetness, which thou hast hidden for them that enter this house; which eye hath not seen nor ear heard; neither hath it entered into the heart of man. To them that unlock this house shall be befitting holiness and also length of days, for it is founded upon a sure rock, which cannot be split unless it be anointed with the blood of a most fine buck goat or be smitten three times with the rod of Moses, that water may flow forth in great abundance, that all the people both men and women drink thereof.

815 Clearly this is about solidifying what is weak. The rock stands for the steadfastness of the personality that comes from a long process of assimilating the unconscious. If one has experienced those great ups and downs that are entailed by meeting with the unconscious for long enough, an unshakable kernel is slowly formed. I think that even a psychological cure or development, which is the same thing, does not change any particular conflict or cure any specific problem. What really changes is the ability to stand it better, and that is the real development. The outer situation may sometimes remain unchanged, or certain difficulties in one's character—what we call

[40] Cf. Franz, *Aurora Consurgens*, 314, 317, 319, 323.

character neuroses—may still remain to a certain extent. If, for instance, someone has a very passionate temperament, or a tendency to depression, it will generally continue for a long time. It will take at least 20 years to educate that out of the system; it cannot be changed at once, for it is ingrained in one's nature. But the first step is to be able to stand it better, not to be dissolved by it, to be detached and have a standpoint, to know that it is one's weakness to which one does not intend to give way, and that it will pass.

816 The essential step is that one is no longer identical with one's own mad spots. For example, if a paranoiac says, "I believe that ... but forgive me, it may not be so, that ..." it shows he has now something of a rock behind his paranoid system; though he has not yet got rid of his fantasy, at least he is able to say he may be imagining it. That is the beginning of the formation of solid earth; outside of the conflict, something has managed to escape from the devil.

817 Or if one has always been swept off one's feet by the animus or some emotion, and there begin to be periods when one becomes reasonable, even though afterward one may again fall back into the passionate possession, those moments are the beginning of the formation of the inner rock. The small piece of solid ground on which one stands becomes stronger and stronger and slowly becomes something solid, so that more and more one feels that, come what may, this will probably not be destroyed again.

818 One can describe it more pessimistically, but it is still the same positive thing: One has suffered so much, or has fallen so deeply into one's own hell that, thank God, one cannot fall any lower, and that gives one a certain sense of security. If you have touched the bottom of hell, there is nothing further down, and that is where the solid rock begins. Or someone may come and say they have always been afraid of going mad, but having reached the age of 40 without doing so, they probably never will now, to which one can generally agree with good conscience. If they have come so far without snapping, they are not likely to do so because something has coagulated within and become solid. One is able, and this is the aim of the work, to

retire into the inner house of wisdom that is built on a rock and "shall not be moved forever"—as it says in the third parable.

819 You may ask if that is not a hardening, is it not rigidity once more? Is that not becoming immune? But the answer is no, for from such a rock flows the water of life; it is the rock from which Moses miraculously obtained the water of life. It is a rock that is also a well, and therefore it is the most liquid thing and the very opposite of rigidity or hardening. It means being flexible, but unshakable. Jung says if the process of individuation goes on unconsciously, it makes the individual cruel and hard toward his fellow creatures; if it is a conscious process, it leads to the *lapis philosophorum*—not to a hardening of the personality but to a firmness in the positive sense of the word. One is no longer easily dissociated and swept away by emotion, losing one's point of view through collective pressure and so on, but that would not mean a hardening which cannot be influenced. This is probably what is meant by the rock on which the house of Wisdom is built.

820 As the text says, the vision of the fullness of the sun and moon takes place in this house. This refers to the motif that in this house the *coniunctio* takes place. It is also therefore alluded to as the alchemical vessel, which is the house in which sun and moon unite.

821 In our chapter, the house is built on fourteen pillars.[41] The pillars stand for the 14 qualities the alchemist must have. These qualities are not only ethical but include all sorts of qualities a human being should have: health, humility, holiness (from the description, this apparently means wholeness or purity), chastity, virtue (this means effectiveness or true efficiency), victoriousness (the ability to overcome), faith (the capacity to trust, or to understand spiritual qualities that cannot be seen), hope (one of the worst things concerning inner work is hopelessness; it is terrible when people give up and declare that they are hopeless; this is one of the animus's stereotypical gramophone records), charity, compassion, goodness (a kind of benevolence), patience (which is very important),

[41] Ibid., 331.

temperateness (a balance between the opposites), discipline or spiritual insight, and obedience.

822 In this connection, it says that the 12th stone or pillar is *temperantia*, meaning a balanced temperament that nourishes and keeps people in good health. "For as long as the elements are in temperance, the soul delighteth in the body, but when they are in discord, the soul abhorreth to dwell in it."[42] Therefore, balance refers to the right mixture of the elements, of warm and coldness, of dry and moist, so that the one does not overpower the other. This is why the philosophers say to watch out that the mystery does not evaporate or the acid turn into steam. "Beware lest ye put to flight the king and his consort with too much fire."[43]

823 The inner process can be overdone with too much fire. This happens to those who strive after the process of individuation. They are not able to go to a summer party because they have to stay home and paint their mandalas. It is the desire to force the process, but one cannot force a process of growth. It is foolish to storm at a little oak tree that it should grow more quickly; that goes against nature. It would be better to water it and put some dung at its roots. There are things in the inner process that cannot be speeded up, and it is pointless being impatient.

824 So the instruction not to burn the king and queen means to not try and force the inner *coniunctio*. One's ego is always behind this: a greedy, immature attitude that naturally leads to a wrong result. This is why the alchemists always warn against overheating the process. Some even recommend that one should never have greater warmth than that of fresh horse dung, which would be about the temperature of the human body, the temperature of the interior of warm-blooded creatures. It should be adequate for a human being. Everything that is *extra modum*, as the text says, that is beyond measure, is wrong. Even what is good—if it is beyond measure, it becomes wrong. Everything that contains an infantile pushing accent is wrong. It can

---

[42] Ibid., 336.
[43] Ibid.

be felt, and one knows it will lead nowhere, even if the intention is good. Those are the stones of the house of Wisdom.

825 The sixth parable is "Of Heaven and Earth and the Arrangement of the Elements."[44] Here, there is a cosmogonic myth that describes the birth of the whole cosmos. Psychologically speaking, what the alchemists call the union of the cosmic world means getting beyond the microcosm of the individual human being and being open to life itself, through being related to the whole of life by watching the process of synchronicity. Even the highest and most important occupation connected with one's own inner development has a narcissistic quality; it has to be so. For a time, one has to be shut up in the vessel and attend to one's own business, and to some extent not be open toward life during that period; this is inevitable. But in the state described now, the whole nature of the cosmos is again included, and this means being connected to God.

826 The seventh and last parable is "Of the Confabulation of the Lover with the Beloved."[45]

827
> Be turned to me with all your heart and do not cast me aside because I am black and swarthy, because the sun hath changed my colour and the waters have covered my face and the earth hath been polluted and defiled in my works; for there was darkness over it, because I stick fast in the mire of the deep and my substance is not disclosed. Wherefore out of the depths have I cried, and from the abyss of the earth with my voice to all you that pass by the way. Attend and see me, if any shall find one like unto me, I will give into his hand the morning star. For behold in my bed by night I sought one to comfort me and I found one, I called and there was none to answer me.[46]

828 You see, here again he begins with the deepest depression.

---

[44] Ibid., 339–361.
[45] Cf. ibid., 362-404.
[46] Ibid.

> Therefore will I arise and go into the city, seeking in the streets and broad ways a chaste virgin to espouse, comely in face, more comely in body, most comely in her garments, that she may roll back the stone from the door of my sepulchre and give me wings like a dove, and I will fly with her into heaven and then say: I live for ever, and will rest in her, for the queen stood on my right hand in gilded clothing, surrounded with variety. Hearken therefore O daughter and see and incline thine ear to my prayers, for I have desired thy beauty with all the desire of my heart.[47]

829 This is the bridegroom calling from his tomb. He wants to be resurrected; he is buried in his tomb, and now he calls for his bride, who is a birdlike being who has feathers and flies in Heaven. So she is a ghost, a spiritual being.

830

> O I spoke with my tongue, Make known to me my end and what is the number of my days, that I may know what is wanting to me, for thou hast made all my days measurable and my substance is as nothing before thee. For thou art she who shall enter through the ear, through my domain, and I shall be clothed with a purple garment from thee and from me, I will come forth as a bridegroom out of his bride-chamber, for thou shalt adorn me round about with shining and glittering gems and shalt clothe me with the garments of salvation and joy to overthrow the nations and all mine enemies, and shalt adorn me with a crown of gold engraved with the sign of holiness.[48]

831 Entering the ear is something very strange. It is an allusion to certain medieval theories that Christ was conceived through the ear of the Virgin Mary. The angel of the Annunciation appeared and told her she would conceive and bear a child, and some theologians took this

[47] Ibid.
[48] Ibid.

to mean that Christ was supernaturally conceived through the word entering her ear. This was called the *conceptio per aurem*, conception by the ear.

832 There is a dead bridegroom in the abyss, in despair in the tomb, and now he calls for his bride, who flies in Heaven with wings. Firstly, she will open his tomb and then will enter his ear; then he will resurrect, and she will give him a garment of resurrection and joy. We see here very clearly that it is an inner process of the *coniunctio*; it is union with the anima. She goes in through the ear, and she is understood and integrated, and that emanates as a new attitude. In alchemical terms, this is the beginning of the *rubedo*. First, there is the *nigredo* or blackness, then the *albedo*, and now begins the *rubedo*, the red, the red state. This is why the bridegroom gets a crimson garment here.

833 The problem is, who is the bridegroom? Here he is compared to Christ Himself, for the words "I will come forth as a bridegroom out of his bride-chamber" allude to Christ.[49] At the same time it is clearly the author. Here again we have this strange fact that the process of the *coniunctio* is described in a way that has the author involved with his divine part. In other words, this is a genuine documentation of what Jung referred to as an individual's experience of Christification.[50] The individual here himself becomes a Son of God, and therefore a bridegroom of the Wisdom of God. It is a mystical union with the Godhead, and the Godhead is, apparently, feminine. He begs her to tell him who she is so that everyone may know, and she replies:[51]

> 834 Hear all ye nations, give ear all ye inhabitants of the world; my beloved, who is ruddy, hath spoken to me, he hath sought and besought: I am the flower of the field and the lily of the valleys, I am the mother of fair love and of knowledge and of holy hope. As the fruitful vine I have brought forth a pleasant odour, and my flowers are the fruit of honour and riches. I

---

[49] *Ps.* 19:5-6.

[50] Jung, *Mysterium Coniunctionis*, vol. 14, *CW*, § 530.

[51] Von Franz, *Aurora Consurgens*, 376-80, 383-5.

am the bed of my beloved, which threescore of the most valiant ones surrounded, all holding swords upon their thigh because of fears in the night. I am all fair and there is no spot in me; looking through the windows, looking through the lattices of my beloved, wounding his heart with one of my eyes and with one hair of my neck. I am the sweet smell of ointments giving an odour above all aromatical spices and like unto cinnamon and balsam and chosen myrrh. I am the most prudent virgin coming forth as the Dawn, shining exceedingly, elect as the sun, fair as the moon, besides what is hid within. I am exalted as a cedar and a cypress tree on Mount Sion, I am the crown wherewith my beloved is crowned in the day of his espousals and of his joy, for my name is as ointment poured forth. ... I am that chosen vineyard, into which the householder sent his labourers at the first, second, third, sixth, and ninth hours, saying: Go you also into my vineyard, and at the twelfth hour I will give you what shall be just. I am that land of the holy promise ... wherefore have all the philosophers commended me and sowed in me their gold and silver and incombustible grain. And unless that grain falling into me die, itself shall remain alone, but if it die, it bringeth forth threefold fruit. ...For of that bread the poor shall eat and shall be filled, and they shall praise the Lord that seeks him, and their hearts shall live forever.

835 And then come the words of God as in the Bible,[52] from which it is completely manifest that this female being is God:

836 I give and take not back, I feed and fail not, I make secure and fear not; what more shall I say to my beloved? I am the mediatrix of the elements, making one to agree with another; that which is warm I make cold, and the reverse; that which is dry I make moist, and the reverse; that which is hard I

[52] *Rev.* 1:8 and *Jer.* 18: 18.

> soften, and the reverse. I am the end and my beloved is the beginning, I am the whole work and all science is hidden in me. I am the law in the priest and the word in the prophet and counsel in the wise.

837 And now again there is a quotation from the words of God as given in the Bible:[53]

838
> I will kill and I will make to live and there is none that can deliver out of my hand. I stretch forth my mouth to my beloved and he presseth his to me; he and I are one; who shall separate us from love? None and no man, for our love is strong as death.

839 Then he answers:

> O beloved, yea supremely beloved, thy voice hath sounded in my ears, for it is sweet, and thine odour is above all aromatical spices. ...Come, my beloved, and let us go into thy field, let us abide in the villages, let us go up early to the vineyard, for the night is past and the day is at hand; let us see if thy vineyard flourisheth, if thy flowers have brought forth fruits. There shalt thou give thy breasts to my mouth, and I have kept for thee all fruits new and old; let us therefore enjoy them and use the good things speedily as in youth, let us fill ourselves with costly wine and ointments, and let no flower pass by us save we crown ourselves therewith, first with lilies, then with roses, before they be withered.

840 This is very meaningful because it is all from the Bible![54] In the biblical *Book of Wisdom* (2, 6-9) it is written that the sinners, the idiots, the imbeciles, and those who are rejected by God say, "Let us go out into the fields." There, it is the sinners who say this, and here

---

[53] *Deut.* 32:39.
[54] *Pss.* 2:14; 4:1; 4:10; 7:5; 7:3.

it is the bride and bridegroom who say it in the *coniunctio*. One of the monks who copied out the text got so drawn in by the pleasure of it that when he came to the part "let no meadow flower pass by us save we crown ourselves therewith," he translated *partum* (meadow) with *peccatum (sins)*. Thus, he wrote, "No sin shall us pass by save we crown ourselves therewith!" The poor old monk mixed up *peccatum*—sins—with *partum*—meadow, something that could happen very easily in medieval stenography. He made a complex mistake. For someone who knew the Bible, it must have been very shocking when the bridegroom and bride quote the words of the world's sinners. What on earth was this man thinking when he wrote that?

841 The end of the text says:[55]

> Let us leave everywhere tokens of joy, for this is our portion, that we should live in the union of love with joy and merriment, saying: Behold how good and pleasant it is for two to dwell together in unity. Let us make therefore three tabernacles, one for thee, a second for me, and a third for our sons, for a threefold cord is not easily broken. He that hath ears to hear, let him hear what the spirit of the doctrine saith to the sons of the discipline concerning the espousal of the lover to the beloved. For he had sowed his seed, that there might ripen thereof threefold fruit, which the author of the *Three Words* saith to be three precious words, wherein is hidden all the science, which is to be given to the pious, that is to the poor, from the first man even unto the last.

842 Those last words allude to a secret tradition that only the initiated hand on to each other, i.e., the tradition of this union of love. The three tabernacles are an allusion to the announcement in *Revelation* 21, 2-3 that God will live in a tabernacle with man on earth. In *Revelation*, John writes: "And I saw the holy city, new Jerusalem, coming down out of heaven from God, made ready as a bride

[55] Cf. von Franz, *Aurora Consurgens*, 395, 398-99.

adorned for her husband. And I heard a great voice out of the throne saying, Behold, the tabernacle of God is with men, and he shall dwell with them, and they shall be his peoples, and God himself shall be with them, and be their God."

843 So the *coniunctio* ends here with an incarnation of the Divinity. It is God coming down into the human being. Jung has formulated this by saying[56] that what is seen from the human angle as being the process of individuation is, from God's viewpoint, from the viewpoint of a God-image, a process of incarnation.

[56] Jung, *Psychology and Religion*, vol. 11, *CW*, § 233.

Appendix

Bibliography

Abt, Theodor, Wilfred Madelung, and Thomas Hofmeier, eds. *Book of the Explanation of the Symbols: Kitāb Ḥall ar-rumūz by Muḥammad Ibn Umail.* Vol. 1. CALA. Zurich: Living Human Heritage, 2003.

Abt, Theodor. *The Great Vision of Muḥammad Ibn Umail.* Los Angeles: C. G. Jung Institute of Los Angeles, 2003.

Angelus Silesius. *The Cherubinic Wanderer*. Introduction and notes by Josef Schmidt. Translated by Maria Shrady. New York: Paulist Press, 1932.

Ashmole, Elias, ed. *Theatrum Chemicum Britannicum.* Vol. 1. Hildesheim: Olms, 1968.

Berndt, Roland M. *Kunapipi: A Study of an Australian Aboriginal Religious Cult.* New York: International Universities Press, 1951.

Bernoulli, Rudolf. "Seelische Entwicklung im Spiegel der Alchemie und verwandter Disziplinen." In *Westöstliche Seelenführung.* Eranos-Jahrbuch 1935, edited by Olga Fröbe-Kapteyn, vol. 3. Zurich: Rhein-Verlag, 1936.

Berthelot, Marcellin. *Collection des anciens alchimistes grecs.* Vol. 1. Paris: Steinheil, 1887.

---. *Collection des anciens alchimistes grecs: Text grec.* Vol. 1. Paris: Steinheil, 1888.

---. *Collection des alchimistes grecs: Traduction.* Vol. 2. Paris: Steinheil, 1888.

Bonnet, Hans. *Reallexikon der ägyptischen Religionsgeschichte.* 2nd ed. Berlin: Gruyter, 1971.

De Nerval, Gérard. "Aurélie." In *Œuvres.* Vol. 1. Edited by Albert Béguin and Jean Richer. Paris: Gallimard, 1952–1956.

De Wit, Constant. *Le rôle et le sens du lion dans l'Égypte ancienne.* Leiden: Brill, 1951.

Hannah, Barbara. *Encounters with the Soul: Active Imagination as Developed by C. G. Jung*. Boston: Sigo Press, 1981.

Hornung, Erik, ed. and trans. *Die Unterweltsbücher der Ägypter*. Zurich: Artemis, 1992.

Ibn Umail, Mu□ammad. *De Chemia Senioris Antiquissimi Philosophi Libellus*. Strasbourg: Samuel Emmel, 1566.

Jung, C. G. *Bollingen Series XX: The Collected Works of C. G. Jung*. 20 vols. Edited by Herbert Read, Michael Fordham, Gerhard Adler and William McGuire. Translated by R. F. C. Hull.

---. *Aion: Research into the Phenomenology of the Self*. 2nd ed. Vol. 9/II. Princeton, NJ: Princeton University Press, 1978.

---. *Alchemical Studies*. Vol. 13. Princeton, NJ: Princeton University Press, 1983.

---. *The Archetpyes and the Collective Unconscious*. 2nd ed. Vol. 9/I. Princeton, NJ: Princeton University Press, 1980.

---. *Mysterium Coniunctionis: An Inquity into the Separation and Synthesis of Psychic Opposites in Alchemy*. 2nd ed. Vol. 14. Princeton, NJ: Princeton University Press, 1989.

---. *Practice of Psychotherapy*. 2nd ed. Vol. 16. Princeton, NJ: Princeton University Press: 1985.

---. *Psychological Types*. Vol. 6. Princeton, NJ: Princeton University Press, 1990.

---. *Psychology and Alchemy*. 2nd ed. Vol. 12. Princeton, NJ: Princeton University Press, 1993.

---. *Psychology and Religion: West and East*. 2nd ed. Vol. 11. Princeton, NJ: Princeton University Press, 1989.

---. *The Structure and Dynamics of the Psyche*. 2nd ed. Vol. 8. Princeton, NJ: Princeton University Press, 1981.

---. *The Symbolic Life*. Vol. 18. Princeton, NJ: Princeton University Press, 1989.

---. "Exercitia spiritualia." In *Modern Psychology: Notes on Lectures Given at the Eidgenössische Technische Hochschule Zurich*. 2nd ed. Vol. 3 and 4. Privatly printed, 1959.

———. *Nietzche's Zarathustra: Notes of the Seminar Given in 1934–1939*. Vol. 2. Edited by James L. Jarrett. London: Routledge and Kegan Paul, 1989.

———. *Letters*. Vol. 2. Edited by Aniela Jaffé and Gerhard Adler. London: Routledge and Kegan Paul, 1975.

———. *The Psychology of Kundalini Yoga: Notes of the Seminar Given in 1932*. Edited by Sonu Shamdasani. Princeton, NJ: Princeton University Press, 1999.

Marti, Hans. *Urbild und Verfassung: Eine Studie zum hintergründigen Gehalt einer Verfassung*. Bern: Hans Huber, 1958.

Mertens, Michèle, ed. *Les Alchimistes Grecs*. Paris: Les Belles Lettres, 1995.

Neihardt, John G., ed. *Black Elk Speaks: Being the Life Story of a Holy Man of the Oglala Sioux*. Albany, NY: Excelsior Editions, State University of New York Press, 2008.

Oppenheim, A. Leo. *The Interpretation of Dreams in the Ancient Near East: With a Translation of an Assyrian Dream-Book*. Transactions of the American Philosophical Society, vol. 46. Philadelphia: The American Philosophical Society, 1956.

Pauli, Wolfgang, C. A. Meier, and C. G. Jung, eds., *Wolfgang Pauli und C. G. Jung: Ein Briefwechsel, 1932–1958*. Berlin: Springer, 1992.

Platon, "Timaios." In *Hauptwerke*. Edited by Wilhelm Nestle. Leipzig: Kröner, 1931.

Radin, Paul. "The Winnebago Tribe." In *Annual Report of the Bureau of American Ethnology*. Washington, DC: 1923.

———. *The Winnebago Tribe*. Lincoln: University of Nebraska Press, 1970.

Roeder, Günther. *Urkunden zur Religion des alten Ägypten*. 2nd ed. Religiöse Stimmen der Völker, edited by Walter Otto, vol. 4. Jena: Eugen Diederichs, 1923.

Ruska, Julius, ed. *Tabula Smaragdina: Ein Beitrag zur Geschichte der hermetischen Literatur*. Heidelberg: Winter, 1926.

Schärf Kluger, Rivkah. "The Queen of Sheba in Bible and Legends." In *Psyche in Scripture: The Idea of the Chosen People and Other Essays*. Toronto: Inner City Books, 1995.

Suzuki, Daisetz Teitaro. *Essays in Zen Buddhism*. London: Rider and Co., 1927.

Stapleton, H. E., M. Turab 'Ali, and M. Hidayat Husain, "Three Arabic Treatises on Alchemy by Muhammad Ibn Umail (10th Century A.D.)." In *Memoirs of the Asiatic Society of Bengal.* Edited by Turab 'Ali. Vol. 12. Calcutta: Asiatic Society of Bengal, 1933.

Stricker, Bruno Hugo. *La prison de Joseph*. Leiden: Brill, 1943.

Von Franz, Marie-Louise. *Alchemical Active Imagination.* Boston: Shambhala, 1997.

---, ed. with a Commentary. *Aurora Consurgens: A Document Attributed to Thomas Aquinas on the Problem of the Opposites in Alchemy. A Companion Work to C. G. Jung's Mysterium Coniunctionis*. Translated by R. F. C. Hull and A. S. B. Glover. Toronto: Inner City Books, 2000.

---. *Book of the Explanation of the Symbols: Kitāb Ḥall ar-rumūz by Muḥammad Ibn Umail. Psychological Commentary by Marie-Louise von Franz*. Vol. 1A. CALA, edited by Theodor Abt and Wilfred Madelung. Zurich: Living Human Heritage, 2006.

--- . *On Dreams and Death: A Jungian Interpretation*. Translated by Emmanuel Xipolitas Kennedy and Vernon Brooks. Boston: Shambhala, 1986.

---. *The Golden Ass of Apuleius: The Liberation of the Feminine in Man*. Boston: Shambhala, 1992.

---. *Psychotherapy*. Boston: Shambhala, 1993.

---. *Die Visionen des Niklaus von Flüe*. 3rd ed. Zurich: Daimon, 1983.

Von Goethe, Johann Wolfgang. *Faust II*.

Wilhelm, Richard. *The Secret of the Golden Flower: A Chinese Book of Life*. With a Commentary by C. G. Jung. New York: Mariner Books, 1970.

Wilcken, Ulrich, ed. *Urkunden der Ptolemäerzeit (ältere Funde)*. Vol. 1. Berlin: Gruyter, 1922–1957.

Index

M

U

V

W

Made in United States
Orlando, FL
16 September 2026

87759405R00187